# Dictionary of Mechanical Engineering

Dictionary of Mechanical Engineering

# Dictionary
## of
# Mechanical Engineering

**Suman Walia**

Website: www.shubhambooks.com

# K S PAPERBACKS
### NEW DELHI - 110 002

*Published by*
**K.S. PAPERBACKS**
New Delhi-110002

*Marketed by*
**SHUBHAM BOOK DISTRIBUTORS**
88, Chander Nagar Market
Alambagh, Lucknow-226005, Ph. 2453269
email : shubhambooks@sify.com

DICTIONARY OF MECHANICAL ENGINEERING

ISBN : 81-89261-38-9

**Rs. 160**

# Preface

This dictionary has been compiled to include the terms related to various branches of mechanical engineering. Each term has been explained in language which is easy to understand. The terms lend verse to your knowledge in mechanical engineering and they enable you to communicate in idea with brevity and wit.

This dictionary is a must for diploma, degree and A.M.I.E. students. This dictionary is also useful for automobile engineers.

**absolute pressure**
A pressure measured from absolute zero.

**absolute pressure sensor**
A device for sensing pressures from absolute zero.

**absolute rating**
A single eternal explanation for all reality. That point at which all motion in matter ceases, such as absolute zero. Also used in filter ratings to indicate the diameter of the largest particle, normally expressed in micrometers (µm), that will pass through the filter. A filter media with an exact and consistent pore size theoretically has an absolute rating.

**absolute zero**
The lowest temperature on the Kelvin temperature scale (0°K), equivalent to -459.7°F (-273.2°C). Temperature measured from 0°K is an absolute temperature. All molecular motion ceases at 0°K.

**absorb**
To take in by capillary action, as in a sponge.

**absorbent medium**
A material akin to a sponge in that it can draw in fluid and retain it within its structure. In this sense, it can act as a filter to remove (absorb) and retain fluid.

**absorptive lens**

A filter lens designed to reduce the effects of glare, reflection, and stray light.

**ac adapter**

A transformer-type power supply that plugs into an ac (alternating current) power outlet and provides low voltage ac or dc to provide power for accessory equipment.

**A-cam**

Pattern used for grinding pistons in an oval- or cam-shape with 0.005 inch (0.127 mm) difference between the thrust face and the pinhole side.

**acc**

Abbreviation for accessory.

**ACC**

An abbreviation for Automotive Communications Council. An abbreviation for air conditioning compressor signal switch.

**acceleration**

1. An increase in velocity or speed.
2. Rate of change of velocity, either scalar or vector, often with subscripts such as ENU or XYZ to denote the coordinate frame; time derivative of velocity; time integral of jerk; *Symbols:* a, A; *Typical Units:* ft/s-squared, g; *Dimensions:* Length / Time-squared.

**Acceleration analysis**

A mathematical technique, often done graphically, by which accelerations of parts of a mechanism are determined. In high-speed machines, particularly those that include cam mechanisms, inertial forces may be the controlling factor in the design of members. An acceleration analysis, based upon velocity analysis, must therefore precede a force analysis. Maximum accelerations are of particular interest to the designer. Although an analytical solution might be preferable if exact maxima were required, graphical solutions formerly tended to be simpler and to facilitate visualization of relationships. Today, for advanced problems certainly, a computer solution, possibly one based on graphical techniques, is often more effective and can also produce very accurate graphical output.

Accelerations on a rigid link

On link OB (Fig. 1a) acceleration of point B with respect to point O is the vector sum of two accelerations: (1) normal acceleration $A^n_{BO}$ of B with respect to O because of displacement of B along a path whose instantaneous center of curvature is at O, and (2) tangential acceleration of $A^t_{BO}$ of B with respect to O because of angular acceleration __chars/alpha/special/agr/black/med/base/glyph.gif align=bottom>.

Fig. 1  Elementary condition. (a) Point B on rigid member rotates about center O. (b) Vector diagram shows normal, tangential, and resultant accelerations.

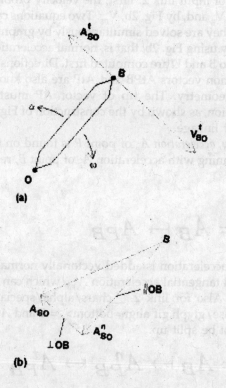

For conditions of Fig. 1a with link OB rotating about O at angular velocity and angular acceleration __chars/alpha/ special/agr/black/med/base/glyph.gif align=bottom>, the accelerations can be written as Eqs. (1) and (2). The vector sum or resultant is ABO (Fig. 1b).

$$A^n_{BO} = (OB)\omega^2 = V^2_B/(OB) \qquad (1)$$

$$A^t_{BO} = (OB)\alpha \qquad (2)$$

Accelerations in a linkage

Consider the acceleration of point P on a four-bar linkage (Fig. 2a) with __chars/alpha/special/agr/black/med/base/ glyph.gif align=bottom>2 = 0 and hence $\omega_2$ = k, the angular velocity of input link 2. First, the velocity problem is solved yielding $V_B$ and, by Fig. 2b, $V_{PB}$. Two equations can be written for AP; they are solved simultaneously by graphical means in Fig. 2c by using Fig. 2b; that is, normal accelerations of P with respect to B and D are computed first. Directions of tangential acceleration vectors AtPB and AtP are also known from the initial geometry. The tip of vector AP must lie at their intersection, as shown by the construction of Fig. 2c. See also: Four-bar linkage.

*Explicitly, acceleration $A_p$ of point P is found on the one hand by beginning with acceleration $A_E$ of point B, represented by Eq. (3).*

$$A_p = A_B \mapsto A_{PB} \qquad (3)$$

To this acceleration is added vectorially normal acceleration $A^n_{PB}$ and tangential acceleration $A^t_{PB}$, which can be written as Eq. (4). Also for link 2, __chars/alpha/special/agr/black/ med/base/glyph.gif align=bottom>$_2$ = 0 and $A^t_B$ = 0; and $A_B$ need not be split up.

$$A_P = A_B \mapsto A^n_{PB} \mapsto A^t_{PB} \qquad (4)$$

Fig. 2   Four-bar linkage. (a) Given are the linkages 2, 3, and 4 between fixed supports 1-1 and the velocity of point $B_1$, $\omega_2 = 0$. (b) A vector polygon is used to determine the velocity at point P. (c) A graphic solution then finds acceleration at P.

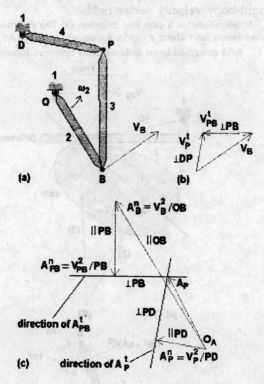

On the other hand, $A_p$ can also be expressed as Eq. (5),

$$A_P = A_P^n \mapsto A_p^t \tag{5}$$

or in Fig. 2c. The intersection of the two tangential components defines the tip of $A_p$. This problem illustrates the generalization that any basic acceleration analysis can be thoroughly performed only after completion of the underlying velocity analysis.

## Acceleration field

Acceleration is a vector and hence has magnitude and direction but not a unique position. A plane rigid body, such as the cam of Fig. 3a, in motion parallel to its plane will possess an acceleration field in that plane differing from, but resembling, a rigid-body velocity vector field.

Fig. 3    Accelerations on a cam and follower. (a) The cam mechanism. (b) The acceleration field about a rigid rotating structure. (c) An acceleration field determining an instantaneous center of rotation.

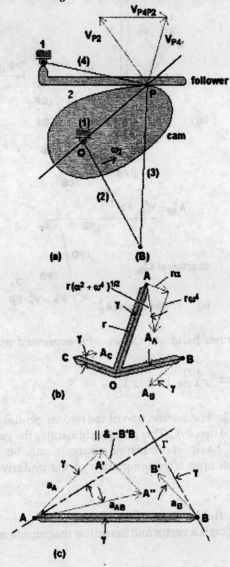

## acceleration east
Aircraft acceleration in true east direction; *Symbols:* A sub E; *Typical Units:* ft/s-squared; *Dimensions:* Length / Time-squared.

## acceleration north
Aircraft acceleration in true north direction; *Symbols:* A sub N; *Typical Units:* ft/s-squared; *Dimensions:* Length / Time-squared.

## acceleration squat
The tendency of the rear part of a vehicle to press down on the rear springs during hard acceleration.

## accelerator
A control, usually a foot-operated pedal, linked to the throttle valve of the carburetor and used to control the flow of fuel into the engine.

## accelerator pedal
A foot-operated device for controlling the flow of fuel into the engine.

## accelerator pedal position sensor
A device designed to send an electrical signal to the central processing unit relative to the position of the accelerator pedal at any given time.

## accelerator pump
A pump in the carburetor connected by linkage to the accelerator pedal that momentarily enriches the air-fuel mixture when the accelerator is depressed at low speed.

## accelerometer
1. An instrument that measures a vehicle's linear or lateral rate of acceleration in g force or feet per second.
2. An inertial device for measuring acceleration, usually in three orthogonal axes (lateral X, longitudinal Y, and vertical Z); accelerometers usually consist of a mass, spring, and damper; accelerometers are usually included in inertial sensors, such as AHRS and INS.

**accept**

To allow to proceed, for example with a position update, usually by an operator; *Compare:* reject.

**acceptable weld**

A weld that meets all the requirements and the acceptance criteria prescribed by the welding specifications. access fitting A service port or service valve. Also may refer to an access valve.

**access slot**

An opening that permits access to a device, such as the openings in the backing plates of a brake system that allow access to the star wheel adjuster.

**access time**

The time that is required to retrieve information from a system's memory.

**access valve**

A service port or service valve. Also may refer to an access fitting.

**accidental ground**

A condition that exists when a wire, connected to the positive battery terminal, contacts a grounded metal part of the car.

**ACCS**

An abbreviation for air conditioning cycling-clutch switch.

**accumulator**

A tank located in the outlet of the evaporator to receive the refrigerant that leaves the evaporator. A component used to store or hold liquid refrigerant in an air-conditioning system. This device is constructed to ensure that no liquid refrigerant enters the compressor.

A device that cushions the motion of a clutch and servo action in an automatic transmission.

A register or storage location that forms the result of an arithmetic or logic operation. Commonly used when a series of calculations are to be totaled.

**acetic acid**

An activator that is used in RTV/silicone sealants to make them more rubber-like in composition.

**acetone**

1. A highly flammable liquid sometimes used as a racing-fuel additive. Acetone CH3COCH3 helps to prevent other chemicals in a fuel mixture from separating.
2. A powerful ketone-type lacquer solvent.
3. Used as a solvent to clean parts.

**acquire**

To begin reception of useful data.

**acetylene**

A highly flammable gas (C2H2) used for metal cutting, welding, and brazing.

**acid**

Hydrogen (H) compounds that yield hydrogen ions when dissolved in water. There are many types of organic and inorganic acids. Though acids are the most important and useful of all the chemicals, acids are not wanted in some environments.

**ACID**

An acronym for a four-mode, driving-test cycle used to test exhaust emissions or vehicle driveability; the modes are Accelerate, Cruise, Idle, and Decelerate.

**acid rain**

Corrosive rain formed when sulfur (S) emissions from motor vehicles and industrial plants combine with hydrogen (H) and oxygen (O) in the atmosphere to form sulfuric acid (H2SO4). The mixture of these chemicals with water (H2O) produces an acid solution that is found in rain. Not only is it corrosive to anything it may come into contact with, it also raises the acidity of lakes and ponds, often to the point that fish and other aquatic life cannot survive.

**Ackerman principle**

The geometric principle used to provide toe-out on turns. The ends of the steering arms are angled so that the inside wheel turns more than the outside wheel when a vehicle is making a turn, without scrubbing the tire treads on the road surface.

**Ackerman steering**

A term often used for Ackerman principle.

**ACL**

An abbreviation for automatic chassis lubrication.

**ACM**

An abbreviation for air-control module.

**ac power supply**

A source of alternating current (ac), such as an ac outlet, transformer, inverter, or an alternator (ac generator).

**ACRL**

An abbreviation for American City Racing League.

**ACRS**

An abbreviation for air-cushion restraint system.

**ACR3**

An abbreviation for an Air Conditioning and Refrigeration Refrigerant Recovery, Reclaim, and Recycle system.

**acrylic**

A polymer-based coating acrylic ($CnH2n-2O2$) widely used for automotive topcoats. Its physical properties can be controlled in part by the choice of the alcohol used to make the ester.

**active plate material**

The sponge lead in an automotive battery that is spread over the negative-plate grid or the lead peroxide that is spread over the positive-plate grid.

**active restraint**
> A vehicle occupant restraint, such as a lap belt and/or shoulder harness, that must be attached or connected by the person using it.

**active solvent**
> A liquid that can dissolve a paint binder when used alone.

**active spring coil**
> Active coils in the center of the spring operate during the complete range of spring loading. Also, see inactive spring coil and transitional spring coil.

**active suspension system**
> Also known as computer-controlled suspension system, a computerized system able to control body roll, body pitch, brake dive, acceleration squat, and ride height. Suspension systems that are controlled by double-acting hydraulic cylinders or solenoids (actuators) mounted at each wheel. The actuators support the vehicle's weight, instead of conventional springs or air springs.

**Actual Cash Value (ACV)**
> The true value of a product, such as a used vehicle.

**actual throat**
> A welding term indicating the shortest distance between the weld root and the face of a fillet weld.

**ACV**
> An abbreviation for air-control valve.
> An abbreviation for actual cash value.

**adapter**
> 1. Any of various pieces of hardware that permits non-matching parts to connect, mesh, or function together.
> 2. A device used to connect an engine and a transmission not originally designed to be used together.
> 3. Welds under a spring seat to increase mounting height of the fit seal to the axle.

**adaptive memory**

The feature of a computer memory that allows the microprocessor to automatically compensate for changes in the dynamics of the process being controlled. Anything stored in adaptive memory is lost when power to the computer is interrupted, such as when the battery is disconnected.

**additive**

Any material added to a lubricating grease or oil to improve its suitability for service. It may improve a property that the lubricant already possesses or give it properties that it does not naturally possess.

Any material added to the cooling system to inhibit rust, increase the boiling point, and/or decrease the freezing point. Any one of a number of special chemicals added to a paint to bring about special effects.

**add-on**

Any device or system added to a vehicle by the dealer, independent garage, or owner.

A component or device added to a computer system to increase its storage capacity, to modify its architecture, or to upgrade its performance; circuitry or system that can be attached to a computer.

**adhesive bonding**

A technique for bonding metals and/or plastics together during assembly of panels and bodies.

A process used to attach aftermarket body kits, such as rocker panels and spoilers.

**adiabatic engine**

An engine having combustion chambers insulated with a high-temperature material. Heat loss is kept at a minimum and is retained rather than being allowed to dissipate through the cooling and exhaust systems. This results in a higher proportion of thermal energy being converted to useful power.

**adjust**

To bring the parts of a component, system, or device to a specific relationship, dimension, temperature, or pressure.

**adjustable shock absorber**
A shock absorber having an external means of adjustment to calibrate it precisely for a specific operating condition.

**adjustable strut**
A strut with a manually operated adjustment for strut firmness. The strut adjusting knob, usually accessible without raising the vehicle, varies the strut orifice opening. Also see travel-sensitive strut.

**adjustable torque arm**
A member used to retain axle alignment and, in some cases, control axle torque. Normally one adjustable and one rigid torque arm are used per axle so the axle can be aligned. This rod can be extended or retracted for adjustment purposes.

**adjusting cam**
Eccentric bolts that are used to automatically or manually adjust the brake shoe-to-drum clearance. Positioned in the backing plate of drum brakes, the cam positions the shoe(s) closer to the drum.

**adjusting shim**
A metal shim, available in various thicknesses, used to change the valve clearance in some overhead cam engines.

**adjusting sleeve**
An internally threaded sleeve located between the tie rod ends. The sleeve is rotated to set toe in/toe out.

**adjustment**
To make a necessary or desired change in clearance, fit, or setting.

**adsorb**
To collect a very thin layer on the surface of a material.

**adsorbent media**
Generally used in filters for the removal of odors, smoke,

fumes, and some impurities. The chief adsorptive granular media used for filters are activated charcoal and similar forms of carbon, Fuller's earth, and other active clays. Also see canister filter and filter.

### adsorption

The attraction and/or retention of particles by molecular attraction or electrostatic forces present between the particles and a filter medium.

### advance curve

A term generally relating to spark advance curve.

### advisory

A signal to indicate safe or normal configuration, condition of performance, operation of essential equipment, or to attract attention and impart information for routine action purposes (from MIL-STD-1472D); an annunciator that is the least critical (less than a caution or a warning).

### aerodynamic

The ease with which air can flow over the vehicle during higher speed operation. An aerodynamically sound vehicle has very little wind resistance.

### aerodynamic resistance

Resistance of the air against an object, such as a vehicle, trying to pass through it. The result of four factors; coefficient of drag, frontal area, vehicle speed, and air density. Also referred to as air drag, air resistance, and aerodynamic drag.

### AESMC

An abbreviation for the Automotive Exhaust Systems Manufacturing Council.

### A/F

An abbreviation for air/fuel ratio.

**AFCS**
Automatic flight control system.

**aiding**
A process by which one or more sensors provide data to another sensor to produce results better than any single sensor; aiding occurs at the data source level or at the physical device level, depending upon specific implementation of the device and the data source (choice of implementation is transparent above the data source); aiding is automatically controlled by software without input from an operator; a basic control to a data source from navigation, radio navigation, or other devices *Compare:* update.

**aileron**
A control surface on fixed-wing aircraft, usually mounted on the aft edge of wings, that controls roll, and is controlled by the wheel; *Symbols:* delta sub A; *Typical Units:* rad, deg.

**aiming screws**
Self-locking screws for adjusting the headlamp in horizontal and vertical positions and for retaining the proper position.

**air**
The combination of gases that make up the earth's atmosphere: nitrogen (76–78%), oxygen (18–21%), and small amounts of carbon dioxide, argon, and other gases. When air is drawn into an engine, the oxygen combines with the fuel during combustion, producing carbon dioxide and water vapor.

**AIR**
An acronym for air-injection reactor.

**air bag**
Passive restraint with an inflatable air bag located in the steering wheel in front of the driver and in the dash in front of the right front seat passenger.
An inflatable bladder used in the place of a spring in an air suspension system. Also see air lift.

**air bag igniter**
> A combustible device that converts electric energy into thermal energy to ignite the inflator propellant. The igniter is an integral component of the inflator assembly.

**air bag inflator**
> A term often used for air bag igniter.

**air bag module**
> The air bag and inflator assembly together in a single package. This module is mounted in the center of the steering wheel.

**air bag system**
> The air bag system is designed as a supplemental restraint. In the case of an accident it will deploy a bag from the steering wheel or passenger side dash panel to provide additional protection against head and face injuries.

**air bleed**
> Holes or tubes in the carburetor to allow air to premix with gas flow.

**airborne**
> A term used to describe contaminants floating in air through the engine. The contaminants are light enough to be suspended in the air stream.

**air box**
> An enclosed chamber to direct air into a carburetor or intake manifold.

**air brake**
> 1. A moveable dynamic spoiler that can be raised against the wind to slow a high speed vehicle.
> 2. The braking system on some heavy duty trucks that uses compressed air to expand the brake shoes by cam or wedge against the brake drums.

**air carbon arc cutting**

A carbon arc-cutting process that removes molten metal with a jet of air.

**Air conditioning**

The control of certain environmental conditions including air temperature, air motion, moisture level, radiant heat energy level, dust, various pollutants, and microorganisms.

Comfort air conditioning refers to control of spaces to promote the comfort, health, or productivity of the inhabitants. Spaces in which air is conditioned for comfort include residences, offices, institutions, sports arenas, hotels, factory work areas, and motor vehicles. Process air-conditioning systems are designed to facilitate the functioning of a production, manufacturing, or operational activity. There are many examples. Heat-producing electronic equipment in an airplane cockpit must be kept cool to function properly, while the occupants of the cockpit are maintained in comfortable conditions. A multicolor printing press requires accurate registration of the colors so the environment must be maintained at a constant relative humidity to avoid paper expansion or shrinkage, and press heat and ink mists must be removed as potential health hazards for personnel. Maintenance of conditions within surgical suites of hospitals and in "clean" or "white" rooms of manufacturing plants, where an atmosphere almost free of microorganisms and dust must be maintained, is a specialized subdivision of process air conditioning.

Physiological principles

A comfort air-conditioning system is aesigned to help maintain body temperature at its normal level without undue stress and to provide an atmosphere which is healthy to breathe. The human body produces heat at various rates, depending basically upon the person's weight and degree of activity. Normally more heat is generated than is required to maintain body temperature at a healthful level. Hence, proper air environment is required to permit normal cooling, even in winter. Heating the room air does not heat people; rather it affects the rate at which they lose heat and thereby affects their comfort and health. Since all people do not have the same metabolic rate or wear comparable clothing, some people in a room may feel comfortable while others do not. The acceptable ranges of operative temperatures and relative humidities shown in shaded areas for winter and summer in Fig. 1 were developed by the American Society of Heating, Refrigerating and Air-Conditioning Engineers.

**Fig. 1** Ranges of operative temperature and relative humidity acceptable to at least 80% of sedentary persons in typical summer or winter clothing and doing light activities. In the overlap area, people with summer clothing might feel slightly cool, while those in winter clothing might feel slightly warm.

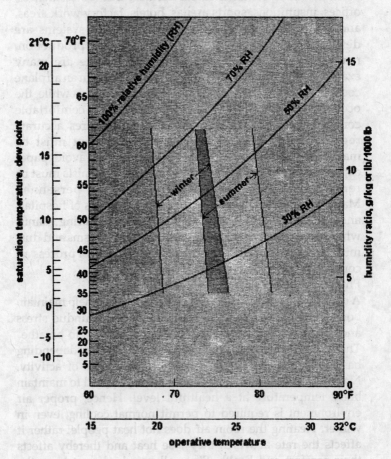

## Human metabolic rate at typical activities*

| Activity | Metabolic rate, met units |
|---|---|
| **Resting** | |
| Sleeping | 0.7 |
| Reclining | 0.8 |
| Seated, quiet | 1.0 |
| Standing, relaxed | 1.2 |
| **Walking (on the level)     mi/h   m/s** | |
| 2     0.89 | 2.0 |
| 3     1.34 | 2.6 |
| 4     1.79 | 3.8 |
| **Miscellaneous occupations** | |
| Bakery (such as cleaning tins, packing boxes) | 1.4-2.0 |
| Brewery (such as filling bottles, loading beer boxes onto belt) | 1.2-2.4 |
| Carpentry | |
| Machine sawing, table | 1.8-2.2 |
| Sawing by hand | 4.0-4.8 |
| Planing by hand | 5.6-6.4 |
| Foundry work | |
| Using a pneumatic hammer | 3.0-3.4 |
| Tending furnaces | 5.0-7.0 |
| Garage work (such as replacing tires, raising cars by jack) | 2.2-3.0 |
| General laboratory work | 1.4-1.8 |
| Machine work | |
| Light (such as electrical industry) | 2.0-2.4 |
| Heavy (such as steel work) | 3.5-4.5 |
| Shop assistant | 2.0 |
| Teacher     1.6 | |
| Watch repairer, seated | 1.1 |
| Vehicle driving | |
| Car     1.5 | |
| Motorcycle | 2.0 |
| Heavy vehicle | 3.2 |
| Aircraft flying routine | 1.4 |
| Instrument landing | 1.8 |
| Combat flying | 2.4 |
| **Domestic work, women** | |
| Housecleaning | 2.0-3.4 |
| Cooking     1.6-2.0 | |

| Washing by hand and ironing | 2.0-3.6 |
| Shopping  1.4-1.8 | |
| Office work | |
| Typing      1.2-1.4 | |
| Miscellaneous office work | 1.1-1.3 |
| Drafting    1.1-1.3 | |
| Leisure activities | |
| Stream fishing | 1.2-2.0 |
| Calisthenics exercise | 3.0-4.0 |
| Dancing, social | 2.4-4.4 |
| Tennis, singles | 3.6-4.6 |
| Squash, singles | 5.0-7.2 |
| Basketball, half court, intramural | 5.0-7.6 |
| Wrestling, competitive or intensive | 7.0-8.7 |
| Golf, swinging and walking | 1.4-2.6 |
| Golf, swinging and golf cart | 1.4-1.8 |

---

*After American Society of Heating, Refrigerating and Air-Conditioning Engineers Standard 55-1981.—chars/dagger/special/dagger/black/med/vsmall/glyph.gif align=bottom>Ranges are for activities which may vary considerably from one place of work or leisure to another or when performed by different people. 1 met = 58.2 W/m$^2$; 50 kcal/h m$^2$; 18.4 Btu/h ft$^2$. Some activities are difficult to evaluate because of differences in exercise intensity and body position.

The comfort chart (Fig. 1) describes average responses to given environmental conditions. Preferences vary considerably from person to person. For instance, in office buildings women may complain of chill or drafts under conditions where men, in different attire, are comfortable. Metabolism rates vary with individuals. Whenever a building budget permits, an engineer designs an air-conditioning system that is flexible enough to allow adjustment by individual occupants of both temperature and air motion in the air-conditioned space. Conditions that would satisfy all persons within the same space have yet to be achieved. See also: Psychrometrics

Control of body temperature is accomplished by control of the emission of energy from the body by radiation, by convection to air currents that impinge on the skin or clothing, by conduction of clothing and objects that are contacted, and by evaporation of moisture in the lungs and of sweat from the skin. Radiant emission from the body is a function of the amount of clothing worn (or blankets used) and the temperature of the surrounding air and objects, so that a body may experience a net loss by radiation to its surroundings or a net gain. Consequently, air-conditioning system operation is affected substantially by the basic construction of the building thermal envelope; cold outer walls induce more body heat loss for the same average room temperature than do warmer walls. Evaporation and convection heat losses are functions of air temperature and velocity. Evaporation is a function, in addition, of relative humidity.

When the amount and type of clothing and the temperature, velocity, and humidity of the air are such that the heat produced by the body is not dissipated at an equal rate, blood temperature begins to rise or fall and discomfort is experienced in the form of fever or chill, in proportion to the departure of body temperature from the normal 98.6°F (37°C) [for individuals this standard may be slightly low or high]. Hence, space conditions to maintain comfort depend upon the degree of human activity in the space, the amount and type of clothing worn, and, to a certain extent, the physical condition of the occupants, because old age or sickness can impair the body's heat-producing and heat-regulating mechanisms.

The heat-dissipating factors of temperature, humidity, air motion, and radiant heat flow must be considered simultaneouly. Within limits, the same amount of comfort (or, more objectively, of heat-dissipating ability) is the result of a combination of these factors in an enclosure. Conditions for constant comfort are related to the operative temperature. The perception of comfort is related to one's metabolic heat production, the transfer of this heat to the environment, and the resulting physiological adjustments and body temperature. The heat transfer is influenced by the environmental air temperature, thermal radiation, air movement, relative humidity, and the personal effects of activity and clothing. The effect of clothing is evaluated by its thermal resistance, or clo value; clo = 0.155 $m^2$ K/W (0.88 $ft^2$ h °F/Btu).

In choosing optimal conditions for comfort and health, knowledge of the energy expended during routine physical activities is necessary, since the production of body heat increases in proportion to exercise intensity. The table gives probable metabolic rates, related to energy costs, for various activities. For an average-size man the met approximates 90 kcal/h (100 W or 360 Btu/h) when sedentary. In the table all energy costs are expressed in multiples of the basic met; they are typical, and are used primarly in engineering planning. For some years, the effective temperature was used to indicate the uniform temperature of a radiantly black enclosure at 50% relative humidity in which an occupant would feel the same comfort, physiological strain, and heat exchange as in the actual environment with the same air motion. The preferred indicator is the operative temperature, the uniform temperature of a radiantly black enclosure in which an occupant would exchange the same amount of heat by radiation plus convection as in the actual nonuniform environment. Operative temperature is the average of the air and mean radiant temperatures weighted by the heat transfer coefficients for convection and radiation. At mean radiant temperatures less than 120°F (50°C) and air speeds of 80 ft/m (0.4 m/s) or less, the operative temperature is approximately the simple average of the air and the mean radiant temperature, and is equal to the adjusted dry bulb temperature.

In practice, most air-conditioning systems for offices, schools, and light-work areas are designed to maintain temperature in the range 68-75°F (20-24°C). In hot weather, in order to minimize the effects of sudden temperature differences when people leave temperature-controlled spaces to go outdoors, higher temperatures are maintained than in cold weather. Lower cold-weather temperatures are used when energy conservation is a factor. Depending on climatic characteristics, in hot weather the relative humidity is reduced to below 50%, while in cold weather it is increased above the 10-15% relative humidity that may occur when no humidification is provided. However, great care must be used in establishing relative humidity limits for each building design and occupancy so that condensation of moisture on and within building components does not create deteriorating conditions, many of which may not be detectable until performance problems occur.

Calculation of loads

Engineering of an air-conditioning system starts with selection of design conditions; air temperature and relative humidity are principal factors. Next, loads on the system are calculated. Finally, equipment is selected and sized to perform the indicated functions and to carry the estimated loads.

Design conditions are selected on the bases discussed above. Each space is analyzed separately. A cooling load will exist when the sum of heat released within the space and transmitted to the space is greater than the loss of heat from the space. A heating load occurs when the heat generated within the space is less than the loss of heat from it. Similar considerations apply to moisture.

Heat generated within the space consists of body heat (see table), heat from all electrical appliances and lights, and heat from other sources such as cooking stoves and industrial ovens. Heat is transmitted through all parts of the space envelope, which includes walls, floor, slab on ground, ceiling, doors, and windows. Whether heat enters or leaves the space depends upon whether the outside surfaces are warmer or cooler than the inside surfaces. The rate at which heat is conducted through the building envelope is a function of the temperature difference across the envelope and the thermal resistance of the envelope (R value). Overall R values depend on materials of construction and their thickness along the path of heat flow, and air spaces with or without reflectances and emittances, and are evaluated for walls and roofs exposed to outdoors, and basements or slab exposed to earth. In some cases, thermal insulations may be added to increase the R value of the envelope.

Solar heat loads are an especially important part of load calculation because they represent a large percentage of heat gain through walls, windows, and roofs, but are very difficult to estimate because solar irradiation is constantly changing. Intensity of radiation varies with the seasons [it rises to 457 Btu/h ft$^2$ (2881 W/m$^2$) in midwinter and drops to 428 Btu/h ft$^2$ (2698 W/m$^2$) in midsummer]. Intensity of solar irradiation also varies with surface orientation. For example, the half-day total for a horizontal surface at 40° north latitude on January 21 is 353 Btu/h ft$^2$ (2225 W/m$^2$) and on June 21 it is 1121 Btu/h ft$^2$ (7067 W/ m$^2$), whereas for a south wall on the same dates comparable data are 815 Btu/h ft$^2$ (5137 W/m$^2$) and 311 Btu/h ft$^2$ (1961 W/m$^2$), a sharp decrease in summer. Intensity also varies with time of day and cloud cover and other atmospheric phenomena. See also: Solar radiation

The way in which solar radiation affects the space load depends also upon whether the rays are transmitted instantly through glass or impinge on opaque walls. If through glass, the effect begins immediately but does not reach maximum intensity until the interior irradiated surfaces have warmed sufficiently to reradiate into the space, warming the air. In the case of irradiated walls and roofs, the effect is as if the outside air temperature were higher than it is. This apparent temperature is called the sol-air temperature, tables of which are available. In calculating all these heating effects, the object is proper sizing and intelligent selection of equipment; hence, a design value is sought which will accommodate maximums. However, when dealing with climatic data, which are statistical historical summaries, record maximums are rarely used. For instance, if in a particular locality the recorded maximum outside temperature was 100°F (38°C), but 95°F (35°C) was exceeded only four times in the past 20 years, 95°F may be chosen as the design summer outdoor temperature for calculation of heat transfer through walls. In practice, engineers use tables of design winter and summer outdoor temperatures which list winter temperatures exceeded more than 99% and 97.5% of the time during the coldest winter months, and summer temperatures not exceeded 1%, 2.5%, and 5% of the warmest months. The designer will select that value which represents the conservatism required for the particular type of occupancy. If the space contains vital functions where impairment by virtue of occasional departures from design space conditions cannot be tolerated, the more severe design outdoor conditions will be selected.

In the case of solar load through glass, but even more so in the case of heat transfer through walls and roof, because outside climate conditions are so variable, there may be a considerable thermal lag. It may take hours before the effect of extreme high or low temperatures on the outside of a thick masonry wall is felt on the interior surfaces and space. In some cases the effect is never felt on the inside, but in all cases the lag exists, exerting a leveling effect on the peaks and valleys of heating and cooling demand; hence, it tends to reduce maximums and can be taken advantage of in reducing design loads.

Humidity as a load on an air-conditioning system is treated by the engineer in terms of its latent heat, that is, the heat required to condense or evaporate the moisture, approximately 1000 Btu/lb (2324 kilojoules/kg) of moisture. People at rest or at light work generate about 200 Btu/h (586 W). Steaming from kitchen activities and moisture generated as a product of combustion of gas flames, or from all drying processes, must be calculated. As with heat, moisture travels through the space envelope, and its rate of transfer is calculated as a function of the difference in vapor pressure across the space envelope and the permeance of the envelope construction.

Years ago engineers and scientists contributed their experiences with moisture migration rates into walls of ordinary houses in ordinary climates; this led to defining a limiting rate of moisture flow that was designated a perm (from permeance). Permeance is the rate of moisture flow through a material or construction as used, whereas permeability is a property of a material that expresses moisture flow rate for a unit thickness. A unit perm was considered the highest rate of water vapor flow into a wall (or roof) that would differentiate the probability of moisture problems from the probability of no moisture problems. As stated above, excessive moisture adversely affects the thermal performance of constructions, and thereby the condition of air for comfort and health of people; in addition, it affects energy waste that could be avoided.

While moisture migrates by diffusion, building designs and the air-conditioning designs must also consider the effects of air infiltration and exfiltration, especially from wind in a particular location.

Another load-reducing factor to be calculated is the diversity among the various spaces within a building or building complex served by a single system. Spaces with east-facing walls experience maximum solar loads when west-facing walls have no solar load. In cold weather, rooms facing south may experience a net heat gain due to a preponderant solar load while north-facing rooms require heat. An interior space, separated from adjoining spaces by partitions, floor, and ceiling across which there is no temperature gradient, experiences only a net heat gain, typically from people and lights. Given a system that can transfer this heat to other spaces requiring heat, the net heating load may be zero, even on cold winter days.

## Air-conditioning systems

A complete air-conditioning system is capable of adding and removing heat and moisture and of filtering airborne substitutes, such as dust and odorants, from the space or spaces it serves. Systems that heat, humidify, and filter only, for control of comfort in winter, are called winter air-conditioning systems; those that cool, dehumidify, and filter only are called summer air-conditioning systems, provided they are fitted with proper controls to maintain design levels of temperature, relative humidity, and air purity.

Design conditions may be maintained by multiple independent subsystems tied together by a single control system. Such arrangements, called split systems, might consist, for example, of hot-water baseboard heating convectors around a perimeter wall to offset window and wall heat losses when required, plus a central cold-air distribution system to pick up heat and moisture gains as required and to provide filtration for dust and odor. See also: Hot-water heating system

Air-conditioning systems are either unitary or built-up. The window or through-the-wall air conditioner (Fig. 2) is an example of a unitary summer air-conditioning system; the entire system is housed in a single package which contains heat removal, dehumidification, and filtration capabilities. When an electric heater is built into it with suitable controls, it functions as a year-round air-conditioning system. Unitary air conditioners are manufactured in capacities as high as 100 tons (1 ton of air conditioning equals 12,000 Btu/h or 76,000 W/m$^2$) and are designed to be mounted conveniently on roofs, on the ground, or other convenient location, where they can be connected by ductwork to the conditioned space.

Built-up or field-erected systems are composed of factory-built subassemblies interconnected by means such as piping, wiring, and ducting during final assembly on the building site. Their capacities range up to thousands of tons of refrigeration and millions of Btu per hour of heating. Most large buildings are so conditioned.

Another important and somewhat parallel distinction can be made between incremental and central systems. An incremental system serves a single space; each space to be conditioned has its own, self-contained heating-cooling-dehumidifying-filtering unit. Central systems serve many or all of the conditioned spaces in a building. They range from small, unitary packaged systems serving single-family residences to large, built-up or field-erected systems serving large buildings.

Fig. 2 Schematic of room air conditioner. (After American Society of Heating, Refrigerating, and Air-Conditioning Engineers, Inc., Guide and Data Book, 1967)

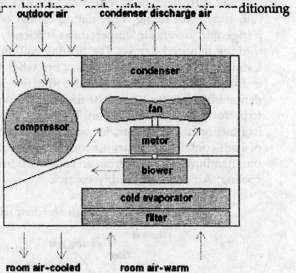

system which is complete except for a refrigeration and a heating source, are tied to a central plant that distributes chilled water and hot water or steam, the interconnection is referred to as a district heating and cooling system. This system is especially useful for campuses, medical complexes, and office complexes under a single management.

Air temperature in a space can be controlled by radiant panels in floor, walls, or ceiling to emit or absorb energy, depending on panel temperature. Such is the radiant panel system. However, to control humidity and air purity, and in most systems for controlling air temperature, a portion of the air in the space is withdrawn, processed, and returned to the space to mix with the remaining air. In the language of the engineer, a portion of the room air is returned (to an air-handling unit) and, after being conditioned, is supplied to the space. A portion of the return air is spilled (exhausted to the outdoors) while an equal quantity (of outdoor air) is brought into the system and mixed with the remaining return air before entering the air handler. See also: Panel heating and cooling

Typically, the air-handling unit contains a filter, a cooling coil, a heating coil, and a fan in a suitable casing (Fig. 3). The filter removes dust from both return and outside air. The cooling coil, either containing recirculating chilled water or boiling refrigerant, lowers air temperature sufficiently to dehumidify it to the required degree. The heating coil, in winter, serves a straightforward heating function, but when the cooling coil is functioning, it serves to raise the temperature of the dehumidified air (to reheat it) to the exact temperature required to perform its cooling function. The air handler may perform its function, in microcosm, in room units in each space as part of a self-contained, unitary air conditioner, or it may be a huge unit handling return air from an entire building. See also: Air cooling; Air filter; Humidity control.

Fig. 3   Schematic of central air-handling unit.

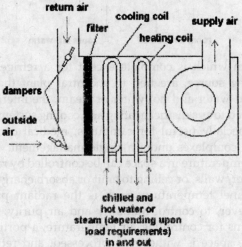

## Air cooling

Lowering of air temperature for comfort, process control, or food preservation. Air and water vapor occur together in the atmosphere. The mixture is commonly cooled by direct convective heat transfer of its internal energy (sensible heat) to a surface or medium at lower temperature. In the most compact arrangement, transfer is through a finned (extended surface) coil, metallic and thin, inside of which is circulating either chilled water, antifreeze solution, brine, or boiling refrigerant. The fluid acts as the heat receiver. Heat transfer can also be directly to a wetted surface, such as waterdroplets in an air washer or a wet pad in an evaporative cooler.

## Evaporative cooling

For evaporative cooling, nonsaturated air is mixed with water. Some of the sensible heat transfers from the air to the evaporating water. The heat then returns to the airstream as latent heat of water vapor. The exchange is thermally isolated (adiabatic) and continues until the air is saturated and air and water temperatures are equal. With suitable apparatus, air temperature approaches within a few degrees of the theoretical limit, the wet-bulb temperature. Evaporative cooling is frequently carried out by blowing relatively dry air through a wet mat (Fig. 1). The technique is employed for air cooling of machines where higher humidities can be tolerated; for cooling of industrial areas where high humidities are required, as in textile mills; and for comfort cooling in hot, dry climates, where partial saturation results in cool air at relatively low humidity.

Fig. 1 Schematic view of simple evaporative air cooler.

## Air washer

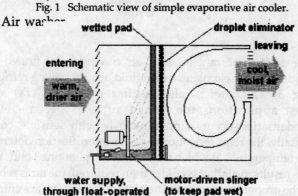

wetted pad

droplet eliminator

leaving

entering

warm, drier air

cool, moist air

water supply, through float-operated fill valve

motor-driven slinger (to keep pad wet)

In the evaporative cooler the air is constantly changed and the water is recirculated, except for that portion which has evaporated and which must be made up. Water temperature remains at the adiabatic saturation (wet-bulb) temperature. If water temperature is controlled, as by refrigeration, the leaving air temperature can be controlled within wide limits. Entering warm, moist air can be cooled below its dew point so that, although it leaves close to saturation, it leaves with less moisture per unit of air than when it entered. An apparatus to accomplish this is called an air washer (Fig. 2). It is used in many industrial and comfort air-conditioning systems, and performs the added functions of cleansing the airstream of dust and of gases that dissolve in water, and in winter, through the addition of heat to the water, of warming and humidifying the air.

Fig. 2  Schematic of air washer.

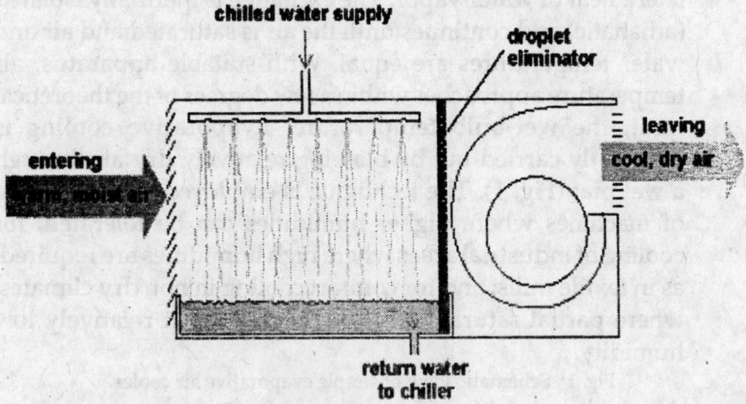

chilled water supply

droplet eliminator

entering

leaving cool, dry air

return water to chiller

### Air-cooling coils

The most important form of air cooling is by finned coils, inside of which circulates a cold fluid or cold, boiling refrigerant (Fig. 3). The latter is called a direct-expansion (DX) coil. In most applications the finned surfaces become wet as condensation occurs simultaneously with sensible cooling. Usually, the required amount of dehumidification determines the temperature at which the surface is maintained and, where this results in air that is colder than required, the air is reheated to the proper temperature. Droplets of condensate are entrained in the airstream, removed by a suitable filter (eliminator), collected in a drain pan, and wasted.

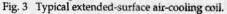

Fig. 3 Typical extended-surface air-cooling coil.

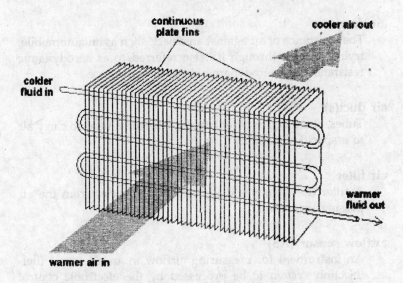

### Air Data Computer (ADC)

A primary navigation data source. A navigation sensor based on atmospheric data sensors; usually measures static pressure, dynamic pressure, and outside air temperature; sometimes computes other atmospheric data, such as indicated airspeed, Mach number, calibrated airspeed As a guidance mode, ADC is least accurate of the listed modes and is used only as a last resort.

### Air data dead reckoning (ADDR)

Dead reckoning navigation based on simple instruments as source (barometric altimeter, magnetic compass, airspeed indicator, known wind conditions); sometimes called dead reckoning.

### air delivery system

The component that contains the air ducts, doors, blower, evaporator core, heater core, and controls that deliver air to the interior via the various outlets.

### air door

A door in the duct system that controls the flow of air in the air conditioner and/or heater.

### air drag

The resistance of air against an object, such as an automobile, trying to pass through it. Also referred to as aerodynamic resistance and aerodynamic drag, air resistance.

### air duct(s)

Tubes, channels, or other tubular structures used to carry air to a specific location.

### air filter

A filter that removes dust, dirt, and particles from the air passing through it.

### airflow sensor (AS)

An instrument for measuring airflow in an electronic fuel-injection system to be processed by the electronic control module with other sensory data to calibrate the air/fuel mixture.

### air foil

The inverted wing of a race car designed to increase downward aerodynamic force and, with it, vehicle traction.

### air/fuel mixture

The proportion of air to fuel provided by a carburetor or fuel-injection system.

### air/fuel ratio (A/F, AFR)

The relative proportions of air and fuel entering an engine's cylinders as produced by the carburetor or fuel-injection system; the measure of the amount of air and fuel needed for proper combustion. The ideal or stoichiometric ratio for gasoline is 14.7: 1 air to fuel by weight. A higher ratio would contain more air and less fuel, and would be considered a lean mixture. A lower ratio with more fuel and less air would be a rich mixture. The air/fuel ratio is determined by the orifice size of the main jets inside a carburetor, the dwell duration of the mixture control solenoid inside a feedback carburetor, or the orifice opening and fuel pulse duration of a fuel injector.

**air gap**
A small space between parts that are mated magnetically or electrically.

**Air-ground ranging (AGR)**
Straight-line distance from the aircraft to a point on the ground.

**air hoist**
A hoisting device using compressed air in a cylinder, acting against a piston, with suitable outside connections, such as a hook.

**air horn**
1. A horn that is actuated by compressed air.
2. A tubular passage containing the choke valves in the atmospheric side of a carburetor venturi through which the incoming air must pass.

**altitude compensation system**
An altitude barometric switch and solenoid used to provide better driveability at more than 4,000 feet (1,219 meters) above sea level.

**altitude**
Height, usually with respect to the terrain below (radar altitude, feet above closest dirt) or fixed earth reference (barometric altitude, feet above mean sea level); *Symbols:* h; *Typical Units:* ft; *Dimensions:* Length.

**altitude error**
A basic output from guidance to flight director, indicating the difference between actual altitude and desired altitude; *Symbols:* DELTA h; *Typical Units:* ft; *Dimensions:* Length.

**altitude error scale factor (KZSF)**
> A guidance control law parameter, generated by the vertical guidance modes; varies control authority of vertical guidance.

**altitude integral gain (KALTINT)**
> A guidance control law parameter, generated by the vertical guidance modes; varies control authority of the altitude integral in vertical guidance, to reduce steady-state errors in altitude error *Typical Units:* ft; *Dimensions:* Length.

**altitude integral input (ALTINTVAL)**
> A guidance control law parameter, generated by the vertical guidance modes; a reference altitude for reducing steady-state errors in altitude error *Typical Units:* ft; *Dimensions:* Length.

**altitude integral limit (INTMAGLIM)**
> A guidance control law parameter, generated by the vertical guidance modes; limits the magnitude of altitude integral value *Typical Units:* ft; *Dimensions:* Length.

**alum**
> A crystallized double sulfate of aluminum (Al) and potassium (K).
> More commonly, an abbreviation for aluminum (Al).

**aluminized coating**
> A metal spray process used to coat engine components subject to high temperatures for long periods of time to increase heat dissipation to the ambient atmosphere.

**aluminized valve**
> A valve with a thin layer of aluminum sprayed on the valve face and, sometimes, on the top of the valve head to provide a thin, hard, corrosion-resistant coating.

**aluminum (Al)**
> A versatile engineering and construction material that is light in weight,

### aluminum cylinder block

An engine block cast of aluminum or aluminum alloy, usually with cast iron sleeves installed as cylinder bores.

### aluminum-killed steel

Steel alloy in which aluminum has been added to kill it in the molten stage and refine its grain structure. A process of stopping molten steel from bubbling and combining with oxygen after being poured into ingots. Also see silicone-killed steel.

### amber lens

The color lens used for turn signals and flashers on modern motor vehicles.

### ambient air

The air that surrounds an object.

### ambient air temperature

The temperature of the air that surrounds an object.

### ambient compressor switch

An electrical switch that energizes the air conditioner compressor clutch when the outside ambient air temperature is 47°F (8.3°C) or above. Similarly, the switch turns off the compressor when the air temperature drops below 32°F (0°C).

### ambient sensor

A sensor used on computerized automatic temperature-control systems that senses the outside air temperature and uses this information as an input to the system; a thermistor used in automatic temperature-control units to sense ambient temperature. Also see thermistor.

### ambient switch

A switch used to control compressor operation by turning it ON or OFF. The switch is regulated by ambient temperature.

### ambient temperature

The temperature of the air surrounding a vehicle.

**ambient temperature sensor**
> A sensor that measures the outside air temperature as it enters
> the evaporator.

**American Automobile Association (AAA)**
> A motor club providing travel information, emergency road
> service, and other services to its members.

**American Automobile Manufacturers Association (AAMA)**
> A trade association of Chrysler, Ford, and General Motors that
> sponsors research, disseminates information, and lobbies on
> behalf of the American automotive industry in the United
> States.

**American City Racing League**
> A racing series sanctioned by the Sports Car Club of America
> (SCCA) for three-car teams representing specific cities and
> running 2000 spec cars with 2.0 liter Ford engines.

**American Hot Rod Association (AHRA)**
> A drag-racing sanctioning body that is no longer in existence.

**American International Automobile Dealers Association
(AIADA)**
> An association of auto dealers and their employees who sell
> and service automobiles manufactured in the United States
> and abroad.

**ammeter**
> An instrument used to determine the amount of amperage
> (current draw) in a circuit by the strength of the magnetic field
> that is created by the current flowing through the wire.

**ammeter shunt**
> A low-resistance conductor used to increase the range of an
> ammeter. It is shunted (placed in parallel) across the ammeter
> movement and carries the majority of the current.

### ampacity
The current-carrying capacity of conductors or equipment, expressed in amperes.

### amperage
The amount of current, expressed in amperes.

### amperage capacity
An indication of the length of time a battery can produce an amperage, or the amount of amperage that a battery can produce before being discharged.

### ampere (A)
A unit of measure for current.

### amp/hour
Amperes per hour; a standard measure for a rate of current flow.

### anaerobic sealants
A chemical sealant placed on a gasket in an engine to aid in sealing and to position the gasket during installation.

### anaerobic sealer
Liquid or gel that bonds two parts together in the absence of air.

### analog computer
A computer that measures continuously changing conditions, such as temperature and pressure, and converts them into quantities.

### analog instrument
An instrument having a needle on a dial used for taking measurements, such as temperature and engine RPM.

### analog-to-digital converter
Mechanical or electrical device used to convert continuous analog signals to discrete digital numbers.

**anaroid tube**
A thermo-mechanical device in a fuel-injection system that regulates the amount of fuel being injected according to differences in temperature and pressure in the intake manifold.

**anchor**
A slang expression for brakes.
A mounting point on a vehicle structure for a stressed, non-structural component, such as a seat belt or a seat.

**aneroid bellows**
An accordion-shaped temperature sensor charged with a small amount of volatile liquid. Temperature change causes the bellows to contract or expand, which, in turn, opens or closes a switch, such as a thermostat.

**angle block**
A cylinder block that does not have a deck at 90 degrees to the cylinders.

**angle mill**
A machining operation to mill the deck surface at a shallow angle on the exhaust side of the engine block in order to increase the compression ratio by decreasing the combustion chamber volume.

**angle plug head**
A cylinder head having spark plugs that are angled toward the exhaust valves.

**angle of attack**
The difference between pitch and the air-referenced flight path angle; the angle between the aircraft center line and the airspeed vector in the vertical plane, positive when the nose is up; *Symbols:* alpha; *Typical Units:* rad, deg.

**angular acceleration**
Rate of change of angular velocity, either scalar or vector, often with subscripts such as XYZ to denote the coordinate

frame; time derivative of angular position; time integral of angular acceleration; *Symbols:* alpha; *Typical Units:* rad/s-squared; *Dimensions:* 1/Time-squared.

## Antifriction bearing

A machine element that permits free motion between moving and fixed parts. Antifrictional bearings are essential to mechanized equipment; they hold or guide moving machine parts and minimize friction and wear. Friction wastefully consumes energy, and wear changes dimensions until a machine becomes useless.

Simple bearings

In its simplest form a bearing consists of a cylindrical shaft, called a journal, and a mating hole, serving as the bearing proper. Ancient bearings were made of such materials as wood, stone, leather, or bone, and later of metal. It soon became apparent for this type of bearing that a lubricant would reduce both friction and wear and prolong the useful life of the bearing. Convenient lubricants were those of animal, vegetable, or marine origin such as mutton tallow, lard, goose grease, fish oils, castor oils, and cottonseed oil. Egyptian chariot wheels show evidence of the use of mutton tallow for bearing lubrication.

The use of mineral oils dates back principally to the discovery of Drake's well at Titusville, Pennsylvania, in 1859. Petroleum oils and greases are now generally used for lubricants, sometimes containing soap and solid lubricants such as graphite or molybdenum disulfide, talc, and similar substances.

Materials

The greatest single advance in the development of improved bearing materials took place in 1839, when I. Babbitt obtained a United States patent for a bearing metal with a special alloy. This alloy, largely tin, contained small amounts of antimony, copper, and lead. This and similar materials have made excellent bearings. They have a silvery appearance and are generally described as white metals or as Babbitt metals. For many decades they have served as the measure of excellence against which other bearing materials have been compared.

See also: Alloy

Wooden bearings are still used, however, for limited

applications in light-duty machinery and are frequently made of hard maple which has been impregnated with a neutral oil. Wooden bearings made of lignum vitae, the hardest and densest of all woods, are still used. Lignum vitae is native only to the Caribbean area. This wood has a density of approximately 80 lb/ft³ (1.3 g/cm³) and has a resin content of some 30% by volume; thus it is remarkably self-lubricating. The grain is closely interwoven, giving the material high resistance to wear and compression and making it difficult to split. Applications are found in chemical processing and food industries where lignum vitae wood can successfully resist the destructive action of mild acids, alkalies, oils, bleaching compounds, liquid phosphorus, and many food, drug, and cosmetic compounds.

About 1930 a number of significant developments began to occur in the field of bearing metals. Some of the most successful heavy-duty bearing metals are now made of several distinct compositions combined in one bearing. This approach is based on the widely accepted theory of friction, which is that the best possible bearing material would be one which is fairly hard and resistant but which has an overlay of a soft metal that is easily deformed. Figure 1 shows actual bearings in which graphite, carbon, plastic, and rubber have been incorporated into a number of designs illustrating some of the material combinations that are presently available.

Fig. 1   Bearings with (*a*) graphite, (*b*) wood, plastic, and nylon (*after J. J. O'Connor, ed., Power's Handbook on Bearings and Lubrication, McGraw-Hill, 1951*); (*c*) rubber (*Lucian Q. Moffitt, Inc.*).

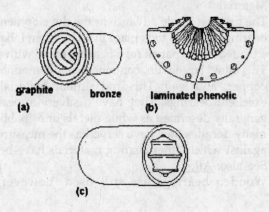

graphite          bronze      laminated phenolic
(a)                 (b)

(c)

Rubber has proved to be a surprisingly good bearing material, especially under circumstances in which abrasives may be present in the lubricant. Rubber bearings have found wide application in the stern-tube bearings of ships, on dredge cutter heads, on a number of centrifugal pumps, and for shafting bearings on deep-well pumps. The rubber used is a tough resilient compound similar in texture to that in an automobile tire. These bearings are especially effective with water lubrication, which serves as both coolant and lubricant. Cast iron is one of the oldest bearing materials. Iron bearings were used in ancient India and China. With the advent of more complicated machinery during the industrial revolution, cast iron became a popular bearing material. It is still used where the duty is relatively light.

Porous metal bearings are frequently used when plain metal bearings are impractical because of lack of space or inaccessibility for lubrication. These bearings have voids of 16-36% of the volume of the bearing. These voids are filled with a lubricant by a vacuum technique. During operation they supply a limited amount of lubricant to the sliding surface between the journal and the bearing. In general, these bearings are satisfactory for light loads and moderate speeds.

In some areas recent research has shown that, surprisingly enough, very hard materials when rubbed together provide satisfactory bearing characteristics for unusual applications. Materials such as Stellite, Carboloy, Colmonoy, Hastelloy, and Alundum are used. Because of their hardness, these bearings must be extremely smooth and the geometry must be precise for there is little possibility that these materials will conform to misalignment through the process of wear.

Lubricants

Petroleum oils and greases have been fortified by chemical additives so that they are effective in reducing wear of highly stressed machine elements such as gears and cams. The additives include lead naphthenate, chlorine, sulfur, phosphorus, or similar materials. In general, compounds containing these elements are used as additives to form__chars/-/special/mdash/black/med/base/glyph.gif align=bottom>through reaction with the metal surfaces__chars/-/special/mdash/black/med/base/

glyph.gif align=bottom>chlorides, sulfides, and phosphides which have relatively low shear strength and protect the surface from wear and abrasion.

The method of supplying the lubricant and the quantity of lubricant which is fed to the bearing by the supplying device will often be the greatest factor in establishing performance characteristics of the bearing. For example, if no lubricant is present, the journal and bearing will rub against each other in the dry state. Both friction and wear will be relatively high. The coefficient of friction of a steel shaft rubbing in a bronze bearing, for example, may be about 0.3 for the dry state. If lubricant is present even in small quantities, the surfaces become contaminated by this material whether it is an oil or a fat, and depending upon its chemical composition the coefficient of friction may be reduced to about 0.1. Now if an abundance of lubricant is fed to the bearing so that there is an excess flowing out of the bearing, it is possible to develop a self-generating pressure film in the clearance space as indicated in Fig. 2.

Fig. 3   Hydrodynamic fluid-film pressures in a journal bearing.

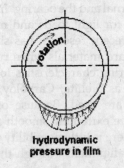

hydrodynamic
pressure in film

Figure 3 shows a schematic of a simple test device which indicates the pressure developed in the converging clearance space of the journal bearing. The position shown where the center of the journal is eccentric to the center of the bearing is that position which the journal naturally assumes when loaded. If the supply of lubricant is insufficient to fill the clearance space completely or if the load and speed of operation are not favorable to the generation of a complete fluid film, the film will be incomplete and there will be areas within the bearing which do not have the benefit of a fluid film to keep the rubbing surfaces apart. These areas will be only lightly contaminated by lubricant.

**Fig. 3** Schematic of a test device for determining pressure in a journal bearing. 1 psi = 6.9 kPa.

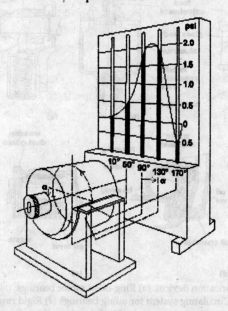

The types of oiling devices that usually result in insufficient feed to generate a complete fluid film are, for example, oil cans, drop-feed oilers, waste-packed bearings, and wick and felt feeders.

Oiling schemes that provide an abundance of lubrication are oil rings, bath lubrication, and forced-feed circulating supply systems. The coefficient of friction for a bearing with a complete fluid film may be as low as 0.001. Figure 4 shows typical devices which do not usually supply a lubricant in sufficient quantity to permit the generation of a complete fluid film. Figure 5 shows devices in which the flow rate is generally sufficient to permit a fluid film to form. Figure 5a, b, and d shows some typical forms of fluid-film journal bearings. The table shows current design practice for a number of bearings in terms of mean bearing pressure. This is the pressure applied to the bearing by the external load and is based on the projected area of the bearing.

Fig. 4   Schematic showing some of the typical lubrication devices. (*a, b*) Drop-feed oilers. (*c*) Felt-wick oiler for small electric motors. (*d*) Waste-packed armature bearing. (*e*) Waste-packed railroad bearing.

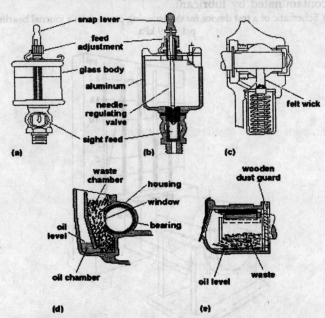

**(a)**            **(b)**            **(c)**

**(d)**                              **(e)**

Fig. 5   Lubrication devices. (*a*) Ring-oiled motor bearings. (*b*) Collar-oiled bearing, (*c*) Circulating system for oiling bearings (*d*) Rigid ring-oiling pillow block

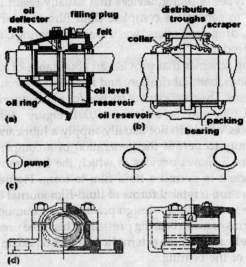

**(a)**                              **(b)**

**(c)**

**(d)**

**arnoid hydrocarbons**
Compounds having carbons linked in a closed ring by alternating single and double bonds.

**articulated vehicle**
Large trucks or buses with two or more wheeled units, so designed for ease of cornering.

**articulating upper coupler**
A bolster plate kingpin arrangement that is not rigidly attached to the trailer but provides articulation and/or oscillation about an axis parallel to the rear axle of the trailer.

**ASA**
An abbreviation for the Automotive Service Association.

**asbestos**
A fiber mineral that is heat resistant and nonburning. Once used in brake linings, gaskets, and clutch facings, it is no longer used due to health hazards.

**Asbestos Information Association (AIA)**
An association to provide industry-wide information on asbestos and health, and on industry efforts to eliminate existing hazards.

**ASE**
An abbreviation and registered trademark of the National Institute for Automotive Service Excellence.

**ASIA**
An abbreviation for the Automotive Service Industry Association.

**A-shim**
A valve spring-adjuster insert with a thickness of 0.060 inch (1.524 mm) used to balance spring pressure and to correct installed height.

**ASME**

An abbreviation for the American Society of Mechanical Engineers.

**aspect ratio**

Also known as tire profile. A measurement of a tire; the percentage of the tire's height to the width.

**asphalt eater**

A top-performing drag car.

**aspirator**

A device that uses suction to move air, accomplished by a differential in air pressure; a one-way valve attached to the exhaust system of an engine that admits air during periods of vacuum between exhaust pressure pulses. Used to help oxidize hydrocarbon (HC) and carbon monoxide (CO), and to supply additional air that the catalytic converter may require. Can be used instead of a belt-driven, air-injection pump in some applications.

**aspirator valve**

A device used to draw out fluids by suction. In this case, a pollution device is used to draw fresh air by suction into the exhaust flow to reduce emissions.

**assembly**

Any unit made up of two or more parts.

**assembly line communications link**

An electrical connector used to check a vehicle's operating system while it is still on the assembly line.

**assembly line data link**

The information processed for use in assembly-line diagnostics.

**assembly lube**

A special lubricant used to coat parts that rub or rotate against each other during initial assembly.

**Association of International Automobile Manufactures (AIAM)**
A trade association of United States subsidiaries of international automobile companies.

**ASTE**
Abbreviation for American Society of Test Engineers.

**ASTM**
Abbreviation for American Society of Testing and Materials.

**astronomical latitude**
Latitude measured with respect to vector of apparent gravity; *Compare:* geocentric latitude, geodetic latitude; *Symbols:* Phi sub A; *Typical Units:* rad, deg,DMS.

**asymmetrical cam**
A camshaft having different profiles for the intake and exhaust lobes.

**asymmetrical rear-leaf spring**
A spring on which the rear axle is not located in its center.

**atmospheric data**
Environmental data related to the atmosphere at some point of interest.

**atmospheric ozone**
As ultraviolet (UV) rays from the sun reach Earth, they are combined with smog and other pollutants to produce atmospheric ozone. Atmospheric ozone, unlike stratospheric ozone, is considered harmful. Whenever possible it is to be avoided.

**auto control**
Another term used for automatic control.

**auto ignition**
Short for automatic ignition.

**automatic**
Having the power of self-motion, self-moving or self-acting.

**automatic adjuster**
A drum-brake mechanism that adjusts the lining clearance as wear occurs. It is commonly actuated on reverse stops or when the parking brake is set.

**automatic chassis lubrication (ACL)**
A system where the chassis is automatically lubricated at predetermined intervals.

**automatic choke**
A mechanism that positions the choke valve automatically in accordance with engine temperature.

**automatic control**
A dial on the instrument panel that is set at a desired temperature level to control the condition of the air automatically.
Any system that reacts to a predetermined condition rather than responding to external commands.
Also known as auto control.

**automatic door locks**
A passive system used to lock all doors when the required conditions are met. Many systems lock the doors when the gear selector is placed in drive, the ignition switch is in RUN, and all doors are properly shut.

**Automatic Direction Finding (ADF)**
A basic guidance mode, providing lateral guidance to a radio station. Equipment that determines bearing to a radio station.

**Automatic flight control system (AFCS)**
An automated system for controlling the primary flight controls, often with built-in functions for guidance and flight director, and sometimes radio navigation; many flight control systems include basic instruments similar to a AHRS; many

flight control systems accept flight director inputs so that its radio navigation, guidance, and flight director can be bypassed.

## automatic temperature control (ATC)
An air-conditioner control system designed to maintain a pre-selected, in-car temperature and humidity level automatically.

## automatic tensioning
The constant tension of a device, maintained at a proper value by some automatic means, to minimize the attention required.

## automatic transmission (AT – A/T)
A transmission in which gear ratios are changed automatically.

## automatic transmission cooler
A device, often found in the radiator, through which automatic transmission fluid circulates to be cooled by surrounding air or engine coolant.

## automatic transmission fluid (ATF)
A red, petroleum-based fluid used to transfer power and control, lubricate, cool, and clean the automatic transmission.

## Automatic Transmission Rebuilders Association (ATRA)
A trade association for transmission repair shops, technicians, and suppliers of transmission repair equipment, parts, and tools.

## automation
Semi-automatic or automatic material handlers, loaders, unloaders, and other labor-saving devices.
Automatic cycle control of machines or equipment by tracer, cam, plugboard, numerical control, or computer.
The application of machinery and equipment to perform and control semi-automatically or automatically and continuously all operations in a manufacturing plant.

## Automobile

A self-propelled land vehicle, usually having four wheels and an internal combustion engine, used primarily for personal transportation. Other types of motor vehicles include buses, which carry large numbers of commercial passengers, and medium- and heavy-duty trucks, which carry heavy or bulky loads of freight or other goods and materials. Instead of being carried on a truck, these loads may be placed on a semitrailer, and sometimes also a trailer, forming a tractor-trailer combination which is pulled by a truck tractor.

### Design

The basic design of the automobile was standardized by 1908, when the Ford Motor Company began production of the Model T. A metal frame served as the main structural member that supported the power train and body. The frame was supported through springs by four wheels and tires. The engine was mounted at the front of the vehicle and transmitted power to the two rear wheels. The body was open, providing little protection from the weather.

By the early 1930s, most automobiles had a closed body made of stamped steel parts that were welded together before attachment to the frame. Improved versions of the front-engine rear-wheel-drive power train dominated automotive production into the 1970s. Until then, this basic configuration was never seriously challenged, although some vehicles had either front-engine front-wheel drive or rear-engine rear-wheel drive.

In the United States, the change from rear drive to front drive was largely necessitated by three acts passed by Congress which established new laws covering automotive air pollution, automotive safety, and automotive fuel economy. The solutions to problems of automotive air pollution and safety were often add-on devices that allowed the conventional automobile to be manufactured in compliance with the new regulations. However, the additional weight and action of some of these devices reduced fuel economy.

When compliance with fuel-economy standards also became a design objective, automotive stylists and engineers began redesigning the car by reducing vehicle weight, downsizing new models, using smaller engines, and changing to lighter, stronger materials. The result was an evolutionary redesign that allowed continuing production while the required new parts and vehicles were developed and phased into each manufacturer's passenger-car fleet.

## Automotive air pollution

Historically, the design and manufacture of automotive vehicles in the United States was an unregulated industry. In 1955, the Department of Health, Education, and Welfare was instructed to begin a study of air pollution. By 1962, the automobile engine had been identified as the source of more than 40% of airborne pollutants, making the automobile the largest single contributor to air pollution. See also: Air pollution

In 1963, Congress passed the Clean Air Act which, together with its subsequent amendments, directed the Environmental Protection Agency (EPA) to promulgate automotive emission standards and to regulate automotive engine fuels and fuel additives. Because of unusual air-pollution problems in Los Angeles, the Clean Air Act permitted the state of California to set more stringent standards than the rest of the nation. See also: Diesel fuel; Gasoline

To comply with automotive emission standards, emission-control devices were developed to reduce or eliminate air pollutants from the engine crankcase, engine exhaust gas, and fuel tank and carburetor. However, some devices reduced fuel economy as well as emissions, resulting in 1968-1974 automobiles having worse fuel economy than earlier models. In 1973, however, the EPA moved toward requiring automobile engines to run on unleaded gasoline (tetraethyllead was formerly used as an additive for motor fuels to reduce engine knock). Beginning in 1975, a stepped phase-down limited the amount of tetraethyllead allowed in gasoline. Tetraethyllead impairs the operation of some engine emission-control devices and, after the additive becomes airborne in the engine exhaust gas, creates a human and environmental health hazard. See also: Lead; Toxicology

## Automotive safety

During the early 1960s, traffic deaths in the United States approached 50,000 per year. Congress began passing legislation in an attempt to reverse the upward trend. The National Traffic and Motor Vehicle Safety Act (1966) required that all new motor vehicles sold in the United States be manufactured in compliance with Federal Motor Vehicle Safety Standards. The first 20 such standards were issued in 1967 and became mandatory on all 1968 models.

Automotive fuel economy

In 1973, Arab nations imposed a total ban on oil exports to the United States. This resulted in a shortage of gasoline and diesel fuel, and caused a consumer demand for smaller cars which were lighter and more fuel-efficient. As the limited amount of fuel that was available rapidly increased in price, the larger, more powerful rear-drive cars built by manufacturers in the United States were gradually replaced by smaller, more fuel-efficient cars imported from Europe and Japan.

To help reduce the dependence of the United States on imported oil, Congress passed the Energy Policy and Conservation Act (1975), which established corporate average fuel economy standards to be met by new cars produced by each automotive manufacturer. To essentially double the fuel economy of the nation's passenger-car fleet in 10 years, Congress established a 1985 corporate average fuel economy standard of 27.5 mi/gal (2 km/liter). This could be achieved by the manufacturers' producing smaller, lighter cars powered by smaller engines.

Weight was reduced by redesigning the basic vehicle structure, eliminating excess material, and continuing the change to lighter and stronger materials. Fuel economy was further improved by introducing more aerodynamic body styles, reducing rolling resistance, and reducing friction and power losses in engines and other components. To maximize these gains, most new car designs had front drive with a transversely mounted integrated power train in which the engine, transmission, final drive, and differential form a single unit. By the 1980s, the downsized front-engine front-drive car had become the most fuel-efficient and widely produced automobile design. However, some data indicated that the new lighter and smaller car had higher personal injury claims and damage repair costs after a collision than the full-size car.

Manufacturing

In automobile manufacturing, production is the making of the thousands of parts, subsystems, and modular assemblies that comprise the automobile, while assembly is the fitting together of these components. Typical assembly of a passenger car begins when the steel pieces that form the side openings for mounting the doors are assembled and spot-welded together by robot welders. The side assemblies are then welded to the underbody, which consists of pieces of galvanized steel that have been welded together to form the floor pan, engine compartment, and luggage compartment. Welding helps prevent noise__chars/-/special/mdash/black/med/base/glyph.gif align=bottom>squeaks, rattles, and vibration__chars/-/special/mdash/black/med/base/glyph.gif align=bottom>that could be caused later by parts moving while the vehicle is on the road. Roof, quarter panels, doors, deck lid, and hood are also welded during fabrication so that a minimum of mechanical fasteners is required.

The body assembly is dipped in a phosphate bath to clean any debris from the surface and then submerged in an anticorrosion solution, such as zinc phosphate. Fillers and sealers are applied to body joints, seams, and cavities that might leak under stress and collect or admit moisture. Sound-deadening material and additional sealer and primer are applied where necessary. A chip-resistant urethane coating is sprayed onto the lower body to provide extra protection against stones flying up from the road. See also: Metal coatings

Robot painters apply the main color, while workers paint spot areas on the body. The paint is sealed with a clear coating to produce a high gloss finish. The hard trim, which includes the instrument panel, steering column, weather stripping, and body glass, is installed. Then, after testing for water leakage, the soft trim is installed. This includes carpeting over a layer of sound-deadening material, seats, door pads, roof insulation, and upholstery. Adhesive bonding may be used, especially when joining various types of nonmetal parts.

The body moves along an assembly line that is above a conveyor line on which the engine and other chassis components are moving (Fig. 1). The chassis is the complete operable vehicle, but without the body. A manufacturer's designation for a specific chassis is often called a platform. Changing outside body panels and interiors allows different models to be built on the same platform. All models built on that platform have the same tread width, but wheelbase may vary.

Fig. 1   Final assembly of the automobile, as the engine and chassis are raised into position and fastened to the body.

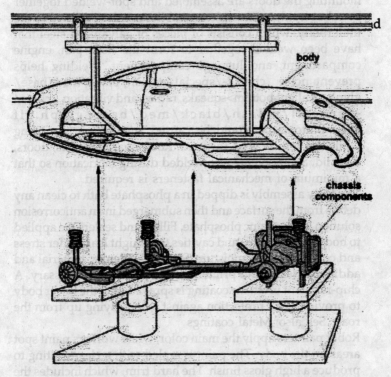

As the engine, complete with transmission or transaxle and exhaust system, is prepared for installation, the fuel tank and bumpers may be fitted to the body. Final assembly occurs when the engine and chassis are raised into position, mounting bolts are installed, and the wheel-and-tire assemblies are attached. Wheel alignment is tested under simulated road conditions as the vehicle undergoes final inspection and drive-away for delivery to a dealer or distribution center.

**Body**

The automobile body is the assembly of sheet-metal, fiberglass, plastic, or composite-material panels together with windows, doors, seats, trim and upholstery, glass, and other parts that form enclosures for the passenger, engine, and luggage compartments. The assembled body structure may attach through rubber mounts to a separate or full frame (body-on-frame construction), or the body and frame may be integrated (unitized-body construction). In the latter method, the frame, body parts, and floor pan are welded together to form a single unit that has energy-absorbing front and rear structures, and anchors for the engine, suspension, steering, and power-train components. A third type of body construction is the space frame which is made of welded steel stampings. Similar to the tube chassis and roll cage combination used in race-car construction, non-load-carrying plastic outer panels fasten to the space frame to form the body. See also: Composite material; Sheet-metal forming; Welded joint

Size and style

Automobiles are built in several sizes and body styles and may be further classified according to the number of doors and the intended usage. Basic body styles include the hatchback, two-door coupe or sedan, roadster, convertible, four-door sedan, and station wagon. Passenger-car sizes range from the largest full-size car to the compact and small sizes. Light-duty trucks, which include pickups, suburbans, vans, minivans, and sport-utility vehicles, also are available in various sizes.

Many full-size cars are two- or four-door sedans that seat from four to six and have a separate luggage compartment. Some smaller cars are hatchbacks, which have two or four doors, no separate luggage compartment, and a rear lid that lifts up for access to the rear of the passenger compartment. For carrying cargo in a hatchback the available space may be enlarged by folding down the rear seat. The station wagon has two or three seats, and a cargo area that may be enlarged by folding down the rear seat in a two-seat wagon, and the center and rear seats in some three-seat wagons.

Roof options

Several roof options are available, including the vinyl roof, popup sunroof, electric slide sunroof, and T roof. The vinyl roof is a covering of colored vinyl that is laid over the finished roof of the car, primarily for decoration. The sunroof is a panel in the roof above the front seat that can be opened for ventilation; it may pop up, or it may slide open when moved by a hand crank or by an electric motor. A T roof has hatch panels above the driver and passenger that can be removed. Each panel fits between the top of the door glass and a center T bar, which runs from the front section of the roof to a point in back of the front seat. Convertibles are made with a soft fabric top and can be operated as open or closed cars. When the top is down, the convertible is basically a car without a roof.

Safety features

Automobile bodies include many safety features to help protect the occupants, such as the windshield, side windows, and rear window, which are made of laminated or tempered safety glass. The side doors have steel cross bars or beams to resist intrusion into the passenger compartment during side impacts. The body design may include an integral steel safety cage to surround and help protect the occupants, as well as crumple zones front and rear to absorb kinetic energy by deforming during an impact. Energy-absorbing front and rear bumpers, with standardized installed height, prevent or minimize vehicle damage resulting from a low-speed impact or collision. See also: Safety glass

Automotive safety features are classified as helping to provide either crash avoidance or occupant protection. Crash-avoidance (active safety) features are often considered more beneficial because in a significant percentage of incidents they help the driver avoid an impending accident or crash. Examples are antilock-braking, traction-control, and vehicle stability control systems; headlights that turn on and off automatically as needed; and electrochromic rear-view mirrors that automatically dim to reduce glare. See also: Automotive brake

Occupant-protection (passive safety) features include the collapsible energy-absorbing steering column, head restraints, seat belts, air bags, and breakaway inside rear-view mirror. Some front-seat shoulder belts are motorized and move into position automatically. In some vehicles, the seat belt may automatically tighten in a crash to provide additional protection. Air bags are balloon-type supplemental restraints that inflate automatically to help protect the driver and front-seat passenger in a crash (Fig. 3). Rapid inflation of the air bag, usually by a pyrotechnic device, prevents the occupant from being thrown forward and injured by striking the steering wheel or windshield. The seat belt and air bag together provide maximum protection against injury in a collision. Additional air bags in the sides of the seatbacks or doors are also used to provide side-impact protection, primarily for the head and torso, of front- and rear-seat passengers.

Fig. 2   Front air bags, which provide protection for the driver and front-seat passenger in a collision.

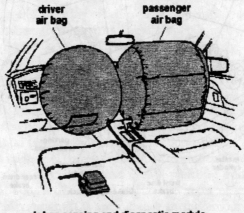

driver air bag      passenger air bag

air bag sensing and diagnostic module

## Automobile Competition Committee for the United States (ACCUS)

With representatives of NASCAR, SCCA, IMSA, and USAC, the American affiliate of FISA, coordinating major United States racing events with the international calendar.

## automotive air pollution

Evaporated and unburned fuel, and other undesirable by-products of combustion that escape from a motor vehicle into the atmosphere.

## automotive battery

An electro-chemical device that stores and provides electrical energy for the operation of a vehicle.

## Automotive brake

Automotive brake system, showing a diagonally split hydraulic system with front disc brakes, rear drum brakes, vacuum booster, and hand-operated parking brake.

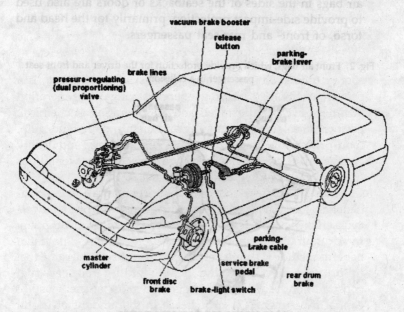

## Steering column
Construction of a rack-and-pinion power-steering gear

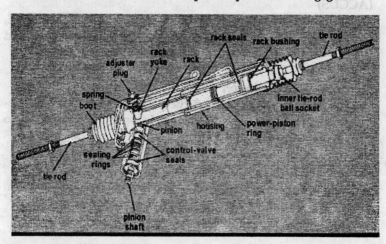

### Wheel alignment

Wheel alignment is the relationship among the wheels, steering parts, suspension angles, and the road that affect the operation and steering of a vehicle. Six basic wheel alignment factors are suspension height, caster, camber, toe, steering-axis inclination, and turning radius or toe-out on turns (Fig.). Alignment of the front wheels with the rear wheels should provide a common vehicle centerline, geometric centerline, and thrust line.

Fig.  Basic factors in wheel alignment. (a) Suspension height. (b) Toe. (c) Caster. (d) Camber. (e) Steering-axis inclination. (f) Turning radius.

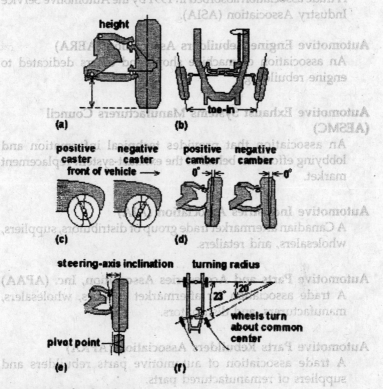

### automotive body shop

A term often used for body shop.

### Automotive Communications Council (ACC)

A professional association of advertising, marketing, and communications executives.

**automotive cooling system**
The many components that operate to absorb and dissipate heat developed in the combustion process, thus maintaining the desired engine-operating temperature.

**Automotive Cooling System Institute (ACSI)**
A Motor and Equipment Manufacturers Association subgroup made up of cooling-system product manufacturers.

**Automotive Electrical Association (AEA)**
A trade association absorbed in 1991 by the Automotive Service Industry Association (ASIA).

**Automotive Engine Rebuilders Association (AERA)**
An association of machine shops and others dedicated to engine rebuilding.

**Automotive Exhaust Systems Manufacturers Council (AESMC)**
An association that provides technical information and lobbying efforts on behalf of the exhaust-system-replacement market.

**Automotive Industries Association (AIA)**
A Canadian aftermarket trade group of distributors, suppliers, wholesalers, and retailers.

**Automotive Parts and Accessories Association, Inc. (APAA)**
A trade association for aftermarket retailers, wholesalers, manufacturers, and distributors.

**Automotive Parts Rebuilders Association (APRA)**
A trade association of automotive parts rebuilders and suppliers of remanufactured parts.

**automotive power brakes**
A brake system having a vacuum and atmospheric air-operated power booster or hydraulic power boost to multiply braking force.

### Automotive Recyclers Association (ARA)

International association of automotive recyclers, owners, and dealers in used car and truck parts.

### Automotive Retailers Association (ARA)

An association of the automotive retailers, sales and service, including collision repairs, mechanical repairs, used car sales, auto wrecking, and towing.

### auxiliary air valve

A device that allows air to bypass a closed throttle during engine start-up and warm-up.

### auxiliary drum parking brake

The incorporation of an auxiliary parking-brake drum inside a rear rotor on some four-wheel drive disc-brake systems.

### auxiliary seal

A secondary seal mounted outside the seal housing:
To prevent refrigeration oil from escaping and entering the clutch assembly.
To aid in the prevention of the loss of fluid from a system.

### auxiliary section

The section of a transmission housing the auxiliary drive gear, main shaft assembly, countershaft, and synchronizer assembly, where range shifting occurs.

### auxiliary shaft

A separate shaft, in an overhead cam engine, that drives devices such as the fuel pump, oil pump, and distributor.

### auxiliary springs

1. A second or third valve spring with a different resonant frequency to cancel out harmonic vibrations that limit engine speed.
2. The spring(s) added to a vehicle, generally in the rear, to support a heavy load.

**auxiliary venturi**
A small secondary venturi mounted inside the main venturi of a carburetor to provide increased air velocity. May also be called a booster venturi.

**available seat miles**
One seat, occupied or not, moved one mile. Used as a measure of airline capacity.

**axis**
1. The center line of a rotating part.
2. One direction in an orthogonal reference frame.

**axle**
1. A cross member supporting a vehicle on which one or more wheels are mounted.
2. A pair of wheels at either end of a vehicle. Some brake repair shops and turnpike tolls charge a per axle rate.

**axle bearing**
A bearing that supports an axle or half shaft in an axle housing.

**axle boot**
The flexible cover that retains grease and/or oil in a transmission or a constant velocity joint.

**axle carrier assembly**
A cast-iron framework that can be removed from the rear-axle housing for service and adjustment.

**axle gears**
Bevel gears that transfer power from the differential pinion gears to the splined axle shafts.

**axle hop**
The tendency of a live axle housing to rotate with the wheels slightly and then snap back during hard acceleration. This action may be repeated several times, creating a loss of traction until the driver releases the accelerator.

## axle housing

Designed in the removable carrier or integral carrier types to house the drive pinion, ring gear, differential, and axle shaft assemblies.

## axle ratio

The ratio between the rotational speed (rpm) of the drive shaft and that of the driven wheel; gear reduction through the differential, determined by dividing the number of teeth on the ring gear by the number of teeth on the drive pinion.

## axle seat

Suspension component used to support and locate spring on the axle. Also known as a spring chair.

## axle shaft

Alloy steel shaft that transfers torque from the differential side gears to the drive wheels. This shaft also supports vehicle weight on most passenger cars.

## axle-shaft end thrust

A force exerted on the end of an axle shaft that is most pronounced when the vehicle turns corners and curves.

## axle-shaft tubes

Tubes that are attached to the axle housing center section to surround the axle shaft and bearings.

## axle tramp

The tendency of a live axle housing to rotate with the wheels slightly and then snap back during hard acceleration. This action may be repeated several times, creating a loss of traction until the driver releases the accelerator.
when mixed in precise proportions, behave like a compound.

## Azimuth

An angle in the horizontal plane, usually measured with respect to body coordinates.

# B

### back to back ticketing

A strategy used to reduce the cost of a round trip involving no Saturday stay when the cost of two excursions is less than the cost of one unrestricted fare. For example, if a traveler wants to fly from New York to Denver on Monday and return Thursday, he would purchase two excursions, one from New York to Denver beginning on Monday and the other from Denver to New York departing on Thursday. The traveler then uses only the outbound portion of each excursion. The itinerary can be designed in such a way that the return portions of each excursion can be used on another trip. This is an illegal practice. Also called "nested excursions".

### backfire

1. An explosion in the exhaust system of a motor vehicle caused when an unburned air/fuel mixture is ignited, usually upon deceleration.
2. An explosion of the air/fuel mixture in the intake manifold, which is evident at the carburetor or throttle body and may be caused by improper ignition timing, crossed spark plug wires, or an intake valve that is stuck open.
3. The momentary recession of the flame into the welding tip, cutting tip, or flame-spraying gun, followed by immediate reappearance or complete extinction of the flame.

### backfire suppression valve

An anti-backfire valve used in the air-injection system of an exhaust emission control.

**backfiring**

1. The pre-explosion of an air/fuel mixture so that the explosion passes back around the opened intake valve, through the intake manifold, and through the carburetor.

2. The loud explosion of over-rich exhaust gas in the exhaust manifold that exits through the muffler and tailpipe with a loud popping noise.

**back flush**

The use of a reverse flow of water, with or without a cleaning agent, to clean out the cooling system of a vehicle.

**backing plate**

Stamped steel plate upon which the wheel cylinder is mounted and the brake shoes are attached; a metal plate that serves as the foundation for the brake shoes and other drum brake hardware.

**back motor**

A mid- or rear-mounted engine.

**back plane**

The main circuit board of a system, containing edge connectors or sockets so other printed circuit boards can be plugged into it.

**back pressure**

1. Resistance of an exhaust system to the passage of exhaust gases. This can have an adverse effect on performance, fuel economy, and emissions. Excessive back pressure may be caused by a clogged catalytic converter, or a dented or crimped pipe.

2. The excessive pressure buildup in an engine crankcase.

**back pressure EGR**

Some emissions-control systems use a back-pressure sensor or diaphragm to monitor back pressure so that exhaust gas recirculating flow can be increased when the engine is under maximum load, and producing maximum back pressure.

**back pressure EGR valve**

A back-pressure-dependent EGR valve. See the specific application; negative-back-pressure EGR valve or positive-back-pressure EGR valve, as applicable.

**back seat**

The position of a valve stem when turned to the left (ccw) as far as possible back seating a two-seat service valve.

**back staging**

Placing a competition vehicle at the start of a drag race behind the usual staging position. Also referred to as shallow staging.

**backup light**

Lamps that illuminate the area behind the vehicle and warn others of the driver's intention to back up. All vehicles sold in the United States after 1971 are required to have such lights.

**backyard mechanic**

An amateur mechanic or one with little training. Often called a shade-tree mechanic.

**bad**

Slang for "Good."

**bad car**

A performance term for an extremely fast car.

**badge engineering**

The act of producing the same car under more than one name.

**bad sector**

A sector on a computer disk that will not read or write correctly. Usually due to a minor physical flaw in the disk.

**baffle**

A barrier used to reduce noise in an enclosed system, such as the exhaust system.

A barrier to prevent splashing of liquid in a tank.

## bail

The spring-steel wire loop used to secure a cover, such as on a master cylinder reservoir.

## balance tube

1. A tube to connect the exhaust pipes in a dual exhaust system to equalize the pressures.
2. A tube to connect the venturis of dual carburetors.

## balancing

The process of proportioning weight or force equally on all sides of an object. Most crankshafts, for example, are balanced both statically and dynamically.

## balancing coil gauge

An indicating device, such as a fuel gauge, that contains a pair of coils in the instrument-panel unit.

## ballast

Material that is added to a racing car chassis to change the weight distribution and/or increase the overall vehicle weight to the minimum class requirement.

## ballast resistor

A term often used for ignition resistor.

## ball bearing

An anti-friction bearing with an inner and outer race having one or more rows of balls between them.

## ball check valve

A one-way valve having a ball and seat.

## ball joint

1. A joint or connection where a ball moves within a socket, allowing a rotary motion while the angle of the rotation axis changes.
2. A suspension component that attaches the steering knuckle to either control arm featuring a ball-and-socket joint to allow pivoting in various directions. Also known as a spherical joint.

**ball joint angle**
  The inward tilt of the steering axis from the vertical.

**ball joint centerline**
  An imaginary line drawn through the centers of the upper and lower ball joints.

**ball joint free play**
  The allowable radial and axial motion between the ball-joint housing, checked with the load removed.

**ball joint inclination**
  The inward tilt of the top of the steering axis centerline through the ball joints as viewed from the front of the vehicle.

**ball joint internal lubrication**
  A ball joint assembly may be pre-lubricated and factory sealed or it may have provision for periodic scheduled lubrication.

**ball joint preload**
  A term relating to certain ball joints, often spring-loaded, having constant friction between the ball-and-joint housing socket.

**ball joint seal**
  A Neoprene rubber seal that fits over a ball-joint stud against the housing to retain lubricating grease and keep unwanted foreign debris, such as sand or dirt, out.

**ball joint slack**
  A term often used for ball joint free play.

**ball joint suspension**
  A type of front suspension in which the wheel spindle is attached directly to the upper and lower suspension arms through the ball joints.

**Ball-and-race-type pulverizer**
  A grinding machine in which balls rotate under pressure to

crush materials, such as coal, to a fine consistency. The material is usually fed through a chute to the inside of a ring of closely spaced balls. In most designs the upper spring-loaded race applies pressure to the balls, and the lower race rotates and grinds the coarse material between it and the balls (see <u>illus.</u>). The finely ground material discharges along the outer periphery of the ball races. For the pulverization of coal, hot air, introduced between the lower race and the pulverizer housing, lifts or carries the fines to a cyclone classifier at the center of the pulverizer. There the finer particles discharge from the pulverizer while the larger particles return to the grinding zone for further reduction in size. Two or more rings of balls can be cascaded in one machine to obtain greater capacity or output. Counterrotating top and bottom rings also are used to increase pulverizer capacity. Such pulverizers are compact and the power required per ton of material ground is relatively low.

Fig.  Coarse raw material is ground by crushing and attrition between balls and races and is then withdrawn from the pulverizer by an airstream.

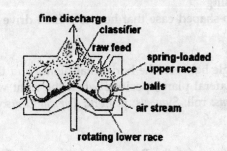

fine discharge
classifier
raw feed
spring-loaded upper race
balls
air stream
rotating lower race

**ball nut**

In a recirculating ball nut steering gear, the ball nut has internal threads that are meshed to the threads of a worm with continuous rows of ball bearings between the two. The ball bearings are recirculated through two outside loops called ball guides. The sliding ball nut has tapered teeth cut on one face that mate with teeth on the cross-shaft sector.

**balloon foot**
A term used to describe a slow driver; one who tends to back off the throttle early.

**ball stud**
A stud with a ball-shaped end.

**band**
1. A hydraulically controlled device installed in an automatic transmission around a clutch drum, used to stop or permit drum turning.
2. A manual or hydraulic device installed around a drum to provide a braking action.

**Band-pass filter (BPF)**
A filter that allows frequencies between two cutoff frequencies to pass while attenuating frequencies outside the cutoff frequencies; a band-pass filter can be constructed as the composition of a low-pass filter and a high-pass filter.

**banjo housing**
A banjo-shaped case that houses a final drive live axle.

**bank angle**
The angle between the horizontal plnase and the right wing in the lateral plane, positive when the right wing is down; *Synonyms:* roll; *Symbols:* phi,Phi; *Typical Units:* rad, deg.

**BAR**
An acronym for the Bureau of Automotive Repair.

**barb fitting**
A fitting that slips inside a hose and is held in place with a gear-type clamp or pressed-on ferrule.

**barefoot charter**
A charter of a boat or yacht which does not include supplies or crew.

**bare electrode**

A filler metal electrode that has been produced as a wire, strip, or bar with no coating or covering other than that which is incidental to its manufacture or preservation.

**bare out**

To strip a car body to its basic shell, generally in preparation for its restoration.

**barge**

A low draft vessel, often towed or pushed, used to transport cargo. A vessel designed for use on inland waterways and canals.

**BARO**

An abbreviation for:
1. Barometric pressure.
2. Barometric-pressure sensor.
3. Barometer.

**barometer**

An instrument used for measuring barometric pressure.

**Barometric altitude**

Height with respect to fixed earth reference (above mean sea level); *Synonyms:* pressure altitude; *Symbols:* h sub b; *Typical Units:* ft; *Dimensions:* Length.

**Barometric altitude select (BALT SEL)**

A basic guidance mode, providing vertical guidance to an operator selected barometric altitude.

**barometric pressure (BARO)**

1. The pressure exerted by the weight of the earth's atmosphere, equal to one bar, 99.97 kPa, or 14.5 psi at sea level. Barometric pressure changes with the weather and with altitude. Since it affects the density of the air entering the engine and ultimately the air/fuel ratio, some computerized emissions-control systems use a barometric pressure sensor so that the spark

advance and exhaust gas recirculate (EGR) valve flow can be
regulated to control emissions more precisely.

2. Height with respect to fixed earth reference (barometric
altitude, feet above mean sea level); *Synonyms:* pressure;
*Symbols:* p sub a; *Typical Units:* in HG,mbar; *Dimensions:* Mass
/Time-squared.

**barometric pressure sensor**

A device that senses barometric pressure and sends an electrical
signal to the CPU for optimum engine control.

**barrel (bbl)**

1. A term sometimes applied to the cylinders in an engine.
2. A term used to refer to the number of throttle bores in a
carburetor.

**barrel faced ring**

A compression piston ring with a rounded contact face.

**barrel finish**

The rounded surface on a piston skirt.

**base fare**

The fare, as of an airline ticket, before tax has been added.
Commissions are calculated on the base fare.

**base metal**

The largest proportion of metal present in an alloy.
A metal that readily oxidizes, or that dissolves to form ions.
The metal or alloy that is welded, brazed, soldered, or cut.
After welding, that part of the metal that was not melted.

**base station**

The bottom section of a station buck that serves as a reference
point in metal working.

**base 10**

A base unit in the metric system. All metric units are increased
or decreased in units of

One meter, for example, has 10 decimeters, 100 centimeters, or 1,000 millimeters.

## basic fuel metering

The amount of fuel delivered to the injectors in a continuous-flow, fuel-injection system,.

## basic fuel quality

The amount of fuel delivered to the injectors, in a pulsed, fuel-injection system, based on airflow sensor readings of engine load and rpm.

## basket of snakes

A tuned exhaust system with individual intertwined headers.

## bass compensation

A circuit in an audio amplifier that increases the output of low-end audio frequencies at low listening levels to compensate for the human ear's loss of sensitivity under these conditions.

## BAT

An abbreviation for battery.

## batch

A group of records or programs that is considered a single unit for processing on a computer.

## bathtub

An auto body design that resembles an inverted bath tub. A combustion chamber in an engine with an area that resembles an inverted bath tub with its valves seated at its base.

## battery acid

An electrolyte used in a battery; a mixture of water ($H_2O$) and sulfuric acid ($H_2SO_4$).

## battery backup

Auxiliary power that is provided to a computer so volatile memory information is not lost during a power failure, or when otherwise disconnected from its normal power source.

## battery capacity
The energy output of a battery measured in amp/hours.

## battery cell
That part of a battery made from two dissimilar metals and an acid solution. A cell stores chemical energy for use later as electrical energy.

## battery charge
The restoration of chemical energy to a battery by supplying a measured flow of electrical current to it for a specified time.

## battery charger
An electrical device that is used for restoring a battery to its original state of charge by passing a current through the battery in a direction opposite of the discharge current flow.

## Battery Council International (BCI)
A professional association of manufacturers, suppliers, and distributors of lead-acid batteries.

## battery efficiency
A battery's ability to vary the current it delivers within a wide range, depending on the temperature and the rate of discharge.

## battery element
A cell.
A group of unlike positive and negative plates assembled with separators.

## battery maintenance
Generally, preventative maintenance, such as visual inspection, adding water, cleaning top and terminals, tightening hold down, and testing.

## battery rating methods
There are several rating methods cold cranking power rating, reserve capacity rating, and twenty-hour rating.

## battery terminal

A means of connecting the battery to the vehicle's electrical system. The three types of battery terminals are post or top, side, and L.

## bayonet socket

A lamp socket having two lengthwise slots in its sides, making a right-angled turn at the bottom. A lamp with two pins may be installed by pushing it into the socket and giving it a slight clockwise turn.

## beam axle

A shaft that does not transmit power but provides a means of fastening wheels to either, or both, ends.

## beam solid-mount suspension

A tandem suspension relying on a pivotal mounted beam, with axles attached at the ends for load equalization.

## beans

Performance term for horsepower.

## bearing

A term used for ball bearing or bushing.

## bearing (BRG)

Direction on a compass; *Synonyms:* direction; *Symbols:* B; *Typical Units:* rad, deg.

## bearing block

The outside surface of a bearing that seats against the housing bore.

## bearing bore

A term often used for housing bore.

## bearing cap

A device that retains the needle bearings that ride on the trunnion of a U-joint and is pressed into the yoke.

### bearing cap register
The cut-out portion of the engine block that keeps the bearing cap aligned to the housing bore.

### bearing crush
The additional height, manufactured into each bearing half, to ensure complete contact of the bearing back with the housing bore when the engine is assembled.

### bearing groove
A channel cut into the surface of a bearing to ensure oil distribution.

### bearing id
The inside diameter of a bearing.

### bearing pre-lubricator
A pressurized oil tank attached to the engine-lubrication provisions to maintain oil pressure when the engine is not running.

### bearing shell
One half of a single rod or main bearing set.

### bearing spacer
A device that is used to hold a bearing in the housing bore.

### bearing spin
A bearing that has rotated in its housing or block, generally due to failure as a result of lack of lubrication.

### bearing spread
The small extra distance across the parting faces of a bearing half in excess of the actual diameter of the bearing bore.

### bearing upper
The bearing shell that is positioned opposite the bearing cap.

**before bottom dead center**
> The position of a piston approaching the bottom of its intake or combustion stroke.

**before top center (BTC)**
> A piston as it is approaching the top of its stroke.

**before top dead center (BTPC)**
> Any position of the piston between bottom dead center and top dead center on its upward stroke.

**Belleville washer**
> A circular disk formed into a conical shape. When a load is applied, the disk tends to flatten, constituting a spring action. May be referred to as a coned-disk spring.

**bell housing**
> A term often used for clutch housing.

**bell-mouthed drum**
> A well-worn brake drum that is deformed so that its open end has a larger diameter than its closed end.

**belly pan**
> Body panel(s) covering the bottom of a competition vehicle to reduce the coefficient of drag.

**belly tank**
> A tear-shaped, World War II aircraft auxiliary fuel tank used as the body for a lakester.

**belt**
> 1. In a tire, the belt(s), generally steel, restrict ply movement and provide tread stability and resistance to deformation, providing longer tread wear and reducing heat buildup in the tire.
> 2. A device used to drive the water pump and/or other auxiliary devices, such as the alternator, off the engine.

**belt-clamping action**
> As related to a continuous variable transmission, the action taking place when the V-pulley sheaves clamp the drive belt.

**belt cover**
> A nylon cover positioned over the belts in a tire that helps to hold the tire together at high speed, and provides longer tire life.
> A rayon, cotton, or nylon cover to protect the interior of a drive belt from the environment and absorb the wear that occurs at the belt-sheave interface.

**belt dressing**
> A prepared solution, generally in spray form, formulated for use on automotive V-belts to reduce or eliminate belt noise. It is not generally recommended for serpentine belts.

**belt-driven cooling fan**
> A rigid or flexible cooling fan is driven by a belt from the crankshaft in vehicles that have longitudinally mounted engines. Usually the belt-driven cooling fan is mounted to the front of the water pump pulley/hub.

**bench seat**
> A full-width seat that can accommodate two or three persons in a vehicle.

**bench test**
> The testing of an engine or component, out of the vehicle, for ease of observation and study.

**bend**
> 1. A curve or angle that has been bent.
> 2. To form a curve or angle by bending.

**bending**
> The forming of a material, usually metal, into a particular shape.

**bending sequence**

The order in which several bends are made so as not to be blocked by a previous bend.

**bending stress**

A stress, while bending, that involves both tensile and compressive forces that are not equally distributed.

**Bendix drive**

A type of starter motor drive that engages, and disengages, the starter and flywheel.

**Bendix Folo-Thru drive**

A starter motor drive engaged by initial rotation of the armature, causing the drive pinion to be twisted outward on a threaded sleeve until it is meshed with the flywheel gear. The gears are disengaged automatically at a predetermined speed of about 400 rpm.

**Bendix screw**

The helix-grooved shaft of a Bendix drive.

**bent**

Not flat or straight, intentionally or unintentionally.

**benzine**

A highly flammable liquid, $C_6H_6$, sometimes found in refined gasoline. Its use, however, is restricted to 3.0% in some areas due to its toxicity.

**benzole**

A mixture of aromatic hydrocarbons with a high percentage of benzine, used as a solvent and as a fuel additive.

**bereavement fare**

A lower airline fare offered to those traveling due to a death or illness in their immediate family.

**berm**

1. A curb-like buildup on the outside of turns on a circular dirt track.

2. The curb-like buildup of dirt along the edges of an unpaved road.

**Bermuda Plan**

A hotel arrangement which includes a full breakfast with the room rate.

**berth**

A bed on a ship, usually attached to the bulkhead. The space on a dock at which a ship or boat is moored.

**bevel gear**

A form of spur gear in which the teeth are cut at an angle to form a cone shape, allowing a gear set to transmit power at an angle.

**bezel**

A trim ring, usually around a gauge, to secure the glass cover.

**bhp**

An abbreviation for brake horsepower.

**bias**

1. A diagonal line of direction.

2. An offset applied to a measurement for error correction; *Synonyms:* offset.

**bias-belted tire**

A tire that has the ply cords placed diagonally across the tire from bead-to-bead, with alternate ply layers cris-crossing diagonally in opposite directions.

**bias-ply tire**

A term used for bias belted tire.

**big arm**
1. The throw of a crankshaft that has been stroked.
2. Sometimes used to identify an engine with a stroked crankshaft.

**big block**
A V–8 engine that displaces more than 400 cubic inches; a muscle car powerplant.

**bigs**
Large rear tires.

**bigs and littles**
A combination of large rear tires and small front tires.

**big three**
The three major United States automobile manufacturers, Chrysler, Ford, and General Motors.

**billet**
A solid bar of metal.

**billet camshaft**
A camshaft machined from a billet of steel.

**billet crankshaft**
A crankshaft machined from a billet of steel, usually used for racing applications.

**bimetal**
A temperature-sensitive strip made up of two metals having different heat expansion rates.

**bimetal engine**
A powerplant with block and head made of different metals, such as a cast iron block and an aluminum head.

**bimetallic**
Two dissimilar metals fused together; these metals expand

and contract at different temperatures to cause a bending effect.

## bimetallic sensing element
Another term used for bimetallic sensor.

## bimetallic sensor
A sensing element having a bimetallic strip or coil.

## bit
1. A character that represents one of the two digits in the number system that has a radix of two.
2. That part of the soldering iron, usually made of copper, that directly transfers heat to the joint.

## black box
A term often used for a central processing unit (CPU).

## black flag
The signal for a driver to return to the pits for consultation with race officials.

## black light
An ultraviolet-light system used to detect flaws in metal parts.

## black smoke
The exhaust that is produced when the air/fuel mixture is too rich.

## block water
Liquid refuse that must be stored on an RV until it can be disposed at a dump station.

## black market
Illegal trade, commerce, or currency exchange which evades taxes, government oversight, or both.

## blacked out, dates, period
Not available. Dates on which tickets or certain fares are not

available. Blackout dates usually coincide with holidays and peak travel seasons.

**blacky carbon**
A term used in disdain for gasoline by drivers using it as a fuel.

**blank**
A term often used for billet.

**bleed**
1. To drain fluid.
2. To remove an air bubble or air lock.
3. To draw air into a system.

**bleed air tanks**
The process of draining condensation from air tanks to increase air capacity.

**bleeder current**
A continuous load placed on a power supply by a resistance load that helps improve regulation and safety.

**bleeder jar**
A glass or transparent plastic container used to detect the escape of air while bleeding brakes.

**bleeder screw**
A small, hollow screw or valve found at drum-brake wheel cylinders, in disc brake calipers, and adjacent to the outlet ports of some master cylinders. It is opened to release pressure and to bleed air and fluid from the hydraulic system.

**bleeding**
1. The slow releasing of pressure in the air-conditioning system by recovering some of its liquid or gas.
2. The act of removing air from a hydraulic brake system.
3. A small leak.
4. When one paint color shows through another.

**bleeding sequence**
The order of bleeding brake systems or other components.

**bleed orifice**
A calibrated orifice in a vacuum system that allows ambient air to enter the system to equalize the vacuum.

**blend air**
The control of air quality by blending heated and cooled air to the desired temperature.

**blend air door**
A door in the duct system that controls temperature by mixing heated and cooled air in correct proportions to achieve the desired effect.

**blinky**
The timing light at the end of a quarter-mile strip.

**blip**
A quick punch to the throttle to rev the engine momentarily.

**blistering**
1. Tire tread separating from the carcass due to high heat.
2. Bubbles or pinholes that appear in paint.
3. To go exceptionally fast, as in a blistering pace.

**blistering pace**
To go exceptionally fast.

**Bloc-Chek**
A device to detect the leakage of exhaust gas into the cooling system.

**Block and tackle**
Combination of a rope or other flexible material and independently rotating frictionless pulleys; the pulleys are grooved or flat wheels used to change the direction of motion

or application of force of the flexible member (rope or chain) that runs on the pulleys. As in a lever, the summation of torques about the axis of rotation of the pulley equals zero for static equilibrium. Tension $T$ in the rope is the same on both sides of the pulley. See also: Lever

For example, in the particular block and tackle in the illustration, at static equilibrium, the summation of forces in any direction equals zero. Each vertical rope carries one-fourth the weight; algebraically $T_1 = T_2 = T_3 = T_4 = W/4$, and therefore the applied force $F$ also equals one-fourth the weight $W$. For this case mechanical advantage $MA$ is shown by the equation below.

$$MA = \frac{W}{F} = \frac{W}{W/4} = 4$$

The block and tackle is used where a large multiplication of the applied forces is desirable. Examples are lifting weights, sliding heavy machinery into position, and tightening fences.

Fig. Block and tackle. (*a*) Actual view. (*b*) Schematic.

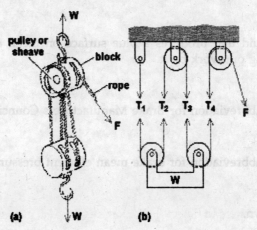

**block**
Main casting of the engine that contains the cylinders; often made of cast iron or aluminum.

**blower relay**
An electrical device used to control the function or speed of a blower motor.

**blower speed controller**
A solid-state control device that operates the blower motor and, sometimes, the compressor clutch based on signals from the microprocessor.

**blower switch**
A dash-mounted device that allows the operator to turn the blower motor ON/OFF and/or to control its speed.

**blown engine**
1. An engine that has a supercharger or turbocharger.
2. A seriously damaged engine.

**blown head gasket**
A broken head gasket that leaks water, oil, or air and reduces engine performance.

**blue streak**
The trade name of a Goodyear high-performance tire.

**bluing**
A fluid that produces a blue surface on metal to assist in laying out work on it.

**BMC**
An abbreviation for Brake Manufacturers Council.

**bmep**
An abbreviation for brake mean efficient pressure.

**bn**
Brown.

**bobbed**
Trimmed and shortened.

**bobtail**
1. A vehicle body with a short-rear overhang.

2. The tractor of a tractor-trailer rig.
3. The results of a modification of a fad car.

**bobweight**
The weight attached to a rod journal to simulate the reciprocating mass when balancing a crankshaft.

**body**
1. The assembly of sheet metal sections and other parts that provide the enclosure of a vehicle.
2. The aircraft, usually referring to a coordinate system.

**body and frame**
The parts of a vehicle that support all components. A frame that supports the engine and drive train and a body that houses the entire vehicle.

**body control module (BCM)**
A component of self-diagnostic systems used to control vehicle function based on monitored inputs.

**body in white**
1. A new, unpainted, and untrimmed body.
2. A body that has been completely stripped.

**body coordinate**
Coordinates referenced to the body of the aircraft; *See Also:* XYZ; *Compare:* earth coordinates, stability coordinates.

**body mounting**
1. Rubber cushions, at strategic locations, to dampen noise and vibration.
2. To place a car body on the chassis.

**body panels**
Sheets of material joined together to form a car body.

**body pitch**
The tendency of a vehicle to dive or squat.

**body roll**
A term often used for roll.

**body shapes**
There are six basic body shapes; sedan, hardtop, convertible top, liftback or hatchback, station wagon, and sports or multipurpose.

**body shop**
A collision-and-damage repair and painting facility.

**body strength**
Body strength depends on the type of vehicle and body structure; factors such as door size and the presence or absence of a center pillar. Also, front body pillar, quarter panels, and roof panels affect how much of an impact is absorbed.

**bog**
1. To lose power and momentarily faulter when coming off the line.
2. To stall or slow due to soft dirt or sand in off-road racing. A mud hole.

**boil tank**
A very large tank of boiling solution used for cleaning large parts, such as engine blocks.

**bolster plate**
The flat, load-bearing surface under the front of a semitrailer, including the kingpin, which rests firmly on the fifth wheel when coupled.

**bolster plate height**
The height from the ground to the bolster plate when the trailer is level and unladen.

**bolt**
A metal rod, usually with a head at one end and a thread at the other, used to secure parts and assemblies.

**bolt circle diameter**
> The diameter of an imaginary line running through the bolt hole centers.

**bolt grade**
> The strength of a bolt.

**bolt hardness**
> The hardness of a bolt is identified by the number of lines on the head of the bolt. The more lines, the stronger the bolt.

**bolt on**
> An aftermarket accessory that can be installed without modification.

**bolt stretch**
> 1. When a bolt is elongated and the shank and/or thread diameter is smaller than specifications.
> 2. When a bolt is torqued as specified and, as a result, is stretched a predetermined amount.

**bolt torque**
> The turning effort required to offset resistance as the bolt is being tightened.

**bomb**
> Performance term for a vehicle that is capable of extraordinary performance.

**bonded lining**
> Brake lining cemented to shoes or bands, eliminating a need for rivets.

**bonding**
> The process of connecting two or more materials using chemicals or heat, or electrical or mechanical forces.

**bonding lining**
> The lining attached to a brake shoe with an oven-cured adhesive.

**Bondo**
A tradename for a plastic two-part body filler.

**bone yard**
A facility that sells used parts for vehicles.

**bonnet**
1. A safety helmet.
2. British term for a vehicle hood.

**Bonneville**
The salt flats in Northwestern Utah; one of the world's most famous courses.

**bookkeeper**
One who keeps record books, prepares invoices, writes checks, makes bank deposits, checks bank statements, and is responsible for tax payments.

**bookmark**
Method by which an internet user can save a Web page so that it can be easily retrieved in the future.

**booking code**
The code used to make a booking on a CRS for a specific fare. Also called a fare code.

**booking fee**
The charge levied by a CRS on a supplier for handling a reservation.

**boondockin'**
Traveling in a remote area, usually with a 4*4 or other off-road vehicle.

**boondocks**
A remote, undeveloped area, often the setting for unauthorized, and illegal, auto competition.

**boonies**
1. A slang term for boondocks.
2. A race driver is off to the boonies if spun off course.

**boost**
The increase in intake-manifold pressure, produced by a turbocharger or supercharger.

**booster battery**
A charged battery connected to a discharged battery in order to start the engine.

**boot**
1. Slang for a tire.
2. A flexible rubber or plastic cover used over the ends of master cylinders, wheel cylinders, transmissions, or constant velocity joints, to keep out water and other matter.
3. The British term for the rear deck or trunk of a car.

**boots**
Performance term for tires.

**Borden tube**
A thermo-mechanical device in the fuel injection system that regulates the amount of fuel being injected according to differences in temperature and pressure in the intake manifold.

**borderline lubrication**
Poor lubrication as a result of greasy friction.
Moving parts coated with a thin film of lubricant.

**bore**
1. The diameter of an engine cylinder.
2. To increase the diameter of a cylinder.

**bore align**
To machine an engine's main bearing journals to assure they are in perfect alignment.

**bore centers**
The center-to-center distance between two bores.

**bored and stroked**
A combination of an enlarged cylinder bore and a lengthened piston stroke to increase an engine's displacement.

**bore in the water**
To bore a cylinder out far enough to brake through the water passage.

**boresight angle**
The angle between the center line of a sensor and aircraft center line, either by design or by misalignment.

**boresighting**
A basic control to a data source from controls and displays to boresight a device; Also, a procedure to align the center line of physical devices, usually update sensors, so that they provide the most accurate results possible; a basic control to a data source from controls and displays; commonly required by FLIR, MMR; boresight procedures commonly result in correction factors to be downloaded from the host processor to the device; during boresighting, the device is usually not available; *See Also:* alignment, calibration, initialization.

**boss**
1. The reinforced extension on a part that holds a mounting pin, bolt, or stud.
2. A slang term for outstanding quality.

**bottom**
The underside; the lowest part.
When a vehicle's chassis hits the lowest point allowed by its suspension system.
When the springs are fully compressed.

**bottom dead center (BDC)**
Piston position at bottom of stroke.

**bottom end**

> The crankshaft main bearing and connecting-rod bearing assembly in an engine.

**bottom out**

> If a race car settles down tightly on its springs on an oval track as it travels through a baked turn, centrifugal force tends to push the car downward, toward the track's surface, causing its chassis to bottom out.

**bottom U-bolt plate**

> A plate that is located on the bottom side of the spring or axle and is held in place when the U-bolts are tightened.

**bottom valve**

> A shock absorber component to control the flow of oil into the reservoir during compression and rebound.

**bounce back**

> A condition that occurs when particles of paint sprayed on a body panel bounce away from the surface.

**brake assembly**

> An assembly of the components of a brake system, including its mechanism for the application of friction forces.

**brake band**

> A round, flat metal band with a friction surface on its inner diameter; used primarily in emergency brake systems.

**brake bias**

> An excessive brake force at either end of the vehicle causing the brakes at that end to lock before the other end, often leading to loss of control.

**brake bleeding**

> Procedure for removing air from lines of a hydraulic brake system.

# Brake

A machine element for applying a force to a moving surface to slow it down or bring it to rest in a controlled manner. In doing so, it converts the kinetic energy of motion into heat which is dissipated into the atmosphere. Brakes are used in motor vehicles, trains, airplanes, elevators, and other machines. Most brakes are of a friction type in which a fixed surface is brought into contact with a moving part that is to be slowed or stopped. Brakes in general connect a moving and a stationary body, whereas clutches and couplings usually connect two moving bodies. See also: Aileron; Clutch; Coupling

The limitations on the applications of brakes are similar to those of clutches, except that the service conditions are more severe because the entire energy is absorbed by slippage which is converted to heat that must be dissipated. The important thing is the rate at which energy is absorbed and heat dissipated. With friction brakes, if the temperature of the brake becomes too high, the result is a lowering of the friction force, called fading.

There are also electrical and hydrodynamic brakes. The electrical type may be electromagnetic, eddy-current, hysteresis, or magnetic-particle. The hydrodynamic type works somewhat like a fluid coupling with one element stationary. Another type, used on electric trains, is the regenerative brake. This electrical machine can be used as a motor or a generator. As a generator, it brakes the train and stores the generated electricity in an accumulator. Another type of brake is the air brake (flaps) on an airplane.

Friction types

Friction brakes are classified according to the kind of friction element employed and the means of applying the friction forces. See also: Friction

Single-block

The simplest form of brake consists of a short block fitted to the contour of a wheel or drum and pressed against its surface by means of a lever on a fulcrum, as widely used on railroad cars. The block may have the contour lined with friction-brake material, which gives long wear and a high coefficient of friction. The fulcrum may be located with respect to the lever in a manner to aid or retard the braking torque of the block.

The lever may be operated manually or by a remotely controlled force (Fig. 1*a*).

Fig. 1   Brakes. (*a*) Single-block brake. The block is fixed to the operating lever; force in the direction of the arrow applies the brake. (*b*) Double-block brake. The blocks are pivoted on their levers; force in the direction of the arrow releases the brake. (*c*) External shoe brake. Shoes are lined with friction material. (*d*) Internal shoe brake with lining.

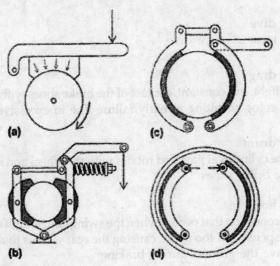

**brake booster**
> A device that uses a supplementary power source to reduce pedal force in a hydraulic brake system.

**brake chamber**
> A unit in which a diaphragm converts pressure to mechanical force for actuation of a brake.

**brake control valve**
> A unit that sends a signal to the computer when the brakes are being applied.

**brake cylinder**
> That part in which a piston converts pressure to mechanical force for actuation of the brake shoes.

**brake disc**
> The parallel-faced, circular, rotational member of a brake, acted upon by the friction material of the shoes.

**brake disc minimum thickness**
> A term sometimes used to indicate disc minimum thickness.

**brake dive**
> A term used for dive.

**brake drag**
> A light, but constant, contact of the brake shoes with the drum or rotor, resulting in early failure due to excessive heat.

**brake drum**
> The cylindrical part that rotates with the wheel and surrounds the brake shoes.

**brake hop**
> A condition that occurs when the swing-arm length of the rear suspension is too short, causing the rear wheels to repeatedly leave the ground during braking.

**brake horsepower (bhp)**
> A measurement of horsepower (hp) delivered at the engine crankshaft. A prony brake or an engine dynamometer is used to determine brake horsepower.

**brake hose**
> A flexible tubular conduit for the transmission of fluid pressure in the brake system.

**brake lights**
> Red lamps at the rear of the vehicle that light up when the brakes are applied.

**brake light switch**
> An electrical switch, operated either mechanically or hydraulically when the brakes are applied, that causes the brake lights to light up.

## brake line
Small-diameter, rigid-steel tubing, or flexible, rubber, reinforced hose, used to channel brake fluid from the master cylinder to the wheel cylinders or calipers when the brakes are applied.

## brake lining
A special friction material that will withstand high temperature and pressure, used for lining the brake shoes or pads, either by riveting or bonding.

## brake lining pad
The friction lining and plate assembly that is forced against the rotor to cause braking action in a disc brake.

## branch circuit
A portion of a wiring system extending beyond the final over-current protective device in a circuit.

## brasserie
A restaurant serving hearty fare, usually with a liquor and coffee bar.

## braze
A weld produced by heating an assembly to above 840°F (450°C) but below the solidus of the base metal.

## break
To damage a car in any way.
To open, as a set of points.

## break before make (BBM)
A switch, such as a headlamp dimmer, that breaks one circuit before making another.

## breaker
A spring-loaded switch in a conventional distributor ignition system that opens (breaks) and closes (makes) the primary circuit.

**breaker cam**
   The rotating part, located near the top of the conventional distributor, that has lobes that cause the breaker points to open and close.

**breakerless system**
   An electronic ignition system that does not use conventional breaker points to time and trigger the primary voltage but retains the distributor for secondary voltage distribution.

**breaker point gap**
   The space between the fully opened breaker points in a conventional distributor.

**breaker points**
   In a conventional ignition system, an electrical switch that opens to interrupt current flow in the primary circuit. Often called contact points.

**breaker trigger system**
   Any ignition system that utilizes conventional breaker contacts to time and trigger the system.

**break-in**
   The operation of a new vehicle at a constant and even speed to assure even initial wear of all engine parts.

**breakout**
   1. The point at which conductor(s) are taken out of a multi-conductor assembly.
   2. The point at which a branch circuit departs from the main wiring harness.

**break rule**
   A regulation in drag racing that permits a car, defeated in an elimination, to return to competition if the car that beat it is not able to get to the line for its next round.

**breathing**

The ability of an engine to draw in air and exhaust gases. The better the breathing, the better the performance.

**brickyard**

The Indianapolis Motor Speedway.

**bridge rectifier**

A full-wave rectifier in which the diodes are connected in a bridge circuit allowing current flow to the load during both positive and negative alternation of the supply voltage.

**Brinell test**

A technique for testing the hardness of a metal.

**brinelling**

A steel-shim head gasket torqued in place on an engine block.

**broach**

A tool used for reshaping or resizing parts.

**brody**

A controlled, rear-wheel skid often used on dirt tracks for fast cornering.

**bronze**

A copper-rich, copper-tin alloy with or without small proportions of other elements such as zinc and phosphorus often used for bearings or bushings.

**bronze guide**

A valve guide made of bronze alloy.

**bronze guide liner**

A thin valve guide, easy to install, but must be broached to stay in place.

**bronzewall**

A type of thread-like, valve-guide repair insert that must be reamed to size after installation.

**browser**

Software program used to travel on the Web. Netscape's Navigator and Microsoft's Internet Explorer are the two major browsers.

**brush**

A block of conducting material, such as carbon, held against an armature commutator or rotor slip ring to form a continuous electrical path.

**brush holder**

Adjustable arms for holding the commutator brushes of a generator against the commutator, feeding them forward to maintain proper contact as they wear and permitting them to be lifted from contact when necessary.

**BSFC**

An abbreviation for brake-specific fuel consumption.

**B-shim**

A valve spring adjuster with a 0.030 inch (0.76 mm) used to balance spring pressure and to correct installed height.

**B-train**

A combination of two or more trailers in which the rear trailer is connected at a single pivot point, commonly a fifth wheel, which is mounted on an extension of the frame of the lead trailer.

**bubble**

The slowest qualifying position for a race.

**bubble balancer**

A wheel balancer using an air bubble to show static balance. The tire and wheel are considered balanced if the bubble is centered in its area.

**bubble gum machine**

Slang for a blue and/or red police-car roof light.

**bubble memory**
>A method by which information is stored as magnetized dots (bubbles), that rest on a thin film of semiconductor material.

**bucket**
>1. The passenger compartment of a roadster.
>2. Overhead camshaft valve lifters.
>3. An individual driver or passenger seat.

**bucket shop**
>A consolidator. Any retail outlet dealing in discounted airfares.

**buckling**
>The bowing or lateral displacement of a compression spring.

**buffing**
>A surface-finishing process that produces a smooth, lustrous appearance generally free of defined line patterns.

**bug**
>1. A minor flaw, imperfection, or malfunction.
>2. A Volkswagen Beetle.

**bug catcher**
>A scoop-like intake on a fuel-injection or blower system.

**build**
>As its name implies; for example, to modify an engine for racing it is to build it.

**buildup time**
>The time required to form a magnetic field around the primary winding of the coil when current is allowed to flow through it in a conventional ignition system.

**Built-in simulation (BIS)**
>Function in avionics software that simulates sensors, aircraft, and pilot, to exercise avionics software (including navigation,

radio navigation, guidance and flight director); BIS is often
used by a development team to check basic operation following
installation of new software or patches; BIS is seldom used by
aircraft flight crews or maintenance crews; *Compare:* real-time
engineering simulation.

## bulb

The glass envelope that contains an incandescent lamp or an
electronic tube.

## bulge

A high spot or crown in stretched metal.

## bullnose

The smooth nose of a hood when the ornament has been
removed and the holes filled in.

## bull ring

A dirt, oval track, generally one-half mile or less.

## bump

To be forced out of a racing lineup by a faster qualifier.

## bumpin'

Cruising in a lowered vehicle, such as a low rider. Some have
hydraulics that assist in bouncing up and down.

## bump steer

The tendency of the steering to veer suddenly in one direction
when one or both of the front wheels strikes a bump.

## Bureau of Automotive Repair (BAR)

A state agency that regulates the auto service and repair
industry in California.

## burette

A glass container used to measure liquid in cubic centimeters
(cc).

## burn

A visible discoloration or sub-surface damage from an excessively high temperature, generally produced by grinding.

## burnout

The moment of final oxidation or combustion of fuel in an engine.

## burn rubber

To accelerate at a rate that the traction tires leave black streaks on the pavement.

## burnt

Permanently damaged material caused by heating conditions producing incipient melting or intergranular oxidation.

## burn time

Time required for a given amount of air/fuel mixture in the combustion chamber to burn.

## bus controller (BC)

Term defining role of device on a MIL-STD-1553 bus as being master; *Compare:* remote terminal.

## bushing

A one-piece sleeve, usually bronze, inserted into a bore to serve as a bearing.

## business coupe

An inexpensive two-door body type with no rear seat, last available in the mid 1940s.

## butane

A gaseous, highly flammable fuel ($C_4H_{10}$) that becomes liquid when it is compressed.

## butterfly

A type of valve used for the choke and throttle valve in a carburetor; a moveable plate that controls the amount of air permitted to enter the carburetor.

## buzzer

An electric sound **generator** that makes a buzzing noise when activated. It operates on the same principle as a vibrating bell. Sometimes used to warn the driver of possible safety hazards, such as when the seat belt is not fastened.

## buzzword

A word or phrase that happens to be a popular cliché of a group of people, such as race car drivers.

## bypass

A passageway between the head and block or behind the water pump that allows a water pump to circulate coolant throughout the cylinder head and engine block before the thermostat opens.

A valve that is used to regulate pressure or control the quantity of a liquid or gas.

## bypass capacitor

A capacitor that provides a low impedance path (usually to ground) to remove unwanted signals from the main signal path.

## bypass control valve

A valve used in a bypass system.

## bypass line

A line or hose used in a bypass system to transfer liquid or gas.

## bypass tube

A tube directly in front of the thermostat. The coolant bypasses the radiator through this tube when cold.

## .com

Internet zone designation used in internet e-mail addresses and Web site URL's associated with commercial content. Others include: .org for a nonprofit organization; .edu for educational and .net for networks.

## caged roller clutch

A one-way clutch having the rollers and springs contained as a unit.

## Calibrated airspeed (CAS)

Indicated airspeed corrected for instrumentation errors, but not for air density; *See Also:* airspeed; *Symbols:* V sub 'CAS'; *Typical Units:* kt,ft/s; *Dimensions:* Length / Time.

## calibration

1. The adjustment of a device or instrument so that output is within a designated tolerance for specific input values.
2. A basic control to a data source from controls and displays for calibrating a device; Also, a procedure to adjust physical devices so that they provide the most accurate results possible; calibration procedures commonly result in correction factors to be downloaded from the host processor to the device; during calibration, the device is usually not available; *See Also:* alignment, boresighting, initialization.

### California Air Resources Board (CARB)

A California agency responsible for regulations intended to reduce air pollution, especially that created by motor vehicles.

### caliper

Non-rotational components of disc brakes that straddle the disc and contain hydraulic components forcing the brake pads against the rotor to slow or stop the vehicle.

### cam

1. The eccentric element of a one-way roller clutch that carries the profiles through which the rollers transmit torque.
2. An abbreviation for camshaft.

### Cam mechanism

A mechanical linkage whose purpose is to produce, by means of a contoured cam surface, a prescribed motion of the output link of the linkage, called the follower. Cam and follower are a higher pair.

**Illustration** Classification of cams. (a) Translating. (b) Disk.

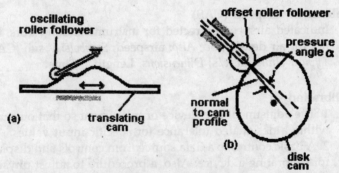

A familiar application of a cam mechanism is in the opening and closing of valves in an automotive engine (Fig. 1). The cam rotates with the cam shaft, usually at constant angular velocity, while the follower moves up and down as controlled by the cam surface. A cam is sometimes made in the form of a translating cam (Fig. 2a). Other cam mechanisms, employed in elementary mechanical analog computers, are simple memory devices, in which the position of the cam (input) determines the position of the follower (output or readout).

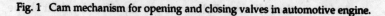

Fig. 1 Cam mechanism for opening and closing valves in automotive engine.

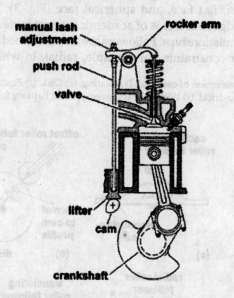

Although many requisite motions in machinery are accomplished by use of pin-joined mechanisms, such as four-bar linkages, a cam mechanism frequently is the only practical solution to the problem of converting the available input, usually rotating or reciprocating, to a desired output, which may be an exceedingly complex motion. No other mechanism is as versatile and as straightforward in design. However, a cam may be difficult and costly to manufacture, and it is often noisy and susceptible to wear, fatigue, and vibration.

Cams are used in many machines. They are numerous in automatic packaging, shoemaking, typesetting machines, and the like, but are often found as well in machine tools, reciprocating engines, and compressors. They are occasionally used in rotating machinery.

Cams are classified as translating, disk, plate, cylindrical, or drum (Fig. 2 ). The link having the contoured surface that prescribes the motion of the follower is called the cam. Cams are usually made of steel, often hardened to resist wear and, for high-speed application, precisely ground.

The output link, which is maintained in contact with the cam surface, is the follower. Followers are classified by their shape as roller, flat face, and spherical face (Fig. 3). The point or knife-edge follower is of academic interest in developing cam profile relationships. Followers are also described by the nature of their constraints, for example, radial, in which motion is

Fig. 2 Classification of cams. (*a*) Translating. (*b*) Disk. (*c*) Positive motion. (*d*) Cylindrical. (*e*) With yoke follower. (*f*) With flat-face follower.

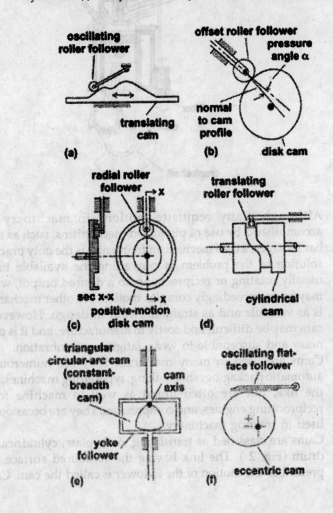

reciprocating along a radius from the cam's axis of rotation (Fig. 1); offset, in which motion is reciprocating along a line that does not intersect the axis of rotation (Fig. 2*b*); and oscillating, or pivoted (Fig. 2*a*. Three-dimensional cam-and-follower systems are coming into more frequent use, where the follower may travel over a lumpy surface.

Fig. 3 Cam followers. (a) Knife edge. (b) Roller. (c) Flat face. (d) Spherical face.

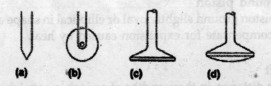

(a)   (b)   (c)   (d)

## cam and kit
A specially ground camshaft, complete with a set of compatible camshaft valve train components, including lifters and springs.

## camber
The outward or inward tilt of the wheels, in degrees, on a vehicle as viewed from the rear or front.

## camber angle
The amount, measured in degrees from the vertical, that the top of a tire is tilted outward (positive) or inward (negative).

## camber compensator
A device that is used to maintain the proper camber of the rear wheels of a vehicle equipped with swing axles.

## cam duration
The amount of time, measured in crankshaft degrees, that a camshaft holds an exhaust or intake valve open.

## camel hump heads
High performance heads by Chevrolet, identified by two humps on the outside end of the casting.

**cam follower**
A term often used for valve lifter.

**cam ground**
Pistons machined to a slightly out-of-round shape to permit them to expand with engine heat without getting stuck against the cylinder walls.

**cam-ground piston**
A piston ground slightly oval or elliptical in shape as a means to compensate for expansion caused by heat.

**cam lift**
The distance, in thousandths of an inch, a cam lobe raises the valve lifter off the base circle.

**cam-lobe face and nose taper**
The slant, about 0.002 inch (0.051 mm), designed across the cam-face contacting surface, from the cam front to rear edge, to promote lifter rotation.

**carburetor spacer**
A steel, aluminum, or plastic plate used to raise the carburetor above the normal opening of the intake manifold.

**carburetor tag**
A tag affixed to the carburetor to identify the model for parts and specifications for service.

**carburetor vacuum**
A ported vacuum, obtained from a carburetor source above the throttle plate, present after the throttle is partially open.

**carburizing flame**
A reducing oxyfuel-gas flame in which there is an excess of fuel gas, resulting in a carbon-rich zone extending around and beyond the cone.

**Car Care Council**
A non-profit organization to educate the general public about the importance of preventive maintenance.

**carcass**
1. A tire casing to which the rubber tread and sidewall are bonded.
2. The inner part of the tire that holds the air for supporting the vehicle.
3. The empty remains of a stripped vehicle.

**carcass plies**
That which surrounds both beads and extends around the inner surface of the tire to provide load-carrying capabilities on the rim.

**carcinogen**
A substance or agent that produces or incites cancer.

**carcinogenic**
A term often used for carcinogen.

**carcinogenic effects**
Causing cancer or increasing the incidence of cancer in the population.

**Cardan joint**
A universal joint having two yokes at right angles to each other, with a cruciform-shaped joint in the middle.

**Cardan universal joint**
A term used for Cardan joint.

**cargo weight rating (CWR)**
A truck's carrying capacity, in pounds.

**Carolina stocker**
A car built for drag racing, without regard for any recognized rules.

## Carrera Panamericana

1. The legendary Mexican road races held in the early 1950s that ran the full length of Mexico.

2. Vintage car races held on the public highways of northern Baja, California.

## carrier housing

Cast-iron rear axle assembly section that contains the working parts of the differential.

## Carryall

A tradename once used for a large station wagon built on a truck chassis; predecessor of the Suburban.

## carry-on

A piece of luggage designed to be taken aboard an airplane and fit in the space allotted for such luggage.

## carry the wheels

To do a wheel stand; a drag-racing term.

## Carson top

A removable, non-folding, padded soft top, used on many customized convertibles and roadsters.

## cartridge filter

A filter media that includes yarns, felts, papers, resin-bonded fibers, woven-wire cloths, and sintered metallic and ceramic structures for cleaning impurities from air or liquid. Performance obtained by a disposable cartridge filter may range from 500 μm to 1 μm or less.

## cartridge roll

A rolled piece of sandpaper used to deburr or blend sharp edges, such as when porting and polishing a head.

## Car Wash Owners and Suppliers Association, Inc. (COSA)

A trade association of car wash manufacturers, operators, and suppliers.

## cascade

Two devices in tandem; the output of one device connected to the input of the other.

## case harden

A heat-treating process that hardens the outer surface of metal, while leaving the core soft and ductile.

## catalyst

A lead-sensitive substance, such as platinum, palladium, or rhodium, that accelerates or enhances a chemical reaction without being changed itself. When used in a catalytic converter, it can reduce the level of harmful pollutants in the exhaust.

## catalytic converter

An automotive exhaust-system component, made of stainless steel, containing a catalyst to reduce oxides of nitrogen (NOX), and/or hydrocarbon (HC), and carbon monoxide (CO), in tailpipe emissions.

## catch can

A container on a race car's radiator or fuel tank to prevent liquid from spilling on the ground during a pit stop.

## catch tank

A term often used for catch can.

## catenary effect

The curve that a length of chain assumes between its suspension points.

## cathode

The negatively charged cell from which current flows in an electrolytic cell.

## cathode ray tube (CRT)

A vacuum tube used in electronic equipment and some electronic readouts to display information.

**caulking compound**
> A thick, viscous material used as a sealer at joints, such as around the windshield.

**caustic**
> 1. A salt-based chemical for cleaning engine parts.
> 2. A cleaner that may be used for most metals, except aluminum.

**caution**
> A signal which alerts the operator to an impending dangerous condition requiring attention, but not necessarily immediate action (from MIL-STD-1472D); an annunciator that is more critical than an advisory but less critical than a warning.

**caution flag**
> A yellow flag displayed to race-car drivers to indicate a slow down. Also used to indicate no passing, due to a problem or mishap on the race track.

**cavitation**
> The presence of air in a liquid during pumping, which can inhibit the flow of the liquid.

**cc**
> 1. An abbreviation for cubic centimeter.
> 2. The measure of the volume of a combustion chamber.
> 3. An abbreviation for close cup, a method of determining the flash point of a flammable liquid.

**C-cam**
> The pattern used to grind pistons in an oval or cam shape, with a 0.009 inch (0.23 mm) difference between the thrust face and pinhole side.

**CCCA**
> An abbreviation for the Classic Car Club of America.

**CCEC**

An abbreviation for constant current electronic control.

**CCFOT**

An abbreviation for cycling clutch fixed orifice tube.

**CC-grade oil**

An American Petroleum Institute (API) specification standard for diesel motor oil.

**cc-ing**

To measure or calculate the volume of a combustion chamber in cubic centimeters.

**C-clip**

1. A term often used to describe an outside snap ring.
2. A C-shaped clip used to retain the drive axles in some rear-axle assemblies.
3. A clip used to secure a pin in linkage, such as for carburetion.

**CCOT**

An abbreviation for cycling clutch orifice tube.

**ccw**

An abbreviation for counterclockwise.

**Cd**

A symbol for coefficient of drag.

**CD-grade oil**

An API performance-specification standard for diesel motor oil.

**CDI**

An abbreviation for capacitor discharge ignition.

**cementation**

A process for introducing elements onto the surfaces of metals by high-temperature diffusion.

**cemf**
An abbreviation for counterelectromotive force.

**center bolt**
A term that generally refers to a leaf-spring center bolt.

**center electrode**
The insulated part of a spark plug that conducts electricity toward the electrode gap to ground.

**centering cones**
Tapered pieces of metal, designed to slide onto a shaft to align and hold parts perpendicular to the axis of the shaft.

**centerline**
1. To bore align.
2. To blueprint.
3. The axis of an object.
4. Same as intake centerline when referring to a camshaft.
5. A line indicating the exact center.

**center link**
A steering linkage that is connected to the tie-rod ends that transfers the swinging motion of the gear arm to a linear, or back-and-forth, motion.

**center-mount components**
The modular installation of a system, such as heating or air conditioning, whereby the evaporator is mounted in the center of the firewall, on the engine side, and the heater core is mounted directly to the rear in the passenger compartment.

**center of gravity (CG)**
The exact point around which an object, such as a vehicle, is perfectly balanced in every direction.

**center of wheelbase**
The exact point midway between the front and rear wheels of a vehicle.

**center-point steering**
A steering geometry in which the steering axis passes through the center of the tire contact points.

**center to center**
The distance between two centers, usually cylinder bores.

**centigrade**
1. Former name for 100 point Celsius scale, the point at which water (H2O) boils (100°C).
2. A term often used incorrectly to indicate a metric temperature value. The proper term for a metric temperature value is Celsius.

**centimeter**
A metric unit of linear measure equal to 0.3937 inch.

**centipoise (cP)**
A metric unit of dynamic viscosity. It is used by the paint industry to measure the viscosity of paint, and by the oil industry to indicate the low-temperature operating characteristics of oil.

**centistroke**
A metric unit of kinetic viscosity used to indicate the high-temperature operating characteristics of oil.

**central port injection**
An early fuel-injection system installed on the 4.3L Chevrolet Vortec V–6, using one throttle-body, injection-style injector to pulse fuel directly to individual nozzles at the intake ports.

**central processing unit (CPU)**
The component of a computer system with the circuitry to control the interpretation and execution of instructions.

**centrifugal**
A term often used to describe centrifugal force.

**centrifugal advance**

A mechanical means of advancing spark timing in a conventional distributor with flyweights and springs.

**centrifugal clutch**

A clutch that utilizes a centrifugal force to apply pressure against a friction disc in proportion to the speed of the clutch.

**centrifugal filter**

A rotating filter that relies on centrifugal force to separate impurities from the fluid, usually oil.

**centrifugal filter fan**

A fan found on the air-pump drive shaft used to clean the air entering the air pump.

**centrifugal force**

The outward force, away from the center (axis) of rotation, acting on a revolving object, increasing as the square of the speed.

**Centrifugal pump**

A machine for moving fluid by accelerating it radially outward. More fluid is moved by centrifugal pumps than by all other types combined. The smooth, essentially pulsationless flow from centrifugal pumps, their adaptability to large capacities, easy control, and low cost make them preferable for most purposes. Exceptions are those in which a relatively high pressure is required at a small capacity, or in which the viscosity of the fluid is too great for reasonable efficiency.

Centrifugal pumps consist basically of one or more rotating impellers in a stationary casing which guides the fluid to and from the impeller or from one impeller to the next in the case of multistage pumps. Impellers may be single suction or double suction (Fig. 1). Additional essential parts of all centrifugal pumps are (1) wearing surfaces or rings, which make a close-clearance running joint between the impeller and the casing to minimize the backflow of fluid from the discharge to the suction; (2) the shaft, which supports and drives the impeller;

and (3) the stuffing box or seal, which prevents leakage between shaft and casing.

Fig. 1 Views of centrifugal pumps. (a) Section across the axis of a single-suction volute pump. (b) Section along the axis of a single-suction volute pump. (c) Double-suction impeller.

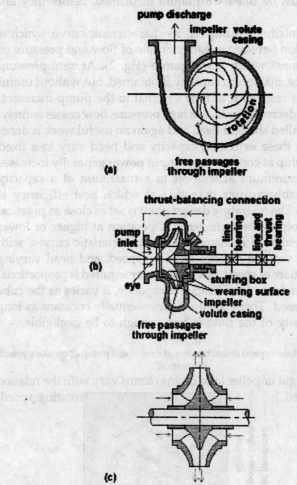

### Characteristics
The rotating impeller imparts pressure and kinetic energy to the fluid pumped. A collection chamber in the casing converts much of the kinetic energy into head or pressure energy before

the fluid leaves the pump. A free passage exists at all times
through the impeller between the discharge and inlet side of
the pump. Rotation of the impeller is required to prevent
backflow or draining of fluid from the pump. Because of this,
only special forms of centrifugal pumps are self-priming. Most
types must be filled with liquid or primed, before they are
started.

Every centrifugal pump has its characteristic curve, which is
the relation between capacity or rate of flow and pressure or
head against which it will pump (Fig. 2). At zero pressure
difference, maximum capacity is obtained, but without useful
work. As resistance to flow external to the pump increases,
capacity decreases until, at a high pressure, flow ceases entirely.
This is called shut-off head and again no useful work is done.
Between these extremes, capacity and head vary in a fixed
relationship at constant rpm. Input power generally increases
from a minimum at shut-off to a maximum at a capacity
considerably greater than that at which best efficiency is
realized. The operating design point is set as close as practical
to the point of best efficiency. Operation at higher or lower
speed results in a change in the characteristic curves, with
capacity varying directly with the speed, and head varying
as the square of speed. Since the power required is proportional
to the product of the head and capacity, it varies as the cube
of the speed. These relations are essentially constant as long
as viscosity of the fluid is low enough to be negligible.

Fig. 2  Some of the typical characteristics of centrifugal pump at constant speed
of rotation.

Centrifugal impeller (and casing) forms vary with the relation
of desired h↑ ↑ ↑        head              rotating speed.

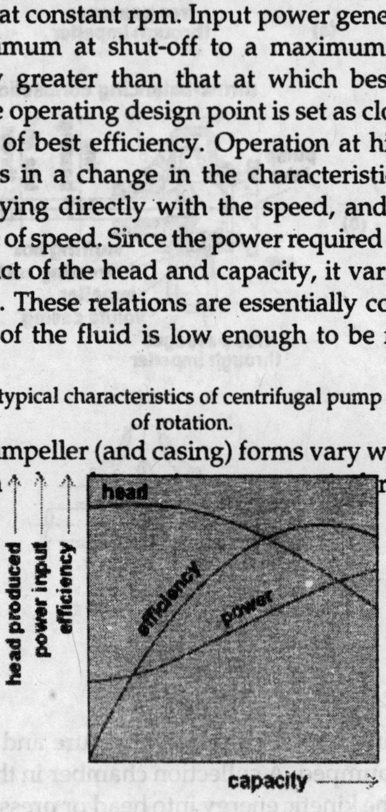

Impellers and pumps are commonly classified as centrifugal, mixed-flow, and axial-flow or propeller (Fig. 3). There is a continuous change from the centrifugal impeller to the axial-flow impeller. For maximum practical head at small capacity, the impeller has a large diameter and a narrow waterway with vanes curved only in the plane of rotation. As the desired capacity is increased relative to the head, the diameter of the impeller is reduced, the width of the waterway is increased, and the vanes are given a compound curvature. For higher capacities and less head, the mixed-flow impeller is used. It discharges at an angle approximately midway between radial and axial. For maximum capacity and minimum head, the axial-flow or propeller-type impeller is used.

Fig. 3  Common classification of impellers. (a) Centrifugal for low speed. (b) Mixed-flow for intermediate speed. (c) Axial-flow or propeller for high speed.

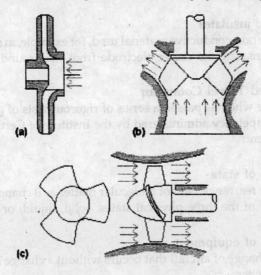

## centrifugal supercharger
A mechanically driven, forced-induction system using centrifugal force to increase air pressure.

## centrifugally disengaging
A one-way roller clutch in which the rollers disengage with the race, in over-running conditions.

**centrifugally engaging**
A one-way roller clutch, in which the rollers make or maintain contact with the race in over-running conditions.

**centrifuge brake drum**
Combining the strength of steel with the friction characteristics of cast iron by spraying a lining of cast iron on the inside of a steel drum while hot.

**century mark**
100 miles per hour.

**Ceramic**
A material composed of silica and earth elements used as an insulator, as in spark plugs.

**ceramic insulator**
The non-conductive material used, for example, in spark plugs, to insulate the center electrode from the ground.

**Certified Travel Counselor**
One who has passed a series of rigorous tests of professional competency administered by the Institute of Certified Travel Agents.

**change of state**
The rearrangement of molecular matter as it changes between any of the three physical states: solid, liquid, or gas.

**change of equipment**
A change of aircraft that occurs without a change in the flight number.

**Chapman strut**
A type of rear suspension having a telescoping strut that is attached to the chassis at the top and to two links at the bottom, restricting lateral and longitudinal movement.

## charcoal canister

A container, usually located in the engine compartment, containing activated charcoal. The charcoal absorbs or traps vapors from a vehicle's sealed fuel system, generally when the engine is turned off. This is a basic component of evaporative emissions control systems.

## charge

1. To fill a battery with electrical energy.
2. To fill an air conditioner with a specific amount of refrigerant or oil by volume or weight.
3. The amount of fuel/air mixture to be burned in a cylinder.
4. To drive aggressively.

## charger

1. A term often used to describe a battery charger.
2. A top performance driver; one who pushes his car to the limit.

## charge temperature sensor

A sensor that sends a signal to the computer causing it to vary the temperature of the intake stream.

## charge the trailer

To fill the trailer air-brake system with air.

## charge tolerance

The accuracy, plus/minus, permitted in the specified amount of liquid or gas that is charged into a system.

## charging

1. The act of placing a charge of refrigerant or oil into an air-conditioning system.
2. The act of refreshing a battery.

## charging cylinder

A container with a visual indicator, for use when a critical or exact amount of fluid must be measured.

**charging hose**
>A small-diameter hose, between the system and source, that is constructed to withstand high pressures.

**charging station**
>A unit containing a manifold and gauge set, charging cylinder, vacuum pump, and leak detector used to service air conditioners.

**chasing threads**
>A manual process using a tap or die to restore threads in a nut or on a bolt.

**chassis**
>The lower structure of a vehicle to which the body and running gear are attached.

**chassis dynamometer**
>A drive-on device, used to measure net road horsepower and torque, delivered by the drive wheels.

**chassis lubrication**
>1. An element of preventive maintenance.
>2. The procedure of applying the correct type and amount of grease to the chassis lubrication points at recommended intervals.
>3. Adding or changing fluids.
>4. Miscellaneous services including tire pressure and safety checks.

**chassis tuning**
>Adjusting the running-gear geometry of a vehicle to compensate for different road conditions.

**chassis waddle**
>A term often used when describing lateral runout or tire waddle.

**chat rooms**
> Discussion groups available on almost any topic. More common on on-line services, but a few are popping up on the Web as well.

**cheater slick**
> A tire that is constructed of the same sticky rubber as a racing tire, but has a shallow tread cut into it to make it street legal.

**check ball**
> 1. A device that maintains air or fuel pressure at a predetermined level.
> 2. A device that permits the flow of fluid or vapor in one direction only.

**check-engine light**
> A warning light, generally located in the instrument cluster, that indicates a potential engine or system problem.

**checker**
> A term often used for checkered flag.

**checkered flag**
> 1. A flag waved at a driver, in closed-course competition, to indicate that he/she has completed the race.
> 2. The first driver shown the flag is the winner of an event.

**check relay**
> A term often used for check-valve relay or vacuum-check relay.

**check-valve**
> 1. A valve that permits the passage of a gas or fluid in one direction, but not in the other.
> 2. A device located in the liquid line or inlet to the drier of some systems to prevent refrigerant flow in the opposite direction when the unit is turned off.

**check-in time**
1. In hotels, the earliest time at which a room will be available.
2. At airline terminals, the latest time at which a passenger may arrive for the flight without the risk of loosing their seat.

**check-valve relay**
An electrical switch to control a solenoid-operated check valve.

**cheek**
The plate-like part of a crankshaft that connects the journals, often serving as a counterweight.

**chemical fire extinguisher**
A type of fire extinguisher that uses dry chemicals that displace oxygen, thereby extinguishing a fire.

**chemical gasket**
A liquid or putty-like substance, similar to RTV, used as a substitute for a solid gasket.

**chemical hazards**
Hazard concerns primarily, but not exclusively, from solvents, fuels, asbestos, and antifreeze.

**chemical instability**
An undesired condition that exists when a contaminant causes a fluid, such as refrigerant, to break down into a harmful chemical.

**chemical milling**
A term often used for acid dip.

**chemical reaction**
The formation of a new substance when two or more substances are brought together.

**chemiluminescence**
The emission of light energy, other than by burning, during a chemical reaction.

**chem mill**
A term used for chemical milling.

**choke**
A manually or thermostatically controlled device mounted to a choke shaft having vanes at the mouth of a carburetor that closes when the engine is cold. This increases the gasoline content in the air/fuel mixture that aids in starting when fuel evaporation is low.

**choke heater**
A device that warms the thermostatic coil of an automatic choke, causing it to open quickly. Later-model carburetors often have an electrical heating element and/or a timer circuit.

**choke piston**
A vacuum-controlled piston used to partially open the choke when the engine starts.

**choke plate**
A butterfly valve that closes at the inlet of the carburetor to enrich the air/fuel mixture, as when starting the engine.

**choke pull-off**
A vacuum motor that opens the choke plate during full acceleration.

**choke rod**
A rod connected to the choke plate.

**choke shaft**
A shaft at the mouth of a carburetor on which the choke plate is mounted.

**choke valve**
A term often used for choke plate.

**chop**
1. To lower the greenhouse of a vehicle.
2. To cut in front of another vehicle in a closed-course race.

**chop, channel, and enamel**
The full restyling treatment of a car.

**chopped flywheel**
To machine the surface of a flywheel to lighten it.

**chop shop**
A facility where stolen vehicles are stripped, dismantled, or otherwise prepared for illegal sale.

**Christmas tree**
The electrical countdown system used in drag racing.

**chrome**
A simple term for chromium.

**chromium**
1. A basic element, Cr.
2. A metal used in alloys to provide a durable and hard surface.
3. An alloy used to plate metal to provide a shining surface.

**city pair**
In airline bookings, the departure and arrival cities on an itinerary.

**city ticket office**
An airline sales and ticketing office located anywhere other than an airport.

**clad**
A metal or material covered with another metal by bonding.

**cladding**
The application of a surfacing material, to impare corrosion and/or heat resistance.

**clad metal**
A metal that is covered with another metal or alloy of different

composition, applied to one or both sides by casting, drawing, rolling, surfacing, chemical deposition, or electroplating.

## class
A group of competition cars with basically the same specifications and performance potentials.

## class F red insulating enamel
A paint that is used to seal the interior of an engine and to aid in rapid oil return to the crankcase.

## classic
1. A fine car.
2. An important racing event, such as the Indy
3. Certain cars built between 1925 and 1948.

## Classic Car Club of America (CCCA)
An organization that is dedicated to the preservation of specific American and European luxury cars manufactured between 1925 and 1948.

## Clean Air Act
A term used for Clean Air Act Amendments (CAAA). A Title IV amendment, signed into law in 1990 by President George Bush, that established national policy relative to the reduction and elimination of ozone-depleting substances.

## Clean Air Performance Professionals (CAPP)
An association of repair shops and technicians promoting inspection and maintenance programs to help protect our environment.

## clean room
An enclosed, ventilated or air-conditioned area, free of airborne particles where delicate components, such as engines and automatic transmissions, can be assembled with minimal risk of contamination.

**clearance ramp**
   The area of a mechanical-lifter camshaft lobe that makes the progression from the base circle to the edge.

**clearance volume**
   The total-volume measurement above a piston at top dead center, (TDC), including the area of the combustion chamber.

**clear coat**
   A hard, transparent coating that is applied to a painted surface to enhance the illusion of visual depth and/or protect the surface.

**clearing time**
   The time it takes a circuit breaker to sense an over current, until circuit interruption.

**clip**
   A major body repair where the front or rear of a vehicle is replaced with the front or rear of another vehicle of the same make and model.

**clock**
   1. A device for telling the time of day.
   2. A term often used for speedometer.
   3. A device that generates a basic periodic signal used to control timing of all operations in a synchronous system or computer.

**clock spring**
   A device, located between the steering column and steering wheel, that conducts electrical signals in an air-bag system to the module, while allowing steering-wheel rotation. This provides electrical continuity in all steering-wheel positions.

**clutch**
   1. A device for connecting and disconnecting the power flow between the engine and standard transmissions, used during starting, shifting, and stopping.

2. A device used to connect two collinear shafts to a driving mechanism such as a motor, engine, or line shaft, and to disconnect them at will.

3. An electromagnetic clutch used to engage and disengage the compressor, to turn the air conditioner on and off.

A coupling device which permits the engagement and disengagement of coupled shafts during rotation. There are four major types: positive, friction, hydraulic, and electromagnetic.

Positive clutch

This type of clutch is designed to transmit torque without slip. It is the simplest of all shaft connectors, sliding on a keyed shaft section or a splined portion and operating with a shift lever on a collar element. The jaw clutch is the most common type of positive clutch. This is made with square jaws (Fig. 1a) for driving in both directions, or spiral jaws (Fig. 1b) for unidirectional drive. Engagement speed should be limited to 10 revolutions per minute (rpm) for a square-jaw clutch and 150 rpm for a spiral-jaw clutch. If desengagement under load is required, the jaws should be finish-machined and lubricated.

Fig. 1 Positive clutches. (a) Square-jaw clutch. (b) Spiral-jaw clutch.

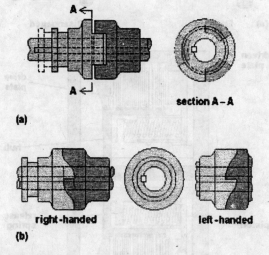

Friction clutch

This type of clutch is designed to reduce coupling shock by

slipping during the engagement period. It also serves as a safety device by slipping when the torque exceeds its maximum rating. The three common designs for friction clutches are cone, disk, and rim, according to the direction of contact pressure.

Fig. 2   Friction clutches. (a) Plate clutch. (b) Multidisk clutch.

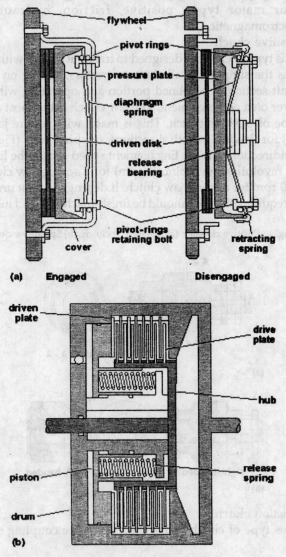

### Cone clutch

This is an axial type clutch. The surfaces of the cone clutch are sections of a pair of cones. This shape uses the wedging action of the mating surfaces under relatively small axial forces to transmit the friction torque. These forces may be established by the compression of axial springs or by the outward displacement of bell-crank levers to apply axial thrust to the conical surfaces.

### Disk clutch

This is also an axial-type clutch. The disk clutch may consist of a single plate or multiple disks (Fig. 2). With the development of improved friction material, disk clutches have become more common than cone clutches, with wide applications in the industrial and automotive fields. Disk clutches are not subjected to centrifugal effects, present a large friction area in a small space, establish uniform pressure distribution for effective torque transmission, and are capable of effectively dissipating the generated heat to the external housing. The disk clutch may be operated dry, as in most automobile drives, or wet by flooding it with a liquid, as in heavier automotive power equipment and in industrial engines. The advantage of wet operation is the ability to remove heat by circulating the liquid enclosed in the clutch housing. Typical friction materials for clutches and design data are shown in the table.

## clutch armature

That part of an electro-magnetic clutch that is attached to the compressor crankshaft and is pulled into contact with the rotor when engaged.

## clutch cable

A cable that actuates the clutch fork of a manual-transmission system.

## clutch coil

A unit consisting of many windings of wire fastened to the front of the air conditioning compressor. When current is applied, a magnetic field is set up that pulls the armature into the rotor to engage the clutch. Also known as clutch field.

**clutch-control unit**
A computer that controls clutch operation.

**clutch-cycle pressure switch**
A pressure activated switch that controls the air-conditioner-compressor clutch action to prevent evaporator icing.

**clutch-cycle switch**
An electrical switch, pressure or temperature actuated, that cuts off the air conditioning compressor at a predetermined evaporator temperature.

**clutch-cycle time (total)**
The time between when an air-conditioner clutch engages and when it disengages, then reengages; a time equal to one on and one off cycle.

**clutch disc**
Circular-shaped component, with a friction facing on each side, that transfers power from the flywheel and pressure plate to the splined clutch shaft.

**clutch field**
A unit consisting of many windings of wire fastened to the front of the air-conditioner compressor. When current is applied, a magnetic field is set up that pulls the armature in to engage the clutch. Also known as clutch coil.

**clutch fork**
A lever in the clutch that actuates the release bearing.

**clutch gear**
A gear or gears found on the clutch shaft.

**clutch housing**
Cast-iron or aluminum shell that surrounds the clutch assembly located between the engine and transmission.

**clutch hub**
A special hub used in certain limited slip-differential

applications, such as single-pack types located between the splined discs and side gear.

## clutch off

To get a fast start by engaging the clutch suddenly, such as at the start of a drag race.

## clutch packs

A series of clutch discs and plates, installed alternately in the clutch housing, to act as a driving or driven unit.

## clutch pedal

A pivoting component inside the vehicle that the driver depresses with his/her foot to operate the clutch.

## clutch piston

An assembly in the multiple-disc clutch drum that is moved by oil pressure to engage the clutch and returned to a released position by mechanical-spring force.

## clutch plate

A pressure plate that forces the clutch disc against the flywheel. A term often used for clutch armature.

## clutch-release bearing

A component, attached to the clutch-release fork, that contacts and then moves the release levers when the clutch pedal is depressed.

## clutch-release fork

A pivoting clutch housing component that transfers motion from the free-play adjusting rod on the clutch linkage to the attached clutch-release bearing.

## clutch-relief check valve

A valve that releases to prevent the buildup of pressure in a multiple-disc clutch assembly.

**coaxial cable**
A cable consisting of two conductors concentric with, and insulated from, each other.

**cockpit**
The driver's compartment of a vehicle.

**code installation**
In general, an installation that conforms to the state and federal regulations and codes to insure safe and efficient conditions.

**Code of Federal Regulations**
Regulations that are generated, published, and enforced by the United States government.

**code sharing**
An agreement whereby airlines permit the use of their CRS code in the flight schedule displays of other airlines.

**co-host carrier**
An airline that pays another to display its flights on a CRS.

**COE**
An abbreviation for cab over engine.

**coefficient of drag (Cx)**
A measure of the air resistance of a moving vehicle; a measure of how much air is moved as the vehicle moves from one point to another.

**coefficient of friction**
The measure of the resistance of one surface moving against another.

**coefficient of water/oil distribution**
The ratio of the solubility of a chemical in water compared to its solubility in oil.

**cog**

A gear, particularly the final drive gear.

## Cogeneration

he sequential production of electricity and thermal energy in the form of heat or steam, or useful mechanical work, such as shaft power, from the same fuel source.

Basic concept

Cogeneration, a direct approach to conserving fuel by improved energy utilization and higher overall system efficiency, is a proven technology offering energy savings. Cogeneration facilities have been installed and are operating at chemical, petrochemical, refinery, mining and metals, paper and pulp, food-processing, district heating and cooling, and utility complexes. These projects can range in electrical power output from several hundred kilowatts to 800,000 kW.

Cogeneration offers economic, environmental, and social benefits. These may be derived from the improved power-cycle efficiency and associated reduction in fuel consumption. In addition to the obvious conservation of energy, potential benefits include (1) higher efficiency by utilizing the same fuel to provide electricity and heat, yielding reduced fuel consumption, reduced fuel costs, and most efficient use of capital investment; (2) an increase in the amount of useful energy produced through the recovery of otherwise wasted heat; (3) fewer effects on the environment as a result of efficient fuel use; (4) through on-site generation, possible reduction of energy losses due to transmission and distribution systems; (5) attainment of plant operation in 1-4 years; (6) economic benefits in the form of tax credits and depreciation.

As an energy conservation technology, cogeneration uses oil, gas, and other alternate fuel resources more efficiently than either typical industrial processes or conventional power plants. Experience has demonstrated that cogeneration facilities are capable of operating in excess of 90% availability with system efficiencies up to 80%. Increased efficiency reduces pollution, fuel consumption, and reliance on imported energy sources. An electric utility requiring additional capacity may look to cogeneration to help defer construction of a new power station. Cogeneration can help a utility to reduce its fuel consumption per kilowatt output, and to count on the availability of cogeneration power during peak-load periods.

Engineering power cycles and applications

Cogeneration projects are typically represented by two basic types of power cycles, topping or bottoming. The topping cycle has the widest industrial application.

The topping cycle (Fig. 1) utilizes the primary energy source to generate electrical or mechanical power. Then the rejected heat, in the form of useful thermal energy, is supplied to the process. The cycle consists of a combustion turbine-generator, with the turbine exhaust gases directed into a waste-heat-recovery boiler that converts the exhaust gas heat into steam which drives a steam turbine, extracting steam to the process while driving an electric generator. This cycle is commonly referred to as a combined cycle arrangement. Combustion turbine-generators, steam turbine-generator sets, and reciprocating internal-combustion-engine generators are representative of the major equipment components utilized in a topping cycle. See also: Generator; Steam turbine; Turbine

Fig. 1  Flow chart of a typical topping cycle.

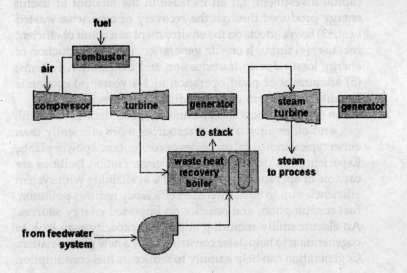

A bottoming cycle (Fig. 2) has the primary energy source applied to a useful heating process. The reject heat from the process is then used to generate electrical power. The typical bottoming cycle directs waste heat from a process to a waste-heat recovery boiler that converts this thermal energy to steam which is supplied to a steam turbine, extracting steam to the process and also generating electrical power.

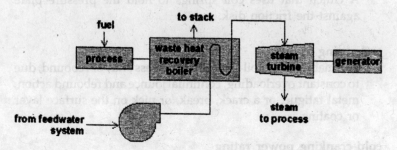

## coil

A term often used to describe a spring or an ignition coil.

## coil bind

A condition where springs are compressed to the point that the coils touch.

## coil failure

1. A defective ignition coil.
2. Also see coil spring failures.

## coil over shock

A suspension component that consists of a shock absorber inside a coil spring.

## coil-preload springs

Coil springs, located in the pressure-plate assembly, made of tempered-steel rods formed into a spiral that resists compression.

## coil spring

A spring-steel bar or rod that is wound into the shape of a

coil to provide an up-down springing effect. Found on most vehicle suspensions, these springs are used to support the car's weight, maintain height, and correctly position all other suspension parts, but are little help in supporting side-to-side or lateral movement.

## coil-spring clutch

A clutch that uses coil springs to hold the pressure plate against the friction disk.

## coil-spring failures

The inability of a coil spring to compress and/or rebound, due to constant overloading, continual jounce and rebound action, metal fatigue, or a crack, break, or nick on the surface layer or coating.

## cold-cranking power rating

The number of amperes that a fully charged battery will deliver for 30 seconds at 0°F (-17.8°C) without the terminal voltage dropping below 7.2 volts.

## cold drawn

A process where metal is drawn or rolled into a particular shape or size.

## cold-engine lockout switch

A switch that sends a signal to the body-control module, or controller, to prevent an action, such as blower-motor operation, until the coolant in the engine has risen to a predetermined temperature.

## cold soak

To place a component in a cool area to allow it to cool to ambient temperature for twelve or more hours.

## cold-solder joint

A loose or intermittent electrical connection, caused by poor soldering techniques.

## cold-start test

A prescribed federal test procedure for measuring emissions before an engine has warmed up after a 12-hour cold soak at 68°F to 78°F (20°C to 25.6°C).

## cold-start valve

A valve that permits additional air into the intake manifold during a cold start on a fuel-injected engine.

## cold-weather modulator

A thermostatically controlled check valve that traps vacuum in the vacuum motor circuit when the car is accelerated hard at any temperature below 55°F (12.8°C), to prevent hesitation by allowing heated air to enter the engine.

## cold weld

A method of repairing small cracks in blocks and heads by using tapered plugs to fill the cracks.

## cold working

The deformation of metallic material at a temperature below the recrystallization temperature, resulting in strain hardening of the material.

## collapsible steering column

An energy-absorbing steering column that is designed to collapse if the driver is thrown into it due to a heavy collision.

## collective

A flight control operated by moving up or down with hand in rotary-wing aircraft, primarily to control lift (altitude); controls collective (total) pitch of the rotors on a rotary-wing aircraft.

## collective cue

A vertical flight director cue for rotary-wing aircraft, primarily to control altitude, by changing power; *Compare:* yoke cue; *Symbols:* Gamma sub 'VERT'; *Typical Units:* percent,in.

## collector

1. A device that collects exhaust gases from the primary tubes and channels them into a single exhaust pipe.
2. The tank of a radiator that receives the fluid before it passes through the radiator.

## collector tank

The tank that collects coolant from the engine, containing a baffle plate to aid in even distribution of coolant through the core.

## color code

A means of identifying conductors or vacuum hoses by the use of color.

## color-code chart

A chart listing the colors of wire insulation and, sometimes, wire sizes for a particular automobile.

## color sanding

Color-blending by lightly sanding to smooth surface imperfections, using 1000 grit or higher paper.

## combination brake system

A dual-brake system that uses disc brakes at the front wheels and drum brakes at the rear wheels.

## combination valve

An H-valve, used in some early air-conditioning systems, combining a suction throttling valve and an expansion valve.

## combined emissions-control system

An early General Motors transmission-controlled spark system that uses the solenoid valve's plunger as an auxiliary throttle stop.

## combustion

The burning of the air/fuel mixture in an engine.

## combustion chamber

Area above a piston at TDC, primarily distinguished by a recessed cylinder head, where combustion takes place.

## combustion emission control (CEC)

An exhaust emission-control system that combines a transmission-controlled spark system and a deceleration throttle-position device.

## combustion knock

A term often used for knock.

## combustion pressure

The pressure in the cylinder from expanding gases immediately after the air/fuel mixture is ignited, which is about four times greater than compression pressure.

## complementary filter

A filter in which the complement of the filter is desired, giving the effect of a high-pass filter by implementing a low-pass filter; a filter for combining multiple data sources, usually of different types, by adding filtered values, where the sum of the filters in the frequency domain is unity; a Kalman filter with fixed gains; Complementary filters are often designed in the frequency domain in way that that the filters determined at build time such that the cutoff frequency of the LFP is equal to that of the HPF. This provides the advantages of DNS's long-term accuracy and INS's short-term accuracy, while filtering DNS's high-frequency noise and INS's slow drift. *Compare:* averaging filter, Kalman filter.

## component isolation

To isolate a component from the rest of the system or circuit for testing or replacement.

## component location table

A table or chart, used with an electrical schematic, that describes or illustrates the actual location of the part being investigated.

### composite headlight

A halogen headlight system that uses a replaceable bulb, allowing vehicle manufacturers to produce any style of headlight lens they desire.

### compound low gear

A combination of low gear in the transmission and low range in the transfer case in a four-wheel-drive vehicle with a two-speed transfer case.

### compound gauge

A gauge that registers both above and below atmospheric pressure; used on the low side of an air-conditioning system.

### compression

1. The process of squeezing a vapor (gas) into a smaller space.
2. The upward stroke of a piston that compresses the air/fuel mixture into the combustion chamber prior to ignition. Short for compression ratio.

### compression braking

The slowing of a vehicle utilizing a diesel engine, such as that provided by a Jake brake. It is a misnomer that a gasoline engine will slow the vehicle by compression braking; actually, vacuum causes the braking effect.

### compression height

A distance, as measured from the crown of the piston to the center of the wrist pin.

### compression ignition

The operating system of a diesel engine, where heated air is used to ignite the fuel.

### compression intake valve

A term used for compression valve or intake valve.

### compression-loaded ball joint

A suspension ball joint, mounted above and resting on the

knuckle, so the vehicle weight forces the ball into the joint.

### compression pressure

The highest pressure developed during the compression stroke in an engine, as checked with a compression gauge.

### compression ratio (CR)

A measurement of how much the air/fuel mixture is compressed inside an engine cylinder. If compressed to 1/10 of its original volume, the compression ratio is 10 to 1.

### compression ring

A piston ring that seals pressure during the compression and power strokes. There are usually two compression rings per piston.

### compression stroke

The movement of the piston from BDC to TDC, immediately after the intake stroke.

### compression valve

A calibrated valve, located at the base of the shock absorber, providing variable resistance to fluid flow during compression.

### compressive strength

The maximum compressive stress that a material can withstand without significant plastic deformation or fracture.

### compressor

1. A component of the refrigeration system that pumps refrigerant and increases the pressure of the refrigerant vapor.
2. A device used to pump air.

### compressor crankshaft seal

A term used for compressor shaft seal.

### compressor-discharge pressure switch

A pressure-operated electrical switch that opens the compressor-clutch circuit during high-pressure conditions.

**compressor-protection switch**

An electrical switch installed in the rear head of some compressors to stop the compressor in the event of a loss of refrigerant.

**compressor-shaft seal**

An assembly consisting of springs, snap rings, O-rings, seal sets, a shaft seal, and a gasket mounted on the compressor crankshaft to permit the shaft to be turned without a loss of refrigerant or oil.

**computer**

A machine capable of following instructions to alter data in a desirable way and to perform most of these operations without human intervention.

**computer-aided manufacturing**

The use of computer technology in the management, control, and operation of manufacturing.

**computer-command control (CCC)**

A term given a computer that controls the function and operation of an automotive system, or sub system.

**computer-controlled brakes**

A system having a sensor on each wheel, feeding electrical impulses into an on-board computer. As the vehicle is stopped, each wheel is stopped or slowed down at the same rate, reducing sideways skidding during rapid braking.

**computer-controlled suspension system**

A system in which a computer-controlled actuator is positioned in the top of each shock absorber or strut. The shock absorber or strut actuators rotate a shaft inside the piston rod, and this shaft is connected to the shock valve.

**computer cycle**

In a periodic, cyclical computer system, the most basic, fastest timing loop.

**computerese**

The jargon and other specialized vocabulary of those working with computers and information-processing systems.

**computerized reservation system (CRS)**

Any of several proprietary computer systems allowing real-time access to airline fares, schedules, and seating availability and offering the capability of booking reservations and generating tickets.

**computer-generated code**

A term more commonly known as trouble code.

**computerize**

1. To equip a business or organization with computers in order to facilitate or automate procedures.
2. To convert a manual operation into one that is performed by a computer.

**computerized air suspension**

A type of suspension system equipped with rubber air bags controlled by an air compressor to maintain a specific ride height determined by vehicle load and road-surface conditions.

**computerized automatic temperature control**

A microprocessor control system that monitors incoming data and adjusts the temperature and humidity of the air inside the passenger compartment.

**computerized engine control**

A microprocessor-based, engine-management system that utilizes various sensor inputs to regulate spark timing, fuel mixture, emissions, and other functions. Most systems include on-board, self-diagnostic capability and store fault codes to help diagnosis of system problems.

**concave fillet weld**

A fillet weld having a concave face.

**concave side**
An inward-curved depression.

**concealed headlight**
A headlight system that enhances a vehicle's style and aerodynamics by hiding the lamps behind electrically- or vacuum-controlled doors when not in use.

**concentrated hub**
An airport where a single airline controls most of the passenger capacity.

**concentricity**
The condition in which two or more features, in any combination, have a common axis.

**concours d'elegance**
French for contest of elegance, a showing of luxury cars in a plush setting.

**condensate**
Moisture that is removed from air, such as that collected on the surface of an air-conditioning-system evaporator.

**countergear**
An integral cluster of three or more various-sized gears, located in the lower transmission case, that revolve on a countershaft to provide the desired gear ratios, usually for second, low, and reverse.

**countershaft**
1. A shaft used in a V-8 engine to reduce the effects of imbalance. Two shafts used in an I-4 engine to reduce the effects of imbalance.
2. The shaft that supports the cluster-gear set in a manual transmission and rotates in the opposite direction of the clutch and driveshaft.

**countersinking**
A machining process, related to drilling, that bevels or recesses the material around the circumference of a hole.

## counterweight

1. A weight that is cast opposite each offset connecting-rod journal to provide the necessary balance.

2. A weight that is added to a rotating shaft or member to offset vibration by balancing the part.

## coupe de ville

A coupe with an open driver compartment and enclosed passenger compartment.

## coupled

Describes operation of flight director in which automatic flight control system causes flight controls to follow commands from flight director or errors from guidance.

## coupling

An attachment where one mechanism or part drives another mechanism or part, to follow the movements of the first.

mechanical fastening device for connecting the ends of two shafts together. There are three major coupling types: rigid, flexible, and fluid.

Rigid coupling

This connection is used only on shafts that are perfectly aligned. The flanged-face coupling (Fig. 1a) is the simplest of these. For this type of coupling the flanges must be keyed to the shafts. The clamp, or keyless compression, coupling (Fig. 1b)has split cylindrical elements which clamp the shaft ends together by direct compression, through bolts, and by the wedge action of conical sections. This coupling is generally used on line shafting to transmit medium or light loads. See also: Machine key

Fig. 1 Rigid coupling. (a) Flanged-face coupling. (b) Clamp coupling.

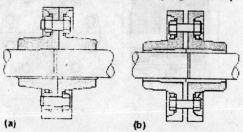

(a)          (b)

Flexible coupling

This connection is used for shafts which are misaligned either laterally or angularly. It also absorbs the impact due to fluctuations in shaft torque or angular speed. The Oldham, or double-slider, coupling (Fig. 2a) may be used to connect shafts that have only lateral misalignment. Because the tongues move about in the slots, the coupling must be well lubricated and can be used only at low speeds. The geared "fast" flexible coupling (Fig. 2b) uses two interior hubs on the shafts with circumferential gear teeth surrounded by a casing having internal gear teeth to mesh and connect the two hubs. Considerable misalignment can be tolerated because the teeth inherently have little interference. This completely enclosed coupling provides means for better lubrication, and is thus applicable for higher speeds. The rubber flexible coupling (Fig. 3a) is used to transmit the torque through a comparatively soft rubber section acting in shear. The type shown in Fig. 3b loads the intermediate rubber member in compression. Both types are recommended for light loads only.

Fig. 2   Flexible coupling. (a) Oldham (double-slider) coupling. (b) Geared "fast" flexible coupling.

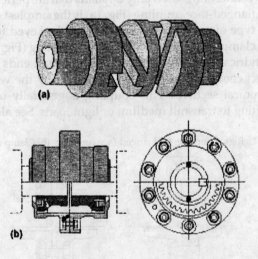

(a)

(b)

Fig. 3   Rubber flexible coupling. (a) Shear type. (b) Compression type.

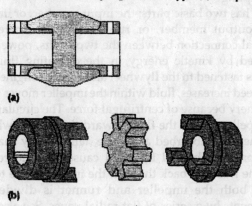

(a)

(b)

## Universal joint

This is a flexible coupling for connecting shafts with much larger values of misalignment than can be tolerated by the other types of flexible coupling. Shaft angles up to 30° may be used. The initial universal joint, credited to Robert Hooke (Fig. 4), was a swivel arrangement by which two pins at right angles allowed complete angular freedom between two connected shafts. However, it suffers a loss in efficiency with increasing angles.

Fig. 4   Hooke's universal joint.

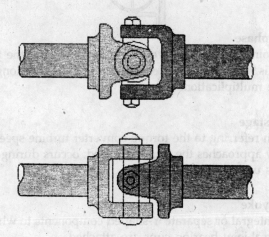

## Fluid coupling

This type has two basic parts: the input member, or impeller, and the output member, or runner (Fig. 5). There is no mechanical connection between the two shafts, power being transmitted by kinetic energy in the operating fluid. The impeller is fastened to the flywheel and turns at engine speed. As this speed increases, fluid within the impeller moves toward the periphery because of centrifugal force. The circular shape of the impeller directs the fluid toward the runner, where its kinetic energy is absorbed as torque delivered by shaft. The positive pressure behind the fluid causes flow to continue toward the hub and back through the impeller. The toroidal space in both the impeller and runner is divided into compartments by a series of flat radial vanes. See also: Fluid coupling; Shafting

Fig. 5   Fluid coupling.

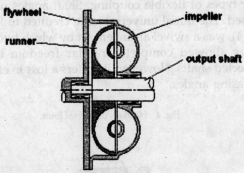

## coupling phase

The point in torque-converter operation where the turbine speed is 90% of the impeller speed, and there is no longer any torque multiplication.

## coupling stage

A term referring to the torque-converter turbine speed, as it closely approaches the impeller speed; occurs during higher speeds under light loads.

## coupling yoke

Two integral or separate Y-shaped components to which the universal-joint bearing cups are attached.

## coupon

1. A piece of metal, of specified size, used for testing.
2. A piece of metal from which a test specimen may be prepared.

## coupon broker

Any person or company that buys and resells airline frequent flyer awards in contravention of airline regulations.

## courier

Any person who accompanies cargo or hand-delivered documents.

## course

Towards a point at a specified course; *Compare:* direct.

## course cut limit (CCLIM)

A guidance control law parameter, generated by the lateral guidance modes; limits the intercept angle of the flight path with a desired course, typically 45deg *Typical Units:* deg, rad.

## courtesy light

Lamps that illuminate the vehicle interior and/or exterior when a door is opened, and are controlled from the headlight and door switches.

## covered electrode

A composite filler metal consisting of a core of bare electrodes or a metal-cored electrode, with a covering sufficient to provide a slag layer on the weld metal.

## cowl

That part of a vehicle between the passenger compartment and engine to which the windshield and dashboard are attached.

## cowl air intake

The inlet at the base of the windshield that allows outside air to enter the heater/air-conditioning system, or driver/passenger compartment of the vehicle.

**CPU**

An abbreviation for central processing unit.

**CR**

An abbreviation for compression ratio.

**cracked**

Broken.

A term often used for the mid-position of a two-way valve.

**crank**

1. A crankshaft.
2. To start an engine.
3. To go fast.

In a mechanical linkage or mechanism, a link that can turn about a center of rotation. The crank's center of rotation is in the pivot, usually the axis of a crankshaft, that connects the crank to an adjacent link. A crank is arranged for complete rotation (360°) about its center; however, it may only oscillate or have intermittent motion. A bell crank is frequently used to change direction of motion in a linkage (see illus.). See also: Linkage (mechanism)

Fig.   Cranks for changing (a) radius of rotation and (b) direction of translation.

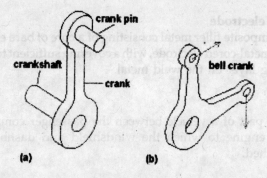

(a)                              (b)

**crankcase**

The lower section of the engine that supports the crankshaft, confined by the lower block casting and the oil pan.

**crankcase breather**
> A tube or vent that allows excessive crankcase pressure to escape.

**crankcase dilution**
> The thinning of oil in the crankcase, caused by the condensation of gasoline due to blow-by, and by seepage past the piston rings.

**crankcase emissions**
> Fumes that leave the crankcase by way of an open or closed ventilation system.

**crankcase fumes**
> Vapors inside the crankcase that could contaminate the air, including unburned fuel vapors, water vapor, or blow-by gases. Also known as crankcase vapors.

**crankcase pressure**
> The pressure produced in the crankcase from blow-by gases.

**crankcase vapors**
> Fumes inside the crankcase, caused by blow-by, that could contaminate the air, including unburned fuel vapors, water vapor, or blow-by gases. Also known as crankcase fumes.

**crankcase ventilation**
> A tube or vent that allows excessive crankcase pressure to escape.

**cranking circuit**
> The starter and its associated circuit, including battery, relay (solenoid), ignition switch, neutral start switch, cables, and wires.

**cranking motor**
> A special high-torque electric motor designed for the purpose of cranking the engine for starting.

**current-draw test**
Starting-system test that determines amperes consumed by the starter motor during operation.

**cursor**
A position indicator on a video display to indicate data or a command to be corrected, repositioned, or entered.
*See:* moding cursor, target cursor

**cut a big one**
To record a particularly high speed or fast time. Also referred to as cut a fat one.

**cutoff frequency**
The frequency at which the gain of a filter is at an edge of a band, usually taken to be when gain is 0.5, or -3.01dB; the frequency at which the output of a filter is half the power of the input; *See Also:* band-pass filter, high-pass filter, low-pass filter; *Symbols:* omega sub c; *Typical Units:* rad/s,Hz; *Dimensions:* 1/Time.

**cutout**
1. To experience a momentary engine miss without a stall.
2. A fuse holder that may be used to isolate part of a circuit.
3. To bypass the exhaust system.

**cutout relay**
An electrical, protective ON and OFF switch between the generator and battery.

**cutting attachment**
A device for converting an oxyfuel-gas welding torch into an oxygen cutting torch.

**cutting brake**
A special type of master cylinder with two brake levers to control how much brake pressure is applied to either of the rear wheels, allowing an off-road vehicle to make a much sharper turn.

**cutting fluid**
Any fluid applied to a cutter or to work being cut, to aid in the cutting operation by cooling and lubricating.

**cutting tip**
The part of a cutting torch from which the gases are emitted.

**cyberspace**
All information in electronic areas. Un delivered e-mail is defined as being lost in cyberspace.

**cycle**
1. The process of discharging and then recharging a battery.
2. A series of repeated events such as the intake, compression, power, and exhaust strokes of an engine.
3. A complete series of events.
4. Short for motorcycle.

**cycle clutch time**
The time from the moment the clutch engages until it disengages, then re-engages. Total time is equal to ON time, plus OFF time for one cycle.

**cycle fenders**
Individual fenders for each wheel of a car.

**cycling clutch**
An air-conditioning, electro-magnetic clutch that is turned on and off to control cabin temperature.

**cycling-clutch fixed orifice tube (CCFOT)**
An air-conditioning system having a fixed-orifice tube in which the air temperature is controlled by starting and stopping the compressor with a thermostat or pressure compressor with a thermostat or pressure control.

**cycling-clutch orifice tube**
A term often used for cycling-clutch, fixed-orifice tube.

## cycling-clutch system

An air-conditioning system in which the cabin air temperature is controlled by starting and stopping the compressor with a thermostat or pressure control.

## Cyclone furnace

A water-cooled horizontal cylinder in which fuel is fired and heat is released at extremely high rates. When firing coal, the crushed coal, approximately 95% of which is sized at 14 in. (0.6 cm) or less, is introduced tangentially into the burner at the front end of the cyclone (see illus.). About 15% of the combustion air is used as primary and tertiary air to impart a whirling motion to the particles of coal. The whirling, or centrifugal, action on the fuel is further increased by the tangential admission of high-velocity secondary air into the cyclone.

Fig.  Schematic diagram of cyclone furnace.

## cylgastos

A gasket made of treated asbestos layers bonded to a metal plate; now obsolete due to personal and environmental hazards associated with asbestos.

## cylinder

1. A storage tank for gases, such as refrigerant.
2. The round hole(s) inside an engine block that provide space for the reciprocating piston(s).

## cylinder arrangement

The way cylinders are placed in an engine, such as in-line, in a row; vee, in two banks or rows at an angle to each other; or flat, pancake.

## cylinder deglazing

The process of removing the glaze from cylinder walls after extended use.

## cylinder head

That part of the engine that covers the cylinders and pistons.

## cylinder-head gasket

The gasket used to seal the head to the block to promote compression and to ensure a leak-free bond.

## cylinder liner

A replaceable cylinder wall.

## cylinder numbering

The order in which the cylinders are numbered cylinder one may be on either front side of a V engine and start with one at the front of in-line engines.

**data processor**
A device that is capable of performing data operations, such as a microcomputer.

**data source object (DSO)**
Software that receives data from a physical device, translates the data into standard units, maintains equipment status, and provides a common interface for each variation of a particular device.

**denatured alcohol**
Ethyl alcohol, used to clean brake systems; contains methanol, rendering it unfit for human consumption.

**denied-boarding compensation**
Payment given passengers who have been bumped from a flight, cruise, or land-tour. May be a free trip, money, or accommodations.

**Depart from hover (dhov)**
A guidance mode providing lateral guidance, longitudinal guidance and vertical guidance for a set heading or bank angle, a set speed, and a set climb rate, altitude or pitch.

**Department of Environmental Regulation (DER)**
A department of the United States Environmental Protection Agency (EPA).

**Department of Transportation (DOT)**
   The United States Department of Transportation, a federal
   agency charged with the regulation and control of the shipment
   of all hazardous materials.

**departure angle**
   The maximum angle, in degrees, of a line running rearward
   and upward from the rear tire contact point to the lowest
   obstruction under the rear of the vehicle.

**departure tax**
   Tax levied on travelers when they leave a country.

**depolarize**
   To remove or eliminate positive and negative poles from an
   item.

**deposited metal**
   Any filler metal that may have been added during a welding
   process.

**depressed park**
   The out-of-sight positioning, below the hood line, of windshield
   wiper blades of some wiper systems.

**depressurize**
   To release or remove pressure.

**depth of fusion**
   The penetration that a weld fusion extends into the base metal,
   or previous bead, from the surface.

**DER**
   An abbreviation for Department of Environmental Regulations.

**derivative**
   Rate of change, usually with respect to time; *Symbols:* x dot,
   x prime, x sup (1), dx/dt, Dx.

**Derrick**

A hoisting machine consisting usually of a vertical mast, a slanted boom, and associated tackle (see illus.). Derricks have a wide variety of forms. The mast may be no more than a base for the boom; it may be a tripod, an A-frame, a fixed column, and so on. Fixed stays may guy it in place. The boom may be fixed, it may pivot at the base of the mast, it may swing horizontally from near the top of the mast, or it may be omitted. The derrick may be permanently fixed, temporarily erected, or mobile on a cart or truck.

Fig.   A boom derrick equipped with a swinging mast and anchored legs.

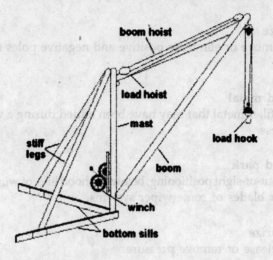

**derived**

Calculated values for which no direct measurement exists; *Compare:* estimated, filtered, measured, raw, selected, smoothed.

**desiccant**

1. A material, such as silica gel, that absorbs moisture from a gas or liquid.
2. A drying agent used in refrigeration systems to remove excess moisture.

**design working pressure**
The maximum pressure under which a specific system or component is designed to work safely and without failing.

**designator, designator code**
A two- or three-digit alphanumeric code uniquely identifying airlines and airports throughout the world. Administered by IATA.

**desired.**
What must be achieved in order to match a plan; *Synonyms:* reference.

**desired altitude (DESALT)**
A guidance control law parameter, generated by the vertical guidance modes; altitude which controlled altitude is attempting to achieve *Typical Units:* ft; *Dimensions:* Length.

**desired path**
A trajectory in space determined by guidance to meet the current mission objectives.

**Desired speed (DESS)**
A guidance control law parameter, generated by the longitudinal guidance modes; speed which controlled speed is attempting to achieve *Typical Units:* ft/s,kt; *Dimensions:* Length / Time.

**desmodromic valves**
A valve system in which positive cam action, not spring action, is used to open and close the intake and exhaust valves.

**detent**
1. A recess to hold the gear selector in the gear range selected.
2. A pin, stud, or lever which initiates or halts an action at a determined time or interval.

**detergent**
A chemical, added to engine oil, that possesses the ability to clean by preventing the accumulation of deposits.

**detergent dispersant**
A chemical component in motor oil that loosens dirt and varnish in an engine.

**detonation**
A phenomenon of internal combustion where the compressed air/fuel charge explodes violently instead of burning smoothly, usually due to the creation of a second flame front in the combustion chamber, away from the spark plug.

**detonation-detection sensor**
A term often used for detonation sensor.

**detonation sensor**
A device, mounted on an engine block, cylinder head, or intake manifold, that generates and sends a small voltage signal to the ECU, to retard timing, when encountering the vibration frequency associated with detonation.

**Detroit locker**
A specific brand of locking rear-end differential.

**deuce**
1. A 1932 Ford.
2. A two-barrel carburetor.
3. A 1962 through 1967 Chevrolet.

**deuce and a half**
A truck having a nominal payload capacity of 2-1/2 tons.

**deuce and a quarter**
The Buick Electra 225, particularly the 225-inch-long 1959 model.

**diagnosis**
A standard procedure that is followed to locate and identify the cause of a malfunction.

**diagnostician**
A person who determines the cause of problems when given all the signs and symptoms.

**diagonal brake system**
A dual-brake system with separate hydraulic circuits connecting diagonal wheels together; right front to left rear and left front to right rear.

**diagonal cross check**
In preparation for oval-track racing, the measure of weight distribution between the right-front and left-rear wheels and between the left-front and right-rear wheels.

**dial**
An instrument with an analog-gauge indicator.

**dial in**
1. To set the Christmas tree for drag racing events, with the interval between starting times for vehicles with different indexes.
2. To set up a car with the right combination for maximum performance for any particular racing condition.

**dial under**
A practice allowed under NASCAR rules in handicap eliminations for Stock and Super Stock classes where the breakout rule is in effect.

**diameter**
The cross-section measurement of a round or circular object.

**diaphragm**
1. A flexible membrane in a speaker or microphone where electrical signals are converted to sound vibrations and vice versa.
2. The flexible membrane found in a temperature- or pressure-control device that seals in an inert fluid from the atmosphere while allowing a mechanical movement.

**diaphragm clutch**
A clutch having a shallow, cone-shaped spring disc to provide pressure to the plate.

**diaphragm spring**
A spring shaped like a disk with tapered fingers pointed inward.
A spring shaped like a wavy disk.

**diaphragm-spring clutch**
A clutch in which a diaphragm spring applies pressure against the friction disk.

**dice**
A tight contest between two cars on an oval track or road course generally battling for a specific position.

**dichlorodifluoromethane**
The proper chemical name for Refrigerant-12.

**dielectric**
1. An insulator.
2. A term referring to the insulation between the plates of a capacitor.

**die out**
To stall or stop running.

**diesel cycle**
An engine operating cycle where the air is compressed and the fuel is injected at the end of the compression stroke, causing ignition.

**diesel engine**
A compression-ignition engine.
In internal combustion engine operating on a thermodynamic cycle in which the ratio of compression ($Rv = 15$) of the air charge is sufficiently high to ignite the fuel subsequently injected into the combustion chamber. Compared to an engine

operating on the Otto cycle, the diesel engine utilizes a wider variety of fuels with a higher thermal efficiency and consequent economic advantage under many service applications (Fig. 1).

Fig. 1 Cross section of a slow-speed two-stroke diesel engine.

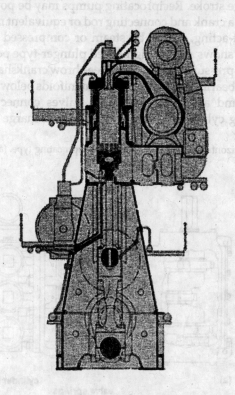

## Diesel Engine Manufacturers Association (DEMA)
A professional association of diesel-engine manufacturers.

## dieseling
A condition in which a carbureted engine continues to run after the ignition is shut off.

## Displacement pump
A pump that develops its action through the alternate filling and emptying of an enclosed volume.

## Reciprocating types

Positive-displacement reciprocating pumps have cylinders and plungers or pistons with an inlet valve, which opens the cylinder to the inlet pipe during the suction stroke, and an outlet valve, which opens to the discharge pipe during the discharge stroke. Reciprocating pumps may be power-driven through a crank and connecting rod or equivalent mechanism, or direct-acting, driven by steam or compressed air or gas. Figure 1 shows a small high-speed plunger-type power pump for high-pressure service. The three-throw crankshaft is carried in roller bearings at each end. The manifolds below the suction valves and above the discharge valves connect the three pumping cylinders to the suction and discharge piping.

Fig. 1   Horizontal triplex power pump of reciprocating type. (a) Plan. (b) Elevation.

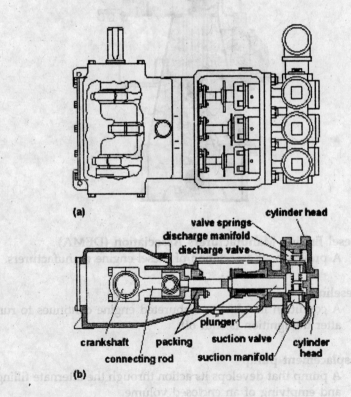

(a)

(b)

Power pumps are frequently built with one or two throw cranks and double-acting liquid ends, or with five, seven, or even nine cranks where smoother flow is desirable. Power-driven reciprocating pumps are highly efficient over a wide range of discharge pressures. Except for some special designs with continuously variable stroke, reciprocating power pumps deliver essentially constant capacity over their entire pressure range when driven at constant speed. In some applications this is an advantage, but in others it complicates the controls required.

Direct-acting steam types

A reciprocating pump is readily driven by a reciprocating engine; a steam or power piston at one end connects directly to a fluid piston or plunger at the other end. Direct-acting reciprocating pumps are simple, flexible, low-speed machines which are low in efficiency unless the heat in the exhaust steam can be used for heating. Steam pumps can be built for a wide range of pressure and capacity by varying the relative size of the steam piston and the liquid piston or plunger. The delivery of a steam pump may be varied at will from zero to maximum simply by throttling the motive steam, either manually or by automatic control. Direct-acting pumps are built as simplex, having one steam and one liquid cylinder; and duplex, having two steam and two liquid cylinders side by side. As indicated by Fig. 2, each steam valve of a duplex pump is positively driven by the motion of the opposite piston

Fig. 2 Duplex type of direct-acting steam-driven feedwater pump.

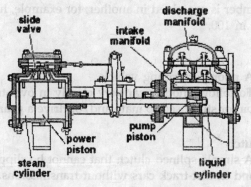

rod by means of cranks and links. In the case of a simplex pump, to avoid stalling at low speed, the valve linkage operates a small pilot valve which in turn controls a piston-thrown main steam valve.

**div**
> An abbreviation for division.

**dive**
> The tendency of the front of a vehicle to press down on the front springs during heavy braking.

**divergent-convergent nozzle end**
> An exhaust-pipe nozzle that is expanded then reduced in size at the end.

**divergent nozzle end**
> An exhaust-pipe nozzle end that expands from the pipe inlet to the end.

**diverter valve**
> A vacuum-operated valve in an air-injection system that directs air-pump output to the atmosphere during high-vacuum deceleration to eliminate backfiring.

**division**
> 1. A branch or department of an organization.
> 2. The mathematic operation to determine how many of one number is contained in another; for example, how many 10s are in 100.

**dog**
> 1. A poor performing vehicle.
> 2. To follow another car very closely in oval-track racing.
> A pin or stub used to mate and/or drive a gear or assembly.

**dog clutch**
> 1. A simple splined clutch that cannot be slipped; generally found in dirt-track cars without transmissions.

2. The mating collars, flanges, or lugs that can be moved as desired to engage or disengage similar collars, flanges, or lugs in order to transmit rotary motion.

## dog house
1. The housing over an engine or transmission.
2. The front fenders, grille, and hood assembly of a vehicle.

## dog leg
A sharp, angular turn.

## dog tracking
Off-center tracking of rear wheels as related to the front wheels.

## DOHC
An abbreviation for dual overhead camshaft.

## do-it-yourself (DIY)
To repair one's vehicle.

## do-it-yourselfer (DIYer)
One known to repair their own vehicles.

## domain name
An identification of an Internet site. Commonly referred to as a "Web address". "casto.com" and "204.255.196.1" are two forms of a domain name.

## domed piston
A piston having a raised crown.

## domestic airline
An air carrier that provides service within its own country. Also called a domestic carrier.

## DOM tubing
An abbreviation for drawn-over mandrel tubing, a type of seamless tubing with precise and consistent inside and outside dimensions, used for race-car chassis construction.

**D-1**
The low forward-drive range of an automatic transmission.

**donuts**
1. A 360-degree tire burnout.
2. Tires, especially big racing slicks.

**dooley**
A Chevrolet pick-up truck with dual rear wheels; generally a term given to any dual-wheel vehicle.

**doorslammer**
A full-bodied drag car with functioning doors.

**doozie**
1. Short for Duesenberg, considered the greatest racing car ever built in the United States.
2. Anything, such as a car, that is truly fine or outstanding.

**doped solder**
Solder containing a small amount of an added element to ensure retention of one or more characteristics of the materials on which it is used.

**doppler**
A technique for measuring velocity by radiating and determining frequency shift.

**Doppler Navigation System (DNS, DPLR)**
A navigation for measuring velocity by radiating and determining frequency shift.

**double filament lamp**
A lamp designed for more than one function; used in the stoplight, tail light, and the turn-signal circuits combined.

**double flare**
A flare on the end of tubing, made by folding it over to form a double face.

## double-groove valve stem
A valve stem having two keeper grooves.

## double-J rim
The double-J shaped safety locks on a rim, used to hold the inner and outer tire beads securely.

## double occupancy rate
The rate charged when two people will occupy a room, suite, apartment, etc. For example, a hotel might charge an individual $100 per night for a room (single occupancy) but charge two people only $130 for double occupancy of the same room.

## double pivot control arm
A term used for control arm.

## double pole double throw (DPDT)
A term used to identify a switch configuration having six terminals that connects one pair to either of the other two pairs of terminals.

## double pole single throw (DPST)
A term used to identify a switch configuration having four terminals that connect or disconnect two pairs of terminals simultaneously.

## double-reduction differential
A differential that contains extra gears to provide additional gear reduction.

## downline
All segments, legs, or cities listed below the originating or headline city (on a schedule or CRS).

## drive axle
An axle or axle shaft that transmits power to the drive wheels.

## drive belt
Flexible belt or belts used to connect a drive pulley on the

crankshaft to the coolant pump and accessories. Two basic types of drive belts are the serpentine or multiple-ribbed belt and the V-belt.

## drive by wire
To use an electronic throttle control rather than mechanical linkage.

## drive coil
A hollow field coil in a positive engaged starter that is used to attract the moveable pole shoe.

## drive gear
In a combination of two operating gears, the first is the drive gear and the other is the driven gear.

## drive line
Assembly of various parts such as the driveshaft, universal joints, and connecting yokes that transmit torque from the transmission to the differential.

## drive-line torque
The transfer of torque between the transmission and the driving axle assembly.

## drive-line windup
A reaction that takes place as a result of the transfer of engine torque through the rear-wheel drive-line.

## driven disk
The friction disk of a clutch.

## driven gear
The gear that receives the driving action from the drive gear.

## driven pinion
A rotating shaft in the differential that transmits torque to another gear.

**drive pinion gear**
> One of the two main driving gears to multiply engine torque located within the transaxle or rear-driving axle housing.

**driver**
> 1. The operator of a vehicle.
> 2. A car for everyday use.

**driver-reaction distance**
> The distance traveled between the point at which the driver perceives a need to brake and the actual start of brake application.

**driving lights**
> A term used for driving lamps.

**drop-center rim**
> A wheel that has a smaller diameter center section, to facilitate tire replacement, designed to prevent the tubeless tire from rolling off the rim when the tire blows out.

**drop-center safety rim**
> A wheel rim with a low center area and raised flanges designed to prevent the tire from accidentally coming off the rim.

**drop-center wheel**
> A conventional wheel that has a space in the center for one bead to fit into while the other bead is being lifted over the rim flange.

**drop head coupe**
> A British term for a two-door convertible.

**drop the hammer**
> To engage the clutch and depress the accelerator suddenly. To suddenly depress the accelerator to the floorboard.

**drop-throttle oversteer**
> A term used for lift-throttle oversteer.

**dropped axle**
A lowered beam axle used on older Fords to dump the front end.

**drop through**
The undesirable sagging or surface irregularity encountered when brazing or welding; caused by overheating with rapid diffusion between the filler metal and the base metal.

**druid**
A term used by a dissatisfied contestant, who has problems with the rules, when referring to a race official.

**drum**
The part of a brake that rotates with the axle hub and that the brake shoes press against to slow or stop the vehicle.

**drum armature**
A generator or motor armature having its coils wound longitudinally or parallel to its axis.

**drum brake**
A type of brake in which stopping friction is created by shoes pressing against the inside of the rotating drum.

**drum-brake fade**
The loss of braking efficiency due to excessive heat.

**drum maximum diameter**
The largest diameter, generally 0.060 inch (1.5 mm) over original, to which a brake drum can be machined or worn before it is considered unsafe.

**dry**
1. The process of changing from a liquid to a solid, as in paint.
2. The process of evaporation, as in water.

**dry-charged battery**
A battery that is filled with electrolyte only when put into service.

**dry deck**
A condition in which the piston crown is at the level of the block deck.

**D-2**
The high, forward-drive range for an automatic transmission.

**dual-area diaphragm**
An automatic transmission shift control that receives its vacuum signal from the intake manifold and the EGR port.

**dual-bed catalytic**
A term used for dual-bed catalytic converter.

**dual-bed catalytic converter**
A catalytic converter that passes different gases through an upper or front chamber coated with platinum and rhodium and a lower or back chamber coated with platinum and palladium.

**dual-bed converter**
A term used for dual-bed catalytic converter.

**dual-brake system**
A brake system that uses two hydraulic circuits; should one fail, the other remains operational.

**dual camshaft**
A type of engine that has two camshafts for opening and closing additional valves.

**dual designated carrier**
Air carrier that uses another airline's code in flight schedule displays.

**ductility**
The property of a material that permits it to be worked by drawing or stretching without rupture.

**duct tape**
  A heavy duty, fiber-backed tape used for emergency repairs to body parts, in all forms of racing.

**duesie**
  1. Anything truly fine or outstanding.
  2. Short for Duesenberg, touted by many to be the finest race car ever built. Also, doozie.

**dummy load**
  An electrical test procedure to simulate actual operating conditions.

**dummy shaft**
  A shaft used as an aid in the assembly or disassembly of a parts group.

**dump**
  1. To lower the front end.
  2. To defeat a competitor in a drag race.
  3. To damage or destroy a component, such as a transmission.

**dumped and tubbed**
  A vehicle that has been lowered in the front and fitted with oversize wheel wells.

**dump station**
  A facility where RV's and others clean their holding tanks.

**dump tubes**
  Straight through exhaust headers.

**dune buggy**
  A small, light-weight, off-road vehicle with little or no body work.

**duo-servo**
  A drum brake design with increased stopping power due to the servo or self-energizing effect of the brake.

**durability**
> The quality of being useful, generally referring to the life of a catalyst or emission-control system.

**Dura Spark ignition**
> An ignition system developed by Ford.

**duration**
> The time, in crankshaft degrees, that a camshaft holds an exhaust or intake valve open.

**dust**
> To overtake or defeat a competitor in a race.

**dust off**
> A term often used for dust.

**dust shield**
> 1. The upper portion of a shock absorber that surrounds the lower twin-tube unit.
> 2. A covering that protects an assembly from the elements.

**duty cycle**
> The percentage of time that a power source, or one of its accessories, can be operated at rated output, without overheating.

**duty solenoid**
> A solenoid on a feedback carburetor that cycles many times per second to control a metering rod, and therefore, the air/ fuel mixture.

**dwell**
> The degree of distributor-shaft rotation while the ignition breaker points are closed.

**dye-penetrant testing**
> A non-destructive, inexpensive method of testing metal for cracks.

**Dyer drive**

A type of starter-motor drive used in heavy-duty applications that provides mechanical meshing means and automatic demeshing.

**dykum blue**

A blue dye used to color metal.

**Dykes ring**

A compression piston ring having an L cross-sectional shape that provides sealing against the cylinder walls.

**dynamically balanced**

1. A term that often refers to a wheel and tire being balanced while spinning.
2. In general terms, the balance of any object when it is in motion.

**dynamo**

An electric DC-current generator.

**dynamometer**

A machine on which a vehicle may be driven, simulating actual driving conditions for emissions and diagnostic purposes.

**dyno**

Short for dynamometer.

**Dytel**

A trade name for a red dye found in some CFC refrigerants.

**Dzus fastener**

A screw-like fastener that may be removed or installed with a quarter turn, ideal for race-car body panels that may have to be replaced quickly.

**E**

**EGR system**
An EGR valve, mounted on the intake manifold, that meters a small amount of exhaust gas into the intake manifold to dilute the air/fuel mixture. This keeps combustion temperatures below 2,500°F and reduces the formation of NOX. The amount of exhaust gas recirculated into the engine is only a few percent.

**EGR valve**
An abbreviation for exhaust gas recirculation valve.

**EGR valve-position sensor**
A potentiometer that keeps the engine control computer informed relative to the EGR valve position.

**EIN**
An abbreviation for engine identification number.

**EL**
An abbreviation for exposure limit.

**elapsed time (ET)**
The time it takes a vehicle to cover a given distance, usually from a standing start, recorded to the thousandths of a second.
  elastic limit: The maximum stress a metal can withstand without exhibiting a permanent deformation on release of the stress.

**elapsed flying time**
 Actual time an airplane spends in the air, as opposed to time
 spent taxiing to and from the gate and during stopovers.

**elastomeric seal**
 A seal made of rubber or a similar material.

**electronic ticket delivery network (ETDN)**
 A network, national or regional, of ticket printing machines
 that are not operated by an ARC-accredited agency but instead
 by a company that sells its ticket distribution services. Also
 called "electronic ticket distribution network." An ETDN
 delivers flight and passenger coupons after an agent generates
 the ticket.

**electric assist choke**
 A choke containing a small electric heating element to warm
 the choke spring.

**electric brakes**
 A brake system having an electro-magnet and armature at
 each wheel to provide the braking action.

**electric car**
 A vehicle having an electric motor as the power source.

**electric current**
 The movement of electrons through a conductor.

**electric defrosting**
 Use of electric-resistance heating coils to melt ice and frost off:
 1. Evaporators.
 2. Rear windows.

**electric-drive cooling fan**
 1. An engine-cooling fan driven by an electric motor.
 2. An electrically controlled fan that cycles ON and OFF with
 the air conditioner control, if predetermined system and/or
 ambient temperatures are exceeded.

## electric engine-cooling fan

A 12-volt, motor-driven fan that is electrically controlled by either, or both, of two methods: an engine-coolant temperature switch (thermostat) and/or the air-conditioner select switch.

## electric fuel pump

A device having either a reciprocating diaphragm or a revolving impeller operated by electricity to draw fuel from the tank to the fuel delivery system.

## electric system

Any of the systems and sub systems that make up the automobile wiring harnesses, such as the lighting system or starting and charging system.

## electric vehicle

A vehicle having electric motors like a power source driven by on-board rechargeable batteries.

## electric welding

A term often used for arc welding.

## electrochromic mirror

A mirror that automatically adjusts the amount of reflectance based on the intensity of glare.

## electrocution

Death caused by electrical current through the heart, usually in excess of 50 ma.

## electrode

1. A component of the electrical circuit that terminates at a gap across which current must arc.
2. A rod used in welding.

## electrohydraulic pressure actuator

A valve that will provide a continuous adjustment of fuel pressure in certain fuel-injection systems.

**electrolyte**

A substance in which the conduction of electricity is accompanied by chemical action.

**electron**

An element of matter that surrounds the nucleus and helps determine the chemical properties of an atom.

**electronically controlled transmission (ECT)**

A transmission that is electronically linked to the vehicle's electronic control system.

**electronic air suspension (EAS)**

A suspension system having provisions to adjust to road and/or load conditions to ensure a comfortable ride. May also include automatic level control.

**electronic brake control module (EBCM)**

A system having a monitor at each wheel to sense conditions and feed an electrical impulse into an onboard computer to reduce sideways skidding during rapid braking action.

**electronic climate control (ECC)**

A system used to regulate the temperature and humidity of a vehicle's cabin.

**electronic computer control system (ECCS)**

A term used for electronic control assembly (ECA).

**electronic control assembly (ECA)**

A device that receives signals, processes them, makes decisions, and gives commands. More commonly referred to as a computer.

**electronic controlled transmission (ECT)**

A transmission that has electronic sensors to monitor throttle position, engine speed, torque converter turbine speed, and other drive-train operations that effect shifting, leading to fuel economy.

## electronic control module (ECM)
An electronic device used to control some engine functions.

## electronic control unit (ECU)
A digital computer that controls engine and transmission functions based on data that it receives from sensors, relative to engine rpm and temperature, air temperature, intake-manifold vacuum, and throttle position.

## electronic cycling-clutch switch
An electronic switch that prevents the evaporator from freezing by signaling various electronic control devices when the evaporator reaches a predetermined low temperature.

## electronic engine control (EEC)
A system that regulates an engine's electrical functions.

## electronic distributorless ignition system (EDIS)
An obsolete term for an ignition system that relies on a computer to time and route the electrical spark to the proper spark plug at the proper interval. Now known as electronic ignition (EI) system.

## electronic feedback carburetor (EFC)
A carburetor that controls the air/fuel mixture according to commands from the engine control computer.

## electronic fuel control (EFC)
A fuel system that uses electronic devices to monitor engine functions to ensure that the proper air/fuel ratio reaches the combustion chamber for optimum engine performance under any operating condition.

## electronic fuel-injection system
A fuel-injection system that injects gasoline into a spark-ignition engine that includes an electronic control to time and meter the fuel flow.

**electronic ignition (EI)**
> An ignition system where a solid state device has replaced mechanical breaker points.

**electronic ignition system**
> An ignition system controlled by the use of small electrical signals and various semiconductor devices and circuits.

**electronic leak detector**
> An electrically (AC or DC) powered leak detector that emits an audible and/or visual signal when its sensor is passed over a refrigerant leak.

**electronic level control (ELC)**
> A device that automatically regulates the ride height of a vehicle under various load conditions.

**electronic mail (e-mail)**
> The process of sending, receiving, storing, and forwarding messages in digital form over telecommunication facilities.

**electron optics**
> Electronics that apply the behavior of moving electrons under the influence of electrostatic or electromagnetic forces to devices or equipment.

**electronics**
> The branch of science pertaining to the study, control, and application of currents of free electrons, including the motion, emission, and behavior of the currents.

**electronic spark control (ESC)**
> A system that controls and governs the vacuum signal to the distributor to assure proper distributor retard-advance under various engine-load conditions.

**electronic spark timing (EST)**
> An electronic system that, based on input signals, provides the correct spark timing for a given engine condition.

**electroplating**

A process for depositing metal on a conductive surface that is made by the cathode in an electrolytic bath containing dissolved salts of the metal being deposited.

**electrostatic shield**

A shield that protects a device or circuit from electrostatic energy, but not necessarily from electromagnetic energy.

**element**

A substance that cannot be further divided; the smallest of matter.

**elephant foot**

A valve-adjusting screw having a ball that swivels when it contacts the valve stem.

**elephant motor**

The Chrysler Hemi 425 cid engine.

**elevation**

An angle in the vertical plane through a longitudinal axis; height above mean sea level, usually of terrain.

**elevator**

A control surface on fixed-wing aircraft, usually mounted on the aft edge of stabilizers, that controls pitch, and is controlled by the yoke; *Symbols:* delta sub E; *Typical Units:* rad, deg.

**eliminations**

A series of matches between two cars at a time, the winner advancing to the next race.

**eliminator**

The fastest drag car in its class.

**Elky**

The Chevrolet El Camino.

**Elliot axle**
   A solid-bar front axle on which the ends span the steering knuckle.

**endurance limit**
   The maximum stress that a metal can withstand without failure, after a specified number of cycles of stress.

**enduro**
   A race of 6 to 24 hours with emphasis on endurance and reliability rather than speed.

**eng**
   An abbreviation for engine.

**engage**
   The mechanical or automatic coupling of two members, like the driving flywheel and pressure plate, to rotate and drive the driven disc of a clutch.

**engagement chatter**
   A shaking, shuddering action that takes place as the driven disc makes contact with the driving members makes contact with the driving members caused by a rapid grip and slip action.

**engine**
   A device that burns fuel to produce mechanical power; to convert heat energy into mechanical energy.

**engine bay**
   The area in a vehicle occupied by the engine.

**engine block**
   A term used for cylinder block.

**engine configuration**
   Relating to the style and type of engine, such as V-8, pancake, and so on.

**engine-coolant temperature (ECT)**
The temperature of the coolant in an engine.

**engine-coolant temperature sensor (ECTS)**
An electronic or electro-mechanical unit for sensing engine-coolant temperature.

**engine cooling fan**
A term used for cooling fan.

**engine cooling system**
A term used for cooling system.

**Engine cooling**
cooling system in an internal combustion engine that is used to maintain the various engine components at temperatures conducive to long life and proper functioning. Gas temperatures in the cylinders may reach 4500°F (2500°C). This is well above the melting point of the engine parts in contact with the gases; therefore it is necessary to control the temperature of the parts, or they will become too weak to carry the stresses resulting from gas pressure. The lubricating oil film on the cylinder wall can fail because of chemical changes at wall temperatures above about 400°F (200°C). Complete loss of power may take place if some spot in the combustion space becomes sufficiently heated to ignite the charge prematurely on the compression stroke. See also: Internal combustion engine
Fortunately, a thin protective boundary of relatively stagnant gas of poor heat conductivity exists on the inner surfaces of the combustion space. If the outer cylinder surface is placed in contact with a cool fluid such as air or water and there is sufficient contact area to cause a rapid heat flow, the resulting drop in temperature produced by the heat flow in the inside boundary layer keeps the temperature of the cylinder wall much closer to the temperature of the coolant than to the temperature of the combustion gas. The quantity of heat that crosses the stagnant boundary layer and must be carried away by the coolant is a function of the Reynolds number of the gas

existing in the cylinder. In terms of practical engine quantities, the heat flow to the coolant varies approximately as in the relationship: (charge density piston speed)0.8. At full throttle and normal piston speed, this heat flow amounts to about 15% of the energy of the incoming fuel. See also: Reynolds number

Liquid cooling

If the coolant is water, it is usually circulated by a pump through jackets surrounding the cylinders and cylinder heads. The water is circulated fast enough to remove steam bubbles that may form over local hot spots and to limit the water's temperature rise through the engine to about 15°F (8°C). In most engines in automotive and industrial service, the warmed coolant is piped to an air-cooled heat exchanger called a radiator (Fig. 1). The airflow required to remove the heat from the radiator is supplied by an electric or engine-driven fan; in automotive applications the airflow is also supplied by the forward motion of the vehicle. The engine and radiator may be separated and each placed in the optimum location, being connected through piping. To prevent freezing, the water coolant is usually mixed with ethylene glycol.

Fig. 1 Cooling system of a V-8 automotive spark-ignition engine. The arrows show the direction of coolant flow through the engine water jackets and cooling system.

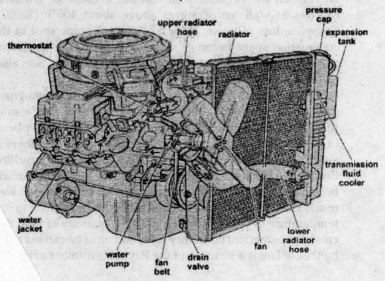

## engine displacement
The volume swept within an engine as its cylinders make one stroke, generally expressed in cubic inches, cubic centimeters, or liters.

## engine dynamometer
Device to measure engine horsepower at the flywheel.

## engine dyno
A term used for engine dynamometer.

## engineering plastics
Thermoset and thermoplastic materials, such as polycarbonate, ABS, and nylon. Their characteristics and properties enable them to withstand mechanical loads, such as tension, impact, flexing, vibration, and friction, combined with temperature changes, making them suitable for application in structural and load-bearing product design elements.

## engine fan
A bladed device found at the front of the engine used to draw air through the radiator and across the engine.

## engine identification number (EIN)
A code to identify the type of engine found stamped on the cylinder block.

## engine idle compensator
A thermostatically controlled device on the carburetor that prevents stalling during prolonged hot weather periods, while the air conditioner is operated.

## Engine lubrication
In an internal combustion engine, the system for providing a continuous supply of oil between moving surfaces during engine operation. This viscous film, known as the lubricant, lubricates and cools the power transmission components while removing impurities, neutralizing chemically active products of combustion, transmitting forces, and damping vibrations.

**Lubricant**

Automotive and other four-stroke Otto-cycle engines are generally lubricated with petroleum-base base oils that contain chemical additives to improve their natural properties. Synthetic oils are used in gas turbines and may be used in other engines. See also: Otto cycle

Probably the most important property of oil is the absolute viscosity, which is a measure of the force required to move one layer of the oil film over the other. If the viscosity is too low, a protecting oil film is not formed between the parts. With high viscosity too much power is required to shear the oil film, and the flow of oil through the engine is retarded. Viscosity tends to decrease as temperature increases. Viscosity index (VI) is a number that indicates the resistance of an oil to changes in viscosity with temperature. The smaller the change in viscosity with temperature, the higher the viscosity index of the oil. See also: Viscosity

**Lubricating system**

Small two-stroke cycle engines may require a premix of the lubricating oil with the fuel going into the engine, or the oil may be injected into the ingoing air-fuel mixture. This is known

Fig.    Pressurized lubricating system for an automobile engine. Arrows show the flow of oil through the engine.

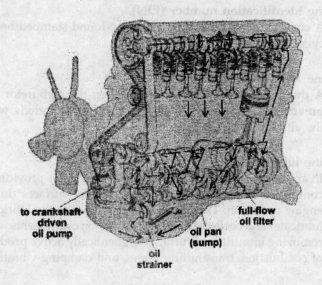

to crankshaft-
driven
oil pump

full-flow
oil filter

oil pan
(sump)

oil
strainer

as a total-loss lubricating system because the oil is consumed during engine operation.

Most automotive engines have a pressurized or force-feed lubricating system in combination with splash and oil mist lubrication (see illus). The lubricating system supplies clean oil cooled to the proper viscosity to the critical points in the engine, where the motion of the parts produces hydrodynamic oil films to separate and support the various rubbing surfaces. The oil is pumped under pressure to the bearing points, while sliding parts are lubricated by splash and oil mist. After flowing through the engine, the oil collects in the oil pan or sump, which cools the oil and acts as a reservoir while the foam settles out. Some engines have an oil cooler to remove additional heat from the oil.

**engine-management system**

An electronic device that monitors, adjusts, and regulates the ignition and fuel-injection systems to maintain engine control under varying operating conditions.

## Engine manifold

Fig. Cross-sectional view of a fuel-injected spark-ignition engine showing the intake and exhaust manifolds. Arrows show the flow of the air through the intake manifold and of the exhaust gases through the exhaust manifold.

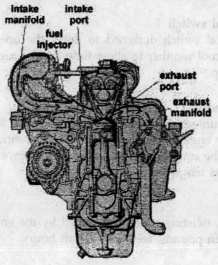

An arrangement or collection of pipes or tubing with several inlet or outlet passages through which a gas or liquid is gathered or distributed. The manifold may be a casting or fabricated of relatively light material. Manifolds are usually identified by the service provided, such as the intake manifold and exhaust manifold on the internal combustion engine (see illus.). Some types of manifolds for handling oil, water, and other fluids such as engine exhaust gas are often called headers. In the internal combustion engine, the intake and exhaust manifolds are an integral part of multicylinder engine construction and essential to its operation. See also: Internal combustion engine

### engine overhaul
To perform more than minor repairs on a powerplant, though not as extensive as an engine rebuild.

### engine paint
A paint specially formulated to withstand engine heat.

### engine rebuild
To perform an extensive engine repair including machining, reboring, and honing to factory-stock specifications.

### engine thermal switch
An electrical switch designed to delay the operation of a system in cool weather to allow time for the engine coolant to warm up.

### engine thermostat
A temperature-sensitive mechanical device found at the coolant outlet of an engine that expands (opens) or contracts (closes) to control the amount of coolant allowed to leave the engine, based on its temperature.

### engine torque
A rotating, twisting action developed by the engine that is measured in pounds, feet, or kilowatt hours.

**engine tuneup**
> The inspection, testing, and adjusting of an engine; the replacement of any parts required to ensure maximum performance.

**Englishtown (E-Town)**
> A town in New Jersey; the site of the annual NHRA Summernationals.

**Environmental Hazards Management Institute (EHMI)**
> An educational organization that provides materials to teenagers and adults relative to responsible management and recycling of hazardous waste materials.

**Environmental Protection Agency (EPA)**
> An agency of the United States government charged with the responsibility of protecting the environment and enforcing the Clean Air Act of 1990.

**Escalator**
> A continuous, moving stairway that transports passengers between two levels. Most escalators are installed to service floors less than 20 ft (6 m) apart, but some escalators have been constructed to rise 100 ft (30 m) or more between floors.
> The modern escalator consists of a series of steps, fastened to an endless chain running in a track system that extends up an incline. The steps continue around a turnaround at the upper landing, pass back down the incline under the steps available to the passengers, and progress to another turnaround at the lower landing. This chain, known as a step chain, is powered by a machine that is usually connected by a gear, chain, or mechanical coupling to a shaft located at the upper landing turnaround. An alternating-current induction motor, selected for its simplicity and constant speed characteristics, is used to move the steps. Most modern escalators travel at 100 ft/min (0.5 m/s). See also: Induction motor
> The track system is designed to permit the steps to approach the upper and lower landings horizontally and to maintain a horizontal tread surface wherever the steps will be holding passengers. The treads of the steps are provided with cleats

that match a pattern of combs at the landings, and each riser (the vertical front face of the step) is fitted with cleats that mesh with the adjacent step. The cleats are a safety feature, reducing the possibility of objects becoming caught at the landings or between steps.

The escalator has handrails on each side of the moving steps. They move at the same speed as the steps and extend a distance beyond the point where the steps pass under the combs at the landings. This provides support for passengers as they move onto or off the moving steps.

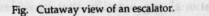

Fig.  Cutaway view of an escalator.

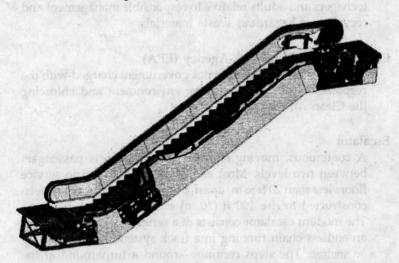

The escalator mechanism is covered with a balustrade that creates a safe environment for the passengers and enhances the product architecturally. There are two types of balustrades, glass and opaque. The glass type has glass panels below the handrails and gives the escalator an open appearance. The opaque type uses nontransparent panels instead of glass. Glass is usually preferred in installations in open atriums found in building lobbies or shopping malls.

The use of escalators is widespread because of their continuous accessibility and their ability to transport large numbers of people. The capacity, in passengers per hour, is determined by the step width and the speed at which the escalator travels. The most common step widths are 24 and 40 in. (60 and 100 cm). The capacity is based on one passenger per 40-in. (100-cm) step or one passenger on every other 24-in. (60-cm) step. These values are reliable for planning the number of escalators required in a building, even though theoretically a larger capacity can be achieved over a short time. Based on such step loading, an escalator running at 100 ft/min (0.5 m/s) can transport 4500 or 2250 passengers per hour with 40- or 24-in. (100- or 60-cm) step widths, respectively.

Movement of people by escalators is very economical. The escalator is a balanced machine when operating empty. As passengers board in the down direction, they offset the friction in the system. When the down load exceeds approximately 10% capacity, power is generated by the escalator so that the total power consumption of the building containing the unit is reduced. Although power is required to carry passengers up, the cost to carry a passenger up one floor on a fully loaded escalator is extremely small, typically less than a fraction of a cent.

## Escapement

A mechanism in which a toothed wheel engages alternate pallets attached to an oscillating member. The escapement is found principally in timepieces but may be employed wherever oscillating motion is required. Its origins are ancient and obscure.

In the simple form of escapement (Fig. 1), oscillating member cc' is an open bar arranged to slide longitudinally in bearings CC, which are attached through a frame (not shown) to the bearing for toothed wheel a. Wheel a turns continuously in

Fig. 1 Simple form of escapement.

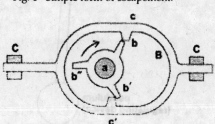

the direction of the arrow, and is provided with three teeth b, b', and b". The oscillating member has two pallets c and c'. In the position shown, tooth b is just ceasing to drive pallet c to the right, and is escaping, while tooth b' is just coming in contact with pallet c', which it will drive to the left.

Although escapements are generally used to convert circular into reciprocating motion, as in the above example, the wheel being the driver, in many cases the action may be reversed. In Fig. 1, if the open slide bar were driven with reciprocating motion, the wheel would be made to turn in the opposite direction from its rotation as the input member. Also, there would be a short interval at the beginning of each stroke of the bar in which no motion would be given to the wheel. The wheel a must have one, three, five, or any other odd number of teeth upon its circumference.

Fig. 2   Anchor recoil escapement.

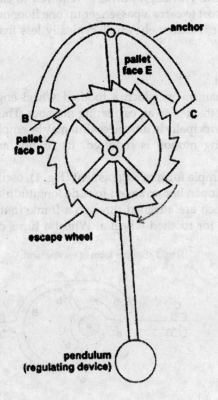

Escapements are also adapted for use in automatic factory equipment to regulate the flow of parts from the magazine or feeder track. Such feeding and spacing devices are of various forms, many being adaptations of the ratchet and pawl.

In a mechanical clock or watch, the escapement intervenes between the energy source (spring or elevated weight) and the regulating device (pendulum or balance wheel). It is acted upon by both. The escape wheel is mounted on the same shaft as the last wheel of the gear train, and impulses are delivered from the escape wheel to operate the regulating device. The regulating device, which has a natural period of oscillation, determines the rate at which it will receive these impulses, and thus regulates the rate of going of the timepiece.

The anchor recoil escapement (Fig. 2) is used with a pendulum and takes its name from the shape of its oscillating member and its action. This type of escapement appeared late in the seventeenth century and has survived, with modifications, to the present. To simplify the explanation, the pendulum is shown attached directly to the anchor, so that the pendulum and anchor swing as one.

In the position shown, pallet B has just received an impulse from the escape wheel, the impulse swinging the pendulum to the left. When pallet B has cleared the tooth, allowing the wheel to escape, pallet C will be in position to arrest the wheel. Recoil, or momentary reversal of the escape wheel, occurs just after it is arrested because the pendulum has not quite completed its swing. The wheel tooth in contact with pallet C will then give the oscillating parts an impulse in the opposite direction.

Deadbeat, an escapement without recoil, has arresting faces of the pallets described by a circular arc whose center is at the pivot point of the anchor. Escape-wheel teeth are contoured to give impulses to these pallet faces, over which they slide without recoil.

Modern watches generally employ a detached-lever escapement (Fig. 3), which has banking pins B to limit the oscillation of the anchor and its lever. An escapement is termed detached when the regulating device, in this case the balance wheel, is given an impulse during only a small part of its operating cycle. When the fork reaches the end of its swing, it is lightly locked by a wheel tooth and remains stationary

until the returning impulse pin E causes sufficient recoil of the
escape wheel to release the pallet. The chronometer escapement
is a detached escapement that furnishes an impulse in only
one direction of the swing of the balance wheel.

Fig. 3  Detached-lever escapement, a type used in watches.

**EST**

An abbreviation for electronic spark timing.

**estimated**

Data that is the result of filtering two or more signals; *Compare:*
derived, filtered, measured, raw, selected smoothed.

**estimator**

The person who determines the cost value of the damage, plus
the price required to repair the damaged vehicle, working
with insurance adjusters or appraisers.

**ESV**

An abbreviation for experimental safety vehicle.

**etching**

The localized attack of metal surfaces causing pitting and/or
deterioration.

**ethane**
C2H6, a minor component of natural gas used as a fuel.

**ethanol**
A form of alcohol, C2H5OH, found in alcoholic beverages and also used as an additive in gasoline to produce gasohol.

**Ethyl**
The trade name for tetraethyl lead, a fuel additive no longer permitted due to environmental hazards.

**ethyl alcohol**
A term often used for ethanol.

**ethylene glycol**
The basic chemical used in automotive antifreeze; mixed with water for cooling-system protection and to increase the boiling point of the coolant.

**ETI**
An abbreviation for Equipment and Tools Institute.

**E-Town**
A popular term for Englishtown.

**Eurailpass**
A special-fare train ticket that entitles the purchaser to unlimited train travel in many European countries for a number of days or weeks.

**Eurostyle**
A custom styling treatment to provide a European flair.

**evacuate**
1. To create a vacuum within a system to remove all traces of air and moisture.
2. A service procedure using a vacuum pump to remove all atmospheric air and moisture from inside an air-conditioning system.

**evap**
   An abbreviation for evaporator.

**evaporation**
   The transformation of a liquid to the vapor state.

**evaporation control system (ECS)**
   A system that prevents fuel vapors from escaping to the atmosphere while the engine is off.

**evaporative emissions**
   Hydrocarbons from fuel that evaporate from a vehicle's fuel tank and carburetor; eliminated by sealing the fuel system and using a charcoal canister to trap vapors from the fuel tank and carburetor.

**evaporative-emissions control (EEC)**
   A canister filled with activated charcoal to reduce raw fuel emissions.

**evaporative-emissions control system (EECS)**
   A system to reduce the amount of raw fuel vapors that are emitted into the ambient air from the fuel tank and carburetor.

**evaporator**
   The heat exchanger of an air-conditioning system that removes heat from the air passing through it.

**evaporator control valve**
   Any of the several types of suction pressure-control valves or devices used to regulate the evaporator temperature by controlling its pressure.

**evaporator core**
   The tube and fin assembly located inside the evaporator housing, where refrigerant fluid picks up heat when it changes into a vapor.

## evaporator housing

The case that contains the evaporator core, diverter doors, duct outlets, and blower mounting arrangement.

## evaporator pressure-control valve

A term used for evaporator control valve.

## evaporator pressure regulator (EPR)

A back-pressure regulated temperature-control device used on some early Chrysler car lines.

## evaporator temperature regulator

A temperature-regulated device used by early Chrysler Air-Temp systems to control the evaporator pressure.

## even fire

A V–6 engine with a 60- or 90-degree block having individual journals on each crankshaft throw staggered in relation to each other to provide even firing.

## everest

A standard model for computing earth data.

## exc

An abbreviation for except.

## except

A word referring to an omitted category or item.

## excess baggage

Luggage that exceeds the allowed limits for weight, size, or number of pieces. Carriers usually charge extra for excess baggage, and in some cases, may have to ship it later rather than with the passenger.

## excess flash

A term used for flash.

**excessive crush**
A condition that exists when a pair of bearings are installed in a bore that is too small, causing them to deform and leading to early failure.

**excursion fare**
A special-price fare that comes with restrictions, such as advance purchase requirements and a minimum stay. Usually a round-trip fare.

**exhaust analyzer**
An automotive test and service device that uses a process involving infrared energy to determine and display the composition of an engine's exhaust gases such as the two-gas type to measure hydrocarbons and carbon monoxide or the four-gas type, which also measures oxygen and carbon dioxide.

**exhaust emissions**
Pollutants identified by clean-air legislation as being harmful or undesirable, including lead, unburned hydrocarbons, carbon monoxide, and oxides of nitrogen.

**exhaust gas**
The burned and unburned gases that remain after combustion.

**exhaust-gas oxygen**
The amount of oxygen present in the exhaust stream, as measured by an oxygen sensor and reported to the computer in closed-loop, feedback systems to aid in the control of the air/fuel mixture.

**exhaust-gas recirculation (EGR)**
An emissions-control system that reduces an engine's production of oxides of nitrogen by diluting the air/fuel mixture with exhaust gas so that peak combustion temperatures in the cylinders are lowered.

**exhaust-gas recirculation valve (EGR valve)**
A valve, generally vacuum operated, to regulate the exhaust gas flow into the intake manifold.

**exhaust-gas speed**
>The speed at which exhaust gases pass through the header pipes, usually at about 200–300 feet (61–91 meters) per second.

**exhaust headers**
>1. A term used for exhaust manifold.
>2. A special exhaust manifold with tubes of equal length from the exhaust ports to the header of the exhaust system.

**exhaust manifold**
>A component, generally of cast iron, with passages of unequal lengths that carry the exhaust gases from the exhaust ports to the header of the exhaust system.

**exhaust pipe**
>A pipe that connects the exhaust manifold, the muffler, or catalytic converter.

**exhaust port**
>In a rotary combustion engine, peripheral opening in the rotor housing that allows the burned gases to leave the engine.

**exhaust stroke**
>The upward motion of the piston forcing burned gases out the open exhaust valve.

**exhaust system**
>The tubing, mufflers, and catalytic converters that direct exhaust gases from the engine to the atmosphere.

**exhaust valve**
>Valve that, upon opening, allows the burned gases to leave the combustion chamber during the exhaust stroke.

**Expanding square search**
>A pattern of progressively larger squares (a "square spiral") followed for searching the ground from an aircraft; *Compare:* creeping line search, sector search.

**expansion control**
> The grinding of a piston in a slightly oval shape so that it becomes round when it expands with heat.

**expansion plug**
> A term used for core plug.

**expansion tank**
> 1. A coolant-recovery tank.
> 2. An auxiliary tank, usually connected to the inlet tank or a radiator, that provides additional storage space for heated coolant.

**expansion tube**
> A metering device used at the inlet of some evaporators to control the flow of liquid refrigerant into the evaporator core.

**expansion valve**
> A term used for thermostatic expansion valve.

**experimental safety vehicle (ESV)**
> A prototype vehicle used to test and evaluate specific safety features.

**explosion-proof cabinet**
> Cabinet used in the automotive shop to store gasoline and other flammable liquids.

**exposure limit (EL)**
> A term often used for permissible exposure limit (PEL).

**extension housing**
> An aluminum or iron casting that encloses the transmission output shaft and supporting bearings.

**external combustion engine**
> An engine that burns the air-fuel mixture in a chamber outside the engine cylinder, such as a steam engine or a Stirling engine.

**external equalizer**
> A term used for equalizer line.

**external in-line filter**
> 1. Filter placed in the transmission-cooler return line outside the transmission housing.
> 2. A supplemental filter placed in the air-conditioning system to prevent system damage after repairs.

**extreme pressure (EP)**
> A much higher-than-average pressure condition.

**extreme pressure lubricant**
> An API-rated lubricant for heavy loads.

**eyeball**
> To make a visual estimation or determination.

**eyes**
> The light beam that operates an electronic, race-timing system.

**eyewash fountain**
> An emergency water fountain that directs water to the eyes for flushing and cleaning.

**F**

**false guide**
> A valve guide used to replace a worn integral-valve guide.

**family buggy**
> 1. The family car.
> 2. A vehicle more than ten years old.

**fan**
> 1. A device having two or more blades attached to the shaft of a motor.
> 2. A device mounted in the heater/air-conditioner duct that causes air to pass over the heater core and evaporator.
> 3. A device having four or more blades, mounted on the water pump, that causes air to pass through the radiator and condenser.
> 4. The spray pattern of a paint spray gun.
> 5. The incorrect technique of applying paint by waving a spray gun back and forth with the wrist.

**fan belt**
> A flexible V-, or flat poly-groove-type drive belt that transfers power from the crankshaft pulley to the water pump and/or accessories, such as the alternator.

**fan blade**
> In an engine cooling-system fan, four to six wings on the fan, usually spaced unevenly to reduce vibration and noise.

**fan clutch**

A device installed between the water-pump pulley and fan of an engine-driven fan that is sensitive to engine speed and underhood temperature.

**fan hub**

The mounting surface for the fan.

**fanning**

The use of pressurized air through a spray gun to facilitate drying, a practice not recommended.

**fanning the brakes**

A term used for brake fanning.

**fan shroud**

Plastic or metal housing inside which the fan rotates; on certain vehicles, this allows the fan to pull more air past radiator finned tubing and prevents air recirculation.

**FAQT**

An abbreviation for Federation of Automotive Qualified Technicians.

**fare basis**

The specific fare for a ticket at a designated level of service; specified by one or more letters or by a combination of letters and numbers. Example: the letter "Y" designates coach service on an airplane. Although the same letters do not always designate the same class on different carriers, the following are generally the same: "F" - first class, "B" & "C" - Business class.

**fare break point**

The destination where a given fare ends. Example: The fare break point for a passenger flying from Washington DC to Kansas City via Cleveland is Kansas City.

**fastback**

An autobody style having a roof line that extends in a single, simple curve from the windshield to the rear bumper.

**fast flush**
> The use of a special machine to clean the cooling system by circulating a cleaning solution.

**fast idle**
> The higher speed, 1,100 to 1,500 rpm, at which an engine idles during warm-up, when first started.

**fast-idle cam**
> A cam-shaped lever on the carburetor that provides fast-idle action when the engine is cold.

**fast-idle screw**
> A screw in the carburetor linkage to adjust fast-idle speed.

**fast-idle solenoid**
> An electro-mechanical device on the carburetor for adjustment of the fast-idle speed.

**fast overdrive**
> A planetary gear set operating with the planetary carrier as input, the sun gear as output, and the ring gear held.

**fast reverse**
> A planetary gear set operating with the planetary carrier held; the ring gear is input, and the sun gear rotates in the opposite direction.

**fat fenders**
> Bulbous fenders, as on vehicles in the 1930s and 1940s.

**fatigue**
> The tendency of a material to break under conditions of repeated stressing considerably below its tensile strength.

**fatigue failure**
> Metal failure due to repeated stress so that the character of the metal is altered and it cracks. This is a condition that

frequently causes engine bearing failure due to excessive engine idling or slow engine-idling speed.

## fatigue strength
The measure of a material's resistance to fatigue.

## faying surface
The mating surface of a member that is in contact or in close proximity with another member to which it is to be joined.

## Fe
The chemical symbol for iron.

## featheredge
The technique of blending the repair of a damaged area into the undamaged area, maintaining the original surface texture and sheen.

## feathering
The technique of modulating the throttle lightly and smoothly for precise, controlled changes in engine speed.

## featherweight leaf spring
A fiber composite spring.

## feature car
A vehicle displayed at a car show for appearance money and not trophy competition.

## federal version
A car that meets the United States' exhaust emission standards, but not California's standards.

## Federation Internationale de l'Automobile (FIA)
An international association of national automobile clubs that sanction and regulate major international auto racing series, such as Formula One.

**Federation Internationale du Sport Automobile (FISA)**
A division of FIA that sanctions and regulates major international auto racing series.

**Federation of Automotive Qualified Technicians (FAQT)**
A professional association that provides life, health, and disability insurance.

**fee-based pricing**
A compensation plan in which a corporation pays its travel agency a portion of the commissions generated by the corporation's travel volume, according to a negotiated schedule.

**feedback**
1. A principle of fuel-system design wherein a signal from an oxygen sensor in the exhaust system is used to give a computer the input it needs to properly regulate the carburetor or fuel-injection system in order to maintain a nearly perfect air/fuel ratio.
2. A signal to a computer that reports on the position of a component, as an EGR valve.

**feedback carburetor**
A carburetor that controls the air/fuel mixture according to commands from the engine control computer, typically through the operation of a duty solenoid.

**feed holes**
The holes to supply coolant or oil to an engine.

**feeder airline**
An air carrier that services a local market and "feeds" traffic to the national and international carriers.

**felt**
Natural felts are produced by compressed wool, hair, wool/hair, or synthetic fibers, yielding a wide range of densities and permeabilities of consistent density, pore size, and mesh geometry so that performance is reasonably predictable.

**felt dust seal**

1. An engine seal made of felt, usually used on the front crankshaft pulley.
2. A compressor-shaft seal made of felt, usually found between the seal face and armature of the clutch.

**female**

The universal designation of a part into which a mating (male) part fits.

**fender cover**

A protective cover placed on the fender when a mechanic works on an engine, preventing damage to the finish.

**fenderside**

A narrow-bed pickup truck.

**Ferguson Formula (FF)**

A four-wheel drive system developed in the 1960s, a forerunner of the AWD and 4WD systems in high-performance cars today.

**ferrite**

An iron compound that has not been combined with carbon in pig iron or steel.

**ferrous metal**

A metal containing iron, such as steel.

**ferrous wheels**

Vehicle wheels made of iron or steel alloy.

**FF**

An abbreviation for:
1. Ferguson Formula.
2. Formula Ford.

**F-head**

An engine design having the intake valves in the head and the exhaust valves in the block.

## F-head engine

An engine with some of its valves in the head and some in the cylinder block, giving an F-shaped appearance.

## Fire-tube boiler

A steam boiler in which hot gaseous products of combustion pass through tubes surrounded by boiler water. The water and steam in fire-tube boilers are contained within a large-diameter drum or shell, and such units often are referred to as shell-type boilers. Heat from the products of combustion is transferred to the boiler water by tubes or flues of relatively small diameter (about 3-4 in. or 7.5-10 cm) through which the hot gases flow. The tubes are connected to tube sheets at each end of the cylindrical shell and serve as structural reinforcements to support the flat tube sheets against the force of the internal water and steam pressure. Braces or tension rods also are used in those areas of the tube sheets not penetrated by the tubes.

Fire-tube boilers may be designed for vertical, inclined, or horizontal positions. One of the most generally used types is the horizontal-return-tube (HRT) boiler (Fig. 1). In the HRT boiler, part of the heat from the combustion gases is transferred directly to the lower portion of the shell. The gases then make a return pass through the horizontal tubes or flues before being passed into the stack.

Fig. 1   Horizontal-return-tube boiler.

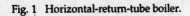

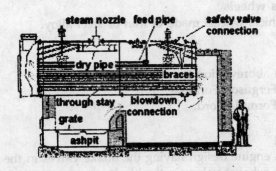

In the Scotch marine boiler, one or more large flues (approximately 18-24 in. or 45-60 cm in diameter) are used for furnaces or combustion chambers within the shell, and the hot gases are returned through groups of small-diameter tubes or flues. The flues that form the combustion chamber are corrugated to prevent collapse when subjected to the water and steam pressure. These boilers may be oil-fired, or solid fuel can be burned on grates set within the furnace chambers. Scotch marine boilers have, with few exceptions, been superseded by water-tube marine boilers.

Gas-tube boilers are sometimes used for the absorption of waste heat from process gases or the exhaust from internal combustion engines, particularly when their installation provides a simple and economical means for the recovery of low-grade heat. The boiler shell may be augmented by an external steam-separating drum and downcomer and riser connections to provide for proper circulation (Fig. 2).

Fig. 2   Fire-tube waste-heat boiler.

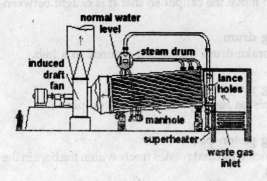

**float bowl**
1. A section of the carburetor main body that acts as a fuel reservoir.
2. The reservoir from which fuel is metered into the passing air.

**float chamber**
The fuel reservoir at the bottom of a carburetor.

**float circuit**
> A circuit that maintains the correct fuel level in the carburetor float bowl.

**floater**
> A term used for full-floating axle.

**floating axle**
> A term used for full- or semi-floating axle.

**floating caliper**
> A disc-brake caliper that has piston(s) on only one side of the disc. The caliper bore moves away from the rotor in order to press the pad on the other side against the disc when the brakes are applied.

**floating-caliper disc brakes**
> A brake system in which only one of the two pads are energized and move the caliper so that it is caught between both pads.

**floating drum**
> A brake drum that is not secured to a hub.

**floating piston**
> A piston having a floating piston pin.

**floating piston pin**
> A piston pin that rotates freely within the bore in the connecting rod.

**float level**
> The float position when the needle valve is against its seat, cutting off the fuel supply.

**float system**
> The system that controls fuel into the carburetor and the fuel level in the float bowl.

**flog**

> To abuse a vehicle by pushing it too hard.

**flood**

> A condition whereby more fuel is in the combustion chamber than can be ignited.

**flooded**

> A condition whereby the air/fuel mixture in a cylinder is too rich to burn.

**flooding**

> A condition caused by:
> 1. Too much liquid refrigerant being metered into the evaporator for evaporation.
> 2. Too much gasoline metered into an engine for combustion.

**floorboard**

> The slanted section of the floor pan immediately behind the firewall.

**floorboard it**

> A term used for floored or floor it.

**floored**

> To run at full throttle. Also floorboard it and floor it.

**floor it**

> To have the accelerator pushed to the floor. Also floorboard it and floored.

**floor pan**

> The panel forming the floor of the interior of the vehicle.

**flopper**

> A funny car with a fiberglass body that flops up in the front to provide access to the engine, chassis, and driver compartment.

## floppy disk

A flexible 5.25- or 3.5-inch disk used widely with microcomputers and minicomputers, providing electronic media storage at a relatively low cost.

## flowability

1. The ability of molten filler metal to flow.
2. The ability of a fluid or vapor to flow.

## flow coating

A method of applying paint by passing parts on a conveyor through a chamber where several nozzles direct a shower of coating material over the parts.

## fluid

Any liquid or gas.

## fluid aeration

Air bubbles formed in a fluid, giving the appearance of foam.

## fluid cooler

1. Small heat-exchanger component in a hydraulic line near the pump to reduce power-steering-fluid temperature.
2. A device inside the radiator to provide cooling for transmission fluid.
3. Any heat exchanger designed to reduce the temperature of a fluid.

## fluid coupling

A device in the power train containing two rotating members, one of which transmits power to the other via fluid.

device for transmitting rotation between shafts by means of the acceleration and deceleration of a hydraulic fluid. Structurally, a fluid coupling consists of an impeller on the input or driving shaft and a runner on the output or driven shaft. The two contain the fluid (Fig. 1). Impeller and runner are bladed rotors, the impeller acting as a pump and the runner reacting as a turbine. Basically, the impeller accelerates the fluid from near its axis, at which the tangential component of absolute velocity is low, to near its periphery, at which the tangential component of absolute velocity is high (Fig. 2). This increase in velocity represents an increase in kinetic energy. The fluid mass emerges at high velocity from the impeller, impinges on the runner blades, gives up its energy, and leaves the runner at low velocity.

Fig. 1  Basic fluid coupling.

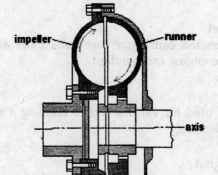

Fig. 2  Hydrokinematic principle.

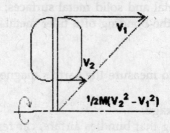

**fluid pressure**
The pressure of a fluid that is invariable and uniform in all directions.

**fluorocarbon**
> Any of a group of chlorofluorocarbon refrigerants, such as R-12.

**flush**
> 1. To use a fluid to remove solid particles such as metal flakes or dirt.
> 2. To purge refrigerant passages with a clean, dry gas, such as nitrogen (N).

**flush bucket**
> An oversized carburetor that feeds more air/fuel mixture than the engine can handle.

**flushing**
> A term used for various acts of cleaning a system, such as brake flushing.

**flushing agent**
> An approved liquid or gas used to flush a system.

**flushing hydraulic system**
> The procedure for replacing old brake fluid with new fluid.

**flux**
> A material to dissolve and prevent the formation of oxides in molten metal and solid metal surfaces; a wetting agent that facilitates the bonding of a filler metal.

**Flux valve**
> A device to measure the earth's magnetic flux; a compass.

**fly-drive package**
> An offering that bundles airfare, car rental, and sometimes, land accommodations into a single package, offered for a fixed price.

**flyboy**
> A drag competitor who races only occasionally as a hobby.

## flying kilometer

The international standard for attempting to set a speed record by entering the measured kilometer after attaining the highest speed possible.

## flying mile

The international standard for attempting to set a speed record by entering the measured mile after attaining the highest speed possible.

## Fly over

A position update by flying directly over a known point.

## flyweight governor

Governor assembly, sensitive to centrifugal force, whose action is controlled by primary and secondary weights.

## flywheel

1. A heavy metal wheel with starter ring gear that is mounted at the rear of the crankshaft. It absorbs energy on power stroke(s), returns energy on other stroke(s), and transfers power to the clutch or torque converter.
2. Front-most part of a clutch assembly that is bolted to the engine crankshaft with a rear surface to provide a smooth friction area for the disc-front facing to contact during clutch engagement.

## flywheel ring gear

A gear, fitted around the flywheel, that is engaged by teeth on the starting-motor drive to crank the engine.

## foaming

1. A condition caused by the churning of oil or other fluids.
2. A term used for shock foaming.

## fog lamp

Auxiliary lamps, often amber, mounted in front of a vehicle to aid visibility during snow dust or fog conditions.

**fold**
>   To bend a material, usually to 180 degrees.

**follower**
>   A term used for lifter.

**following ball joint**
>   A term used for non-load-carrying ball joint.

**FoloThru drive**
>   An inertia-starting motor drive, similar to a Bendix Folo-Thru drive.

**foot (ft)**
>   An English measure equal to 12 inches.

**foot in it**
>   A driver accelerating rapidly and/or refusing to yield during an attempted pass.

**foot in the carburetor**
>   The accelerator pushed to the floor.

**foot-pounds (ft-lb)**
>   An English measure for torque.

**footprint**
>   1. The portion of the contact area of a loaded tire with the ground.
>   2. The bolt pattern of a device.

**foot valve**
>   The foot-operated brake valve that controls air pressure to the service chambers.

**forward clutch**
>   A clutch that is engaged whenever the vehicle moves forward, controlled by the valve-body forward circuit.

**forward rake**
A car having a lower front than rear, to create an extra down force at high speeds.

**forward sensor**
A sensor used in air-bag restraint systems.

**forward shoe**
A term used for leading shoe.

**Forward-Looking Infrared (FLIR)**
Sensor equipment used to supplement AGR, extend the aircraft visual search capability and provide position information for guidance and navigation update capability. Imagery derived from the FLIR sensor is displayed in the cockpit. FLIR pointing can be controlled manually using a tracking handle or automatically by the Mission Computer. FLIR converts a heat image into a video image and determines azimuth, elevation, and sometimes range of a point; *Synonyms:* Infrared Detecting Set.

**fossil fuels**
Fuels formed underground from animal and plant matter by chemical and physical change, such as coal, petroleum, and natural gas.

**foul**
To leave before the green light in drag racing and be disqualified.

**four banger**
1. A four-cylinder engine.
2. A vehicle equipped with a four-cylinder engine.

**four-barrel carburetor**
A carburetor having four venturis.

**four-bolt mains**
A main bearing cap that is held in place with four bolts.

**four by**

A term used for 4*4.

**4*4**

A four-wheeled vehicle with four-wheel drive.

**4*2**

A four-wheeled vehicle with two-wheel drive.

**four cammer**

A V-type engine with dual overhead camshafts on each cylinder bank.

**four cycle**

A term used for four-stroke cycle.

**four-gas analyzer**

An exhaust-gas analyzer able to detect and measure exact amounts of hydrocarbons, carbon monoxide, carbon dioxide and oxygen.

**four on the floor**

A four-speed manual transmission with a floor-mounted shift lever.

**four-point seat belt**

A safety-belt system with two shoulder straps, two lap straps, and a single buckle.

**four speed**

A manual transmission with four forward gears.

**four-speed transmission**

A transmission providing four forward-gear ratios, one reverse ratio, and neutral, permitting closer matching of engine speed to load requirements than a three-speed transmission.

**four-stroke cycle**

1.A cycle of engine operation whereby the combustion occurs

in every cylinder on every second revolution of the crankshaft.
2. A complete cycle includes intake or induction, compression, combustion or expansion, and exhaust.
3. Also known as four cycle.

**freeze crack**
A crack in the engine caused by expansion due to coolant freezing.

**freeze plug**
A term used for core plug.

**freeze protection**
1. The controlling of evaporator temperature so that moisture on its surface does not freeze and block the airflow.
2. An additive added to coolant to prevent freeze-up by lowering its freezing temperature.

**freeze-up**
1. Failure of a unit to operate properly due to the formation of ice at the metering device.
2. A term used for seize.

**frenched**
A body part, normally separate, having been molded together with another body part.

**french seam**
A fabric seam in which the edge of the material is tucked under and sewn on the inner side.

**Freon**
Registered trademark of E.I. duPont, for a group of its refrigerants.

**Freon 12**
The trade term for refrigerant-12 by E.I. duPont.

**frequency**
> The number of complete cycles an alternating electric current, sound wave, or vibrating or rotating object undergoes in a given time.

**frequency valve**
> A valve that is used to stabilize the air/fuel mixture on a fuel-injected engine.

**friction**
> The resistance to motion of two items in contact with each other.

**friction ball joint**
> A term used for non-load-carrying ball joint.

**friction bearing**
> A bearing in which there is a sliding contact between the moving surfaces, such as a connecting rod bearing.

**friction disk**
> A flat disc surfaced with a friction material on one or both sides, such as a clutch disk.

**friction facing**
> A hard-molded or woven material that is riveted or bonded to the clutch-driven disc.

**friction horsepower**
> Engine horsepower losses due to friction from such sources as the engine, transmission, and drive train.

**friction material**
> One of several types of material used for friction surfacing, such as metallic friction material or organic friction material.

**friction-modified fluid**
> Automatic transmission fluid that provides smooth automatic shifts; designed to slip.

### frontal area

The area, in square feet, of the vehicle's cross section, as viewed from the front.

### front and rear suspension systems

The suspension system, with the frame, supplies steering control under all road conditions and maintains proper tracking and directional stability as well as providing proper wheel alignment to minimize tire wear.

### front-axle limiting valve

A valve that reduces pressure to the front service chambers, thus eliminating front wheel lockup on wet or icy pavements.

### front-body structural components

In a perimeter frame design, the front body section is made up of the radiator support, front fender, and front fender apron. These are installed with bolts and form an easily disassembled structure.

### front chute

The front straightaway on a circle race track.

### front clip

The complete replacement of the front bodywork back to the cowl or A-pillar.

### front control arm

Horizontal arms that connect the front wheels to the car and that support the weight of the front of the car.

### front drive

A drive system that transmits power through the front wheels.

### front-end drive

A vehicle having its drive wheels located on the front axle.

### front-end geometry

The angular relationships involving the front suspension, steering system, and tires.

## front engined
A vehicle with the engine in front, ahead of the passenger compartment.

## front idler
A pulley used as a means of tightening the drive belt.

## front-of-dash components
The heating and air-conditioning components that are mounted on the firewall side in the engine compartment.

## front pump
A pump, located at the front of the transmission, driven by the engine through two dogs on the torque-converter housing, to supply fluid whenever the engine is running.

## front-roll center
The center, determined by the front suspension geometry, around which the forward part of a vehicle tends to roll.

## front seating
Closing off the line, leaving the air-conditioner compressor open to the service port fitting, allowing service to the compressor without purging the entire system.

## front steer
A steering gear mounted ahead of the front wheel centerline.

## front straight
A straight area of a race track, such as between turns four and one at the Indianapolis Speedway.

## front suspension
To support the weight of the front of the vehicle.

## front-suspension system
Components that provide support of the vehicle front section, allow wheels to move vertically, and provide adjustments for front wheel alignment. The common parts include upper and

lower ball joints; control arms, shaft bushings and shims; sway bar and bushings; strut rod and bushings; coil springs; stabilizers; shock absorbers; and steering knuckle and spindle.

## front to rear brake bias

The difference in balance of brake pressure between the front and rear brake cylinders or calipers; higher in front due to weight transfer during heavy breaking.

## front-wheel drive

A drive system that transmits power through the front wheels.

## fronty

In early racing, the Chevrolet Frontenac and the Fronty Ford Model T.

## frosting back

The appearance of frost on the air-conditioning suction line extending back as far as the compressor.

## FRP

An abbreviation for fiberglass-reinforced plastic.

## fruit cupper

An amateur driver.

## Fuel pump

Fuel pumps for gasoline engines. (a) In-line mechanical diaphragm pump (b) In-tank electric impeller pum.

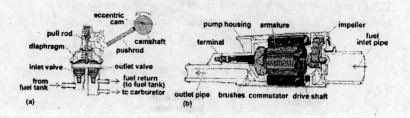

## Fuel system

he system that stores fuel for present use and delivers it as needed to an engine; includes the fuel tank, fuel lines, pump, filter, vapor return lines, carburetor or injection components, and all fuel system vents and evaporative emission control systems or devices that provide fuel supply and fuel metering functions. Some early vehicles and other engines had a gravity-feed fuel system, in which fuel flowed to the engine from a tank located above it. Automotive and most other engines have a pressurized fuel system with a pump that draws or pushes fuel from the tank to the engine. See also: Carburetor; Fuel injection; Fuel pump

### Automobile

The commonly used components for automobile and stationary gasoline engines are fuel tank, fuel gage, filter, electric or mechanical fuel pump, and carburetor or fuel-injection system (Fig. 1). In the past, fuel metering on automotive engines was usually performed by a carburetor. However, this device has been largely replaced by fuel injection into the intake manifold or ports, which increases fuel economy and efficiency while lowering exhaust gas emissions. Various types of fuel management systems are used on automotive engines, including electronically controlled feedback carburetors, mechanical continuous fuel injection, and sequential electronic fuel injection. See also: Automobile

Fig. 1  Components of an automobile fuel system.

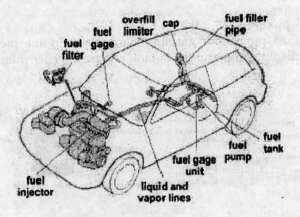

**full trailer**
> A trailer that employs a towbar coupled to a swiveling or steerable running gear assembly at the front and does not transfer any of the load to the towing vehicle.

**fully appointed agency**
> A travel agency that is accredited to sell airline, cruise and other travel services.

**fully oscillating fifth wheel**
> A fifth-wheel type with fore-aft and side-to-side articulation.

**fume**
> The airborne dispersion of minute particles, a byproduct of heating a solid, that may produce an oxide of the solid.

**fundamental tone**
> The tone produced by the lowest frequency component of an audio or radio frequency (RF) signal.

**funny car**
> 1. Any unusual or unorthodox racing vehicle.
> 2. A drag-racing vehicle covered with a lightweight plastic replica of a passenger car body.

**furnace brazing**
> A welding process used to repair complex cast-iron castings.

**fuse**
> 1. A protection device that opens a circuit when the fusible element is severed by heating, due to overcurrent passing through.
> 2. To join two pieces of metal by bonding them together.

**fuse block**
> A box-like enclosure that contains the fuses and circuit breakers for the electrical circuits of a vehicle.

**fuse link**
> A term used for fusible link.

**fuse wire**

Wire made of an alloy that melts at a low temperature.
A term used for fusible link.

**fusible link**

A type of fuse in which a special wire melts to open a circuit
when the current is excessive.

**fusion**

The melting together of filler metal and base metal, or of base
metal only, to produce a weld.

**fusion welding**

Any welding process that uses fusion of the base metal to
make the weld.

# G

**gage**
> 1. A less popular way of spelling gauge.
> 2. An element used to contain and space the rollers in a one-way roller clutch.

**Gaussian radius of curvature**
> Radius of the earth for the best fitting sphere at a given position; *Synonyms:* earth radius best sphere; *Symbols:* rho sub G; *Typical Units:* ft; *Dimensions:* Length.

**gate**
> 1. The money that is collected for admission.
> 2. The starting position for a drag race.
> 3. To take the lead in a drag race right from the start.

**GAWR**
> An abbreviation for gross-axle weight rating.

**GCW**
> An abbreviation for gross combined weight.

**gear**
> A cogged device that mates or meshes with another.

**gear backlash**
> The measurable gap or slack between gears.

**gear carton**
A transmission housing.

**gear drive**
A system of two or more gears, such as one that transmits power from the crankshaft or camshaft.

**geared speed**
A theoretical vehicle speed based on engine rpm, transmission-gear ratio, rear-axle ratio, and tire size, not accounting for slippage.

**gear lubricant**
A type of oil or grease especially formulated to lubricate gears.

**gear oil**
A thick lubricant, generally with an SAE number of 80 or above, used in standard transmissions or differentials. These often contain additives, such as an EP additive, to guard against being squeezed out from between gear teeth.

**gear oil, limited-slip**
A lubricant specified for use in certain limited-slip differentials to prevent chattering during turns and/or abnormal wear to the parts.

**gear pitch**
The number of teeth in a given unit of pitch diameter.

**gear ratio**
The speed relationship that exists between a driving (input) and a driven (output) gear. For example, a driving gear that revolves twice for each driven-gear revolution has a 2 to 1 (2:1) ratio.

**gears**
Mechanical devices containing teeth that mesh that transmit power, or turning force, from one shaft to another.

## gear shift

1. A floor- or steering-wheel-mounted lever used to manually change gears in the transmission.
2. A linkage-type mechanism by which the gears in a transmission are engaged.

## Gear train

combination of two or more gears used to transmit motion between two rotating shafts or between a shaft and a slide. In theory two gears can provide any speed ratio in connecting shafts at any center distance, but it is often not practical to use only two gears. If the ratio is large or if the center distance is relatively great, the larger of the two gears may be excessively large. Moreover, an additional gear may be necessary simply to give the proper direction to the output gear. Belt, rope, and chain drives are frequently used in conjunction with gear trains. See also: Belt drive; Chain drive; Planetary gear train

Classification

Gear train classifications include simple, compound, reverted, epicyclic (planetary), and various combinations. The most important distinction is that between ordinary and epicyclic gear trains. In ordinary trains (Fig. 1a), all axes remain stationary relative to the frame. But in epicyclic trains (Fig. 1b), at least one axis moves relative to the frame. In Fig. 1b gear B, whose axis is in motion, is called a planet. The gears A and C are sun gears.

Fig. 1 Gear trains. (a) Ordinary. (b) Epicyclic.

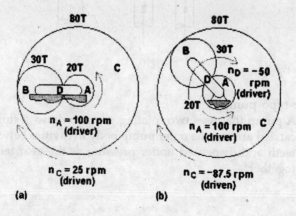

(a)

(b)

An ordinary gear train is a single degree of freedom mechanism: A single input, such as an input to gear A of the train in Fig. 1a, suffices to control the motions of the other moving members. But an epicyclic gear train (Fig. 1b) has two degrees of freedom: Two inputs are necessary. In the epicyclic train of Fig. 1b, the two input members are gear A and the planet carrier, link D. Only if both these members are controlled by external agencies can the motions of gears B and C be predicted. Frequently one gear of an epicyclic train is fixed. This then is one of the input members with a velocity of zero revolutions per unit time. A simple gear train is one in which each gear is fastened to a separate shaft (Fig. 1a). If at least one shaft has two or more gears fastened to it (Fig. 2), the train is compound. The train of Fig. 2 is also a reverted gear train, because the input and output shafts are in line. If the input shaft is not in line with the output shaft, the train is nonreverted.

Fig. 2  Compound reverted gear train.

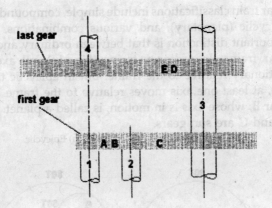

### gear-type pump

A pump that uses two rotating gears to draw in fluid that is carried around the outer pump body in cavities between gear teeth and dispensed under pressure as the gear teeth mesh together.

## gear whine
A high-pitched sound developed by some types of meshing gears.

## gel coat
The first layer that is applied to a female mold for a fiberglass layup, before the mat or cloth layers.

## general engine specifications
Specifications that are used to identify a particular style and type of engine.

## general over-the-road use
A fifth wheel truck designed for pulling multiple standard duty highway equipment such as trailers, flat beds, tankers, and so on.

## general purpose (GP)
A military designation during World War II, for the Willys 4*4; later known as a Jeep.

## generator
An ac or dc electrical-generating device that converts mechanical energy to electrical energy.

## GEN III system
A fuel and engine ignition-management system developed in the late 1980s by General Motors.

## geocentric latitude
Latitude measured with respect to horizontal through mass center of the earth; *Compare:* astronomical latitude, geodetic latitude; *Symbols:* Phi sub C; *Typical Units:* rad, deg.

## Geodetic latitude
Latitude measured with respect to normal to reference ellipsoid; *Compare:* astronomical latitude, geocentric latitude; *Symbols:* Phi sub T; *Typical Units:* rad, deg.

**gerotor**
A term used for gear rotor pump.

**get off it**
To release the accelerator and slow down. Also known as get out of it.

**get out of it**
To release the accelerator and slow down. Also known as get off it.

**g-force**
The force that is exerted on a vehicle during acceleration, deceleration, or cornering, expressed in units of gravity (g's).

**gilhooley**
To spin out on a dirt track.

**Gilmer belt drive**
An accessory drive system using a cogged belt to ensure positive engagement, such as with a supercharger.

**gimbaled inertial sensor**
Accelerometers mounted to a platform which is free to rotate, with gyroscopes to measure rotation and servomotors to maintain a fixed attitude with respect to the earth *Compare:* strapdown inertial sensor.

**gingerbread**
Nonfunctioning visual ornamentation, such as chrome.

**girdle**
A heavy-duty, main-bearing support for a racing engine.

**G.I. spacer**
A device used to space out a piston ring in a piston groove that has been intentionally machined oversize because of wear.

**gladhand**

Connectors between tractor and trailer air lines.

**glass**

1. A term used for fiberglass-reinforced plastic.

2. A hard, brittle, transparent substance composed of silicates mixed with potash or suds and lime; used for windows in a vehicle.

**glass-bead cleaning**

The cleaning of parts and panels using glass beads propelled with the use of compressed air.

**glass beader**

An apparatus for using air-propelled glass beads to clean parts.

**glass-bead test**

A method of determining the absolute rating of a filter and its efficiency by introducing a measured quantity of glass beads of varying, but known, diameter, as a contaminant into the fluid, which is then filtered through the element.

**glass wrapped**

A term used to refer to a vehicle with a fiberglass body.

**glaze**

A smooth, glossy surface.

**glazed**

A very glossy, thin, smooth surface.

**glideslope**

Angle approach a runway; *Symbols:* **Gamma;** *Typical Units:* rad, deg.

**global distribution system (GDS)**

A computer reservations system (CRS), typically owned jointly by airlines in different countries, that includes reservation databases of suppliers in many countries.

**Global Positioning System (GPS)**

A navigation sensor based on satellites; A Global Positioning System (GPS) provides highly accurate navigation data: position, velocity, and time reference. GPS is often aided by the INU, AHRS, and Doppler data. GPS is accurate with four or more properly oriented satellites. Accuracy is degraded with improperly placed satellites or fewer than four satellites visible. GPS-INS is the most accurate of modes listed, with day/night and all weather capability.

**Go Kart**

A term for a specific brand of racing kart, often used as a generic term for any kart.

**gold**

A trophy.

**goodies**

1. Prizes and awards for race-car winners or show-car participants.
2. High performance equipment on an engine.

**goosed moose**

A car having a severe forward rake.

**gourd guard**

A helmet.

**governor**

A device that controls another device, usually on the basis of speed or rpm.2. A speed-sensitive mechanical assembly in the automatic transmission driven by the output shaft, to supply primary control of when shifting is to occur.

**governor assembly**

A vehicle speed-sensing device that produces governor pressure to force the transmission upshift and permit the downshift.

**governor pressure**
The transmission's hydraulic pressure, used to control shift points, which is directly related to output shaft speed.

**governor valve**
A device attached to the output shaft and used to sense vehicle speed.

**gow job**
A term used in the early 1940s to identify a hot rod.

**gow wagon**
A term used in the early 1940s to identify a hot rod.

**gow out**
To accelerate quickly in a gow job.

**GP**
1. An abbreviation for general purpose.
2. An abbreviation for Grand Prix.

**GPH**
An abbreviation for gallons per hour.

**GPM**
An abbreviation for gallons per minute.

**grade**
A hill; generally a steep hill.

**gradeability**
The ability of a truck to negotiate a given grade at a specified GCW or GVW.

**gray-market parts**
Any part that is not covered by a manufacturer's warranty, generally because it was not sold through an authorized dealer.

**gray water**
Used wash water from the kitchen and bathroom of a mobile home or recreational vehicle.

**grease**
Lubricant consisting of a stable mixture of oil, soap thickeners (usually lithium, sodium, or calcium), and other ingredients for the desired physical or operating characteristics.

**grease fitting**
The orifice, having a check valve, that a grease gun fits on during the greasing process.

**grease plug**
A small plug in a lubrication hole where there is a danger of over lubrication by high-pressure equipment. It is removed for lubrication and then reinstalled.

**greasy friction**
The friction between two surfaces coated with a thin layer of oil.

**green:**
1. A color.
2. A term used for green flag.

**green flag**
The flag used to signal the start of a race.

**green goo**
A term used for green Loctite.

**greenhouse**
The upper part of a vehicle body, including the windows, pillars, and roof.

**green Loctite**
A high-temperature anaerobic compound used for securing parts together.

**grenaded motor**
An engine that has blown up.

**grenade motor**
An engine that is expected to deliver a very high horsepower for a short time, before it blows up.

**grid**
1. A wire mesh, such as that used for a grille.
2. The starting position of race cars based on their qualifying order.

**grid north**
Standard aviation term.

**grid growth**
A condition where the battery grid grows little metallic fingers, extending through the separators, shorting out the plates.

**grille**
An ornamental opening in the front of a vehicle through which air is delivered to the radiator.

**grind**
1. To use an abrasive wheel to remove metal.
2. The specific contour of a camshaft lobe, such as a quarter-race grind.
3. A long race with emphasis on endurance rather than performance.

**Grinding mill**
A machine that reduces the size of particles of raw material fed into it. The size reduction may be to facilitate removal of valuable constituents from an ore or to prepare the material for industrial use, as in preparing clay for pottery making or coal for furnace firing. Coarse material is first crushed. The moderate-sized crushings may be reduced further by grinding or pulverizing.
Grinding mills are of three principal types, as shown in the illustration. In ring-roller pulverizers, the material is fed past

spring-loaded rollers. The rolling surfaces apply a slow large force to the material as the bowl or other container revolves. The fine particles may be swept by an airstream up out of the mill. In tumbling mills the material is fed into a shell or drum that rotates about its horizontal axis. The attrition or abrasion between particles grinds the material. The grinding bodies may be flint pebbles, steel balls, metal rods lying parallel to the axis of the drum, or simply larger pieces of the material itself. In hammer mills, driven swinging hammers reduce the material by sudden impacts.

Fig.   Basic grinding mills. (a) Ring-roller mill. (b) Tumbling mill. (c) Hammer mill.

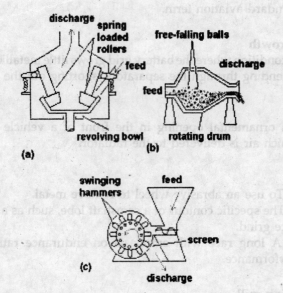

**grip**
   A term used for traction.

**grit**
   Fine dust or dirt.

**grivation**
   *Symbols:* nu sub g ; *Typical Units:* rad, deg.

**grocery getter**

A car used for everyday transportation.

**grommet**

1. A reinforced-metal eyelet through which a fastener is attached.

2. A rubber or plastic eyelet inserted in a hole to protect wires that pass through it.

**groove**

1. The recess in a part to hold a ring or snap ring.

2. Space between two adjacent tread ribs or lugs; the lowered section of the tire tread.

3. The specific path through a turn in an oval track or in road racing.

4. A rut.

**groove weld**

A weld made in a groove between the work pieces.

**gross axle-weight rating (GAWR)**

The maximum allowable fully loaded weight of a given axle.

**gross combination weight (GCW)**

The total weight of a fully equipped vehicle including payload, fuel, and driver.

**gross horsepower**

The maximum engine output as measured on a dynamometer. Also known as gross torque.

**gross torque**

A term used for gross horsepower.

**gross trailer weight (GTW)**

The sum of the weight of the trailer(s) and the payload.

**gross valve lift**

The valve lift, including the running-valve clearance.

**ground-end spring**
> A spring that has flattened ends, usually by grinding, to better fit the perches or retainers.

**grounding**
> he connecting of an electrical unit to the vehicle frame to provide a complete path for electrical current.

**ground-return system**
> A common system of electrical wiring whereby the chassis or frame serves as a part of the electrical circuit.

**groundspeed**
> The speed over the ground; earthspeed projected to a horizontal plane; *Symbols:* V sub g; *Typical Units:* kt,ft/s; *Dimensions:* Length / Time.

**groundspeed select (G/S SEL)**
> A basic guidance mode, providing longitudinal guidance to an operator selected groundspeed.

**Ground track angle (GTA)**
> Direction of ground speed vector with respect to true north; *Synonyms:* true track; *Symbols:* eta; *Typical Units:* rad, deg.

**ground wave**
> An electromagnetic wave that travels along the Earth's surface; usually emitted by a radio transmitter.

**groupie**
> One, especially a female, who follows the racing circuits hoping to be accepted by its members.

**group injection**
> A method of injecting fuel into the manifold areas of several cylinders of an electronic fuel-injection system while at the same time, actually entering each cylinder as its intake valve is opened.

**guard**
A barrier, such as a shroud, that physically prevents entry of the operator's hands or fingers into the point of operation.

**guidance**
System, usually software, that determines state errors of desired state minus current state, typically three states: heading, altitude, and speed.

**guidance control law parameter (GCLP)**
One of several parameters for the guidance control laws, generated by individual guidance modes; *See Also:* altitude error scale factor, altitude integral gain, altitude integral input, altitude integral limit, controlled altitude, controlled speed, course cut limit, crosstrack deviation, crosstrack deviation gain, crosstrack deviation rate, crosstrack deviation rate gain, desired altitude, desired speed, path integral gain, path integral limit, path integral value, reference acceleration, reference acceleration gain, track angle error, track angle error gain, velocity error scale factor.

**gulp valve**
A valve that opens in an air-injection system to admit extra air into the intake manifold upon deceleration, thus leaning out the mixture to prevent backfiring.

**gum**
Residue that remains when gasoline is allowed to sit for a period of time.

**gumballs**
Drag racing tires made of especially soft, sticky compound. The rotating light in a hemispherical housing on top of a police car or emergency vehicle.

**gun-drilled oil holes**
Holes that are drilled to allow oil to be fed to the piston pin.

**gun it**
To rev up an engine suddenly.

**gurgle method**
>A method of adding refrigerant from small cans to a system without running the engine.

**gusset**
>A triangular piece of metal used to add strength to a corner.

**gut**
>To remove non-functional parts of a vehicle in order to reduce its weight.

**guts**
>1. The internal structure of a vehicle.
>2. The essential working parts of a device.

**GVWR**
>An abbreviation for gross vehicle-weight rating.

**gymkhana**
>An individually clocked maneuverability contest for sports cars over an extremely tight course.

**gyroscope (gyro)**
>An inertial device for measuring change of attitude (pitch rate, roll rate, and yaw rate); gyroscopes usually consist of a gimbled, rotating mass; gyroscopes are usually included in inertial sensors, such as AHRS and INS; *See Also*: ring-laser gyro.

...

## hack
1. A taxicab.
2. A passenger car for everyday driving.
3. To cut out a section of body work.

## hand valve
A valve mounted on the steering column or dash, used by the driver to apply trailer brakes independently of the tractor brakes.

## hang a left
To make a left turn.

## hang a right
To make a right turn.

## hang it out
To deliberately throw the rear end into a slide during a turn.

## hang on unit
An under-dash, aftermarket air conditioner. May also refer to other under-dash devices, such as a CB radio.

## hangover
Undesired speaker-cone oscillation caused by a transient signal.

**hard chrome**
A heavy-chrome plating applied to metal to increase its durability and resistance to wear.

**hard copy**
A printed copy of machine output in readable form, such as reports, listings, or graphic images.

**hard dollar savings**
Easily identifiable savings, such as free tickets, reduced rates, or revenue sharing.

**hard edge**
A sharp corner where two surfaces meet.

**hardener**
A chemical component of an epoxy resin that starts a catalytic reaction and causes the mixture to harden.

**hard face**
The application of a hard material, such as chrome, to a surface to increase its durability and wear resistance.

**hardness test**
The technique used to determine the hardness of a material.

**hard parts**
The internal engine parts required to rebuild an engine.

**hard pedal**
1. A loss in braking efficiency so that an excessive amount of pressure is needed to actuate brakes.
2. A condition whereby the load literally overrides the brakes.

**hard spots**
Areas in the friction surface of a brake drum or rotor that have become harder than the surrounding metal.

### hard throttle
A term used when the accelerator is pressed to the floor.

### hardtop
A two- or four-door hardtop convertible body type with front and rear seats, generally characterized by the lack of door or B pillars.

### hardware
The components that make up a computer system, such as a keyboard, a floppy disk drive, and a visual-display terminal. The nuts, bolts, and accessories required to assemble an add-on component.

### hardwired
The physical connection of two pieces of electronic equipment by means of a cable.

### harmonic
The rhythmic vibration of a moving part or assembly.

### Harmonic speed changer
A mechanical-drive system used to transmit rotary, linear, or angular motion at high ratios and with positive motion. In the

Fig. 1  Rotary-to-rotary harmonic speed changer.

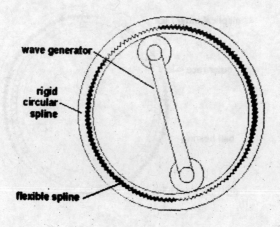

wave generator

rigid
circular
spline

flexible spline

rotary version (Fig. 1), the drive consists of a rigid circular spline, an input wave generator, and a flexible spline. Any one of these can be fixed, used as the input, or used as the output. Any combination (fixed, driver, or driven) may be used.

In Fig. 1 the fixed member is a rigid circular spline with 132 internal teeth. The driven part is a flexible spline, a ring gear with 130 external teeth of same size as on the rigid spline. The driving member is shown as a two-lobed member generating a traveling circular wave on the flexible spline.

The flexible spline meshes with the rigid circular spline at two diametrically opposite regions of the spline, which is shown flexed as an ellipse with its major axis nearly vertical. The teeth on the splines clear each other along the nearly horizontal minor axis.

As the wave generator rotates, the axes of the flexible spline correspondingly rotate along with the regions of contact and clearance between the teeth on the splines. Because the number of teeth on the flexible spline is less than the number of teeth on the fixed and rigid circular spline, when the wave generator rotates one turn, the flexible spline will rotate 2/132 parts of a turn in a direction opposite that of the driving wave generator. The speed reduction is therefore 2:132 (or 1:66). By increasing the number of teeth on the two splines, the flexible spline always having two less (with a two-lobed wave generator) than the number on the circular spline, the speed reduction can be increased correspondingly.

Fig. 2  Diagram of actual construction of a rotary-to-rotary harmonic speed changer.

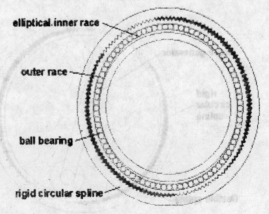

elliptical inner race

outer race

ball bearing

rigid circular spline

**hot drawn**
A process of forming metal by heating it and pulling it through rollers or dies.

**hot gas**
The condition of refrigerant as it leaves the compressor until it gives up its heat and condenses.

**hot-gas bypass line**
The line that connects the hot-gas bypass valve outlet to the evaporator outlet.

**hot-gas bypass valve**
A device used to meter hot gas back to the evaporator, through the bypass line, to prevent condensate from freezing on the core.

**hot-gas defrosting**
The use of high-pressure gas in the evaporator to remove frost.

**hot-idle compensator**
A temperature-sensitive carburetor valve that opens when the inlet air temperature exceeds a certain level to allow additional air to enter the intake manifold, preventing an overly rich air/fuel ratio.

**hot iron**
An early term for a hot rod.

**hot patch**
A patch applied to a tube or tire with the use of heat to vulcanize it onto the damaged surface.

**hot rod**
A passenger car that has been modified and rebuilt for high **performance** and a distinctive appearance used primarily for **straightaway** speed or acceleration racing.

In actual construction (Fig. 2), the wave generator is composed of a ball bearing with an elliptical inner race. In rotating, the inner race flexes the outer race, engaging its external teeth along its major axis with the internal teeth of the rigid spline.

**harmonic balancer**
A balance shaft or wheel that reduces or eliminates harmonics.

**harmonic damper**
A term used for harmonic balancer.

**harmonic vibration**
A rhythmic vibration of a moving part or assembly at a specific speed.

**harness**
A group of electrical conductors laced or bundled in a given configuration, usually with several breakouts.

**harness clip**
A metal or plastic clip used to secure a wiring harness to the car frame or body at various points, providing safe and neat routing.

**harness connector**
An electrical connector at the end of a wire or harness used to connect the conductor to a device or system.

**hat**
A pipe-like housing for the injector on a constant-flow fuel-injection system.

**hatchback**
A passenger-car body style where a full opening hatch, including the rear window, lifts for access to the cargo storage area.

**hauler**
1. A top-performing car.

2. A top-performing driver.

**hauling the mail**
Performance at peak efficiency.

**hazardous waste**
1. Any product used in a system that is considered harmful to people and/or the environment.
2. Any poisonous substance, the byproduct of a poisonous substance, or one that contains carcinogens and is considered unsafe for animal or plant life by the EPA.

**hazard system**
A driver-controlled system of flashing front- and rear-marker lights to warn approaching motorists of a potential hazard.

**H-beam rod**
A connecting rod having an H-beam-shaped cross section.

**HC-CO meter**
A device using an infrared sensor to measure the amount of hydrocarbons, in parts per million, and carbon monoxide, in percent, in the vehicle exhaust.

**HD**
An abbreviation for heavy duty.

**HDMA**
An abbreviation for Heavy Duty Manufacturers Association.

**HDRA**
1. An abbreviation for Heavy Duty Representatives Association.
2. An abbreviation for High Desert Racing Association.

**head**
1. That part of an engine that covers the top of the cylinders and pistons and usually contains the combustion chambers and valve train.

2. That part of a compressor that covers the valve plates and separates the high side from the low side of an air-conditioning system.

**headache rack**
A rack that is provided at the rear of a truck-cab interior to prevent a load from crashing through the rear window.

**head bolts**
The bolts that fasten the cylinder heads to the engine block.

**header**
1. A vehicle crash.
2. A free-flowing exhaust manifold used on high-performance cars.

**header tank**
The top and bottom tanks or side tanks of a radiator in which coolant accumulates or is received.

**head gasket**
A gasket used to seal the cylinder head to the engine block.

**hose clamp**
A device used to attach hoses to the engine, heater core, radiator, and water pump. A popular type of replacement clamp is the high-torque, worm-gear clamp with a carbon steel screw and a stainless-steel band.

**host computer**
A main computer that monitors and controls other computers.

**Hotchkiss drive**
A popular type of drive-line system that features an open or visible drive shaft.

**hot dog**
A top performer in almost all forms of racing.

## hot-rolled steel (HRS)
Steel that is formed while hot.

## hot setup
A combination of modifications and components that enhances maximum performance.

## hot shoe
A top race driver.

## hot soak
A condition that may occur when an engine is stopped for a prolonged period of time after a hot, hard run causing the gasoline to evaporate out of the carburetor.

## hot spot
1. A localized area where excessive heat can build up, such as around a spark plug, that could cause preignition.
2. An area on an auto body where corrosion is most likely to occur.

## hot-tank gloves
Long-sleeved, thick rubber gloves for use in the hot tank.

## Hot-water heating system
heating system for a building in which the heat-conveying medium is hot water. Heat transfer in British thermal units (Btu) equals pounds of water circulated times drop in temperature of water. For other liquids, the equation should be modified by specific heats. The system may be modified to provide cooling.

A hot-water heating system consists essentially of water-heating or -cooling means and of heat-emitting means such as radiators, convectors, baseboard radiators, or panel coils. A piping system connects the heat source to the various heat-emitting units and includes a method of establishing circulation of the water or other medium and an expansion tank to hold the excess volume as it is heated and expands. Radiators and convectors have such different responses that they should not be used in the same system.

Types

In a one-pipe system (Fig. 1), radiation units are bypassed around a one-pipe loop. This type of system should only be used in small installations.

Fig. 1   One-pipe hot-water heating system.

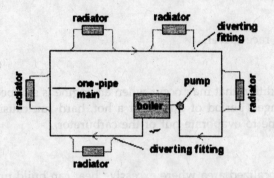

In a two-pipe system (Fig. 2), radiation units are connected to separate flow and return mains, which may run in parallel or preferably on a reverse return loop, with no limit on the size of the system.

Fig. 2   Two-pipe reverse return system.

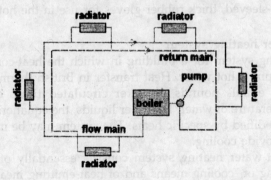

**hot wire**

1. Wire that carries current from the ungrounded terminal of the battery to an electric load.

2. To bypass the ignition switch to start the vehicle.

In actual construction (Fig. 2), the wave generator is composed of a ball bearing with an elliptical inner race. In rotating, the inner race flexes the outer race, engaging its external teeth along its major axis with the internal teeth of the rigid spline.

## harmonic balancer
A balance shaft or wheel that reduces or eliminates harmonics.

## harmonic damper
A term used for harmonic balancer.

## harmonic vibration
A rhythmic vibration of a moving part or assembly at a specific speed.

## harness
A group of electrical conductors laced or bundled in a given configuration, usually with several breakouts.

## harness clip
A metal or plastic clip used to secure a wiring harness to the car frame or body at various points, providing safe and neat routing.

## harness connector
An electrical connector at the end of a wire or harness used to connect the conductor to a device or system.

## hat
A pipe-like housing for the injector on a constant-flow fuel-injection system.

## hatchback
A passenger-car body style where a full opening hatch, including the rear window, lifts for access to the cargo storage area.

## hauler
1. A top-performing car.

2. A top-performing driver.

**hauling the mail**
Performance at peak efficiency.

**hazardous waste**
1. Any product used in a system that is considered harmful to people and/or the environment.
2. Any poisonous substance, the byproduct of a poisonous substance, or one that contains carcinogens and is considered unsafe for animal or plant life by the EPA.

**hazard system**
A driver-controlled system of flashing front- and rear-marker lights to warn approaching motorists of a potential hazard.

**H-beam rod**
A connecting rod having an H-beam-shaped cross section.

**HC-CO meter**
A device using an infrared sensor to measure the amount of hydrocarbons, in parts per million, and carbon monoxide, in percent, in the vehicle exhaust.

**HD**
An abbreviation for heavy duty.

**HDMA**
An abbreviation for Heavy Duty Manufacturers Association.

**HDRA**
1. An abbreviation for Heavy Duty Representatives Association.
2. An abbreviation for High Desert Racing Association.

**head**
1. That part of an engine that covers the top of the cylinders and pistons and usually contains the combustion chambers and valve train.

**hot-rolled steel (HRS)**
Steel that is formed while hot.

**hot setup**
A combination of modifications and components that enhances maximum performance.

**hot shoe**
A top race driver.

**hot soak**
A condition that may occur when an engine is stopped for a prolonged period of time after a hot, hard run causing the gasoline to evaporate out of the carburetor.

**hot spot**
1. A localized area where excessive heat can build up, such as around a spark plug, that could cause preignition.
2. An area on an auto body where corrosion is most likely to occur.

**hot-tank gloves**
Long-sleeved, thick rubber gloves for use in the hot tank.

**Hot-water heating system**
heating system for a building in which the heat-conveying medium is hot water. Heat transfer in British thermal units (Btu) equals pounds of water circulated times drop in temperature of water. For other liquids, the equation should be modified by specific heats. The system may be modified to provide cooling.
A hot-water heating system consists essentially of water-heating or -cooling means and of heat-emitting means such as radiators, convectors, baseboard radiators, or panel coils. A piping system connects the heat source to the various heat-emitting units and includes a method of establishing circulation of the water or other medium and an expansion tank to hold the excess volume as it is heated and expands. Radiators and convectors have such different responses that they should not

be used in the same system.

Types

In a one-pipe system (Fig. 1), radiation units are bypassed around a one-pipe loop. This type of system should only be used in small installations.

Fig. 1  One-pipe hot-water heating system.

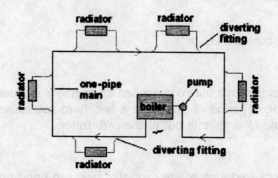

In a two-pipe system (Fig. 2), radiation units are connected to separate flow and return mains, which may run in parallel or preferably on a reverse return loop, with no limit on the size of the system.

Fig. 2  Two-pipe reverse return system.

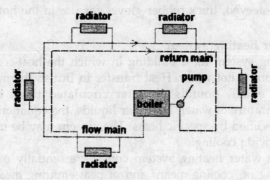

**hot wire**

1. Wire that carries current from the ungrounded terminal of the battery to an electric load.

2. To bypass the ignition switch to start the vehicle.

**hot-wire sensor**
An electrical device inside the mass-airflow meter that measures air flow and density.

**hot working**
The mechanical working of metal at a temperature above its recrystallization point and high enough to prevent strain hardening.

**hough**
A standard model for computing earth data.

**hourglass frame**
A term used for X-frame.

**housekeeping**
The type of safety in the shop that keeps floors, walls, and windows clean, lighting proper, and containers and tool storage correct.

**housing bore**
The inside diameter of a bearing housing.

**housing breather**
A venting device that allows air to enter or leave the axle housing.

**Hover hold (HVR SYM)**
A basic guidance mode, providing lateral guidance and longitudinal guidance to maintain an operator selected north velocity and east velocity; if the selected velocities are zero, then a position is held.

**hybrid**
1. A vehicle having two separate propulsion systems, such as a gasoline engine and an electric motor.
2. A vehicle having its major components from more than one source, such as a Ford engine in a Chevrolet chassis.

**hybrid battery**

A battery that combines the advantages of both the low maintenance and the maintenance-free battery.

**hydraulic brakes**

A braking system using hydraulic pressure to press the brake shoes against the brake drums.

**hydraulic clutch**

A clutch that is actuated by hydraulic pressure.

**hydraulic lifter**

Valve lifter located between the camshaft and pushrod that uses internal oil pressure to cause the lifter to expand lengthwise.

**hydraulic pressure**

A pressure exerted through the medium of a liquid.

**hydraulic principles**

The use of a liquid under pressure to transfer force or motion, or to increase an applied force.

**hydraulics**

Hydraulic ram units, installed in a low rider at each suspension point, to lower or raise the ride height. Also referred to as hydro.

**Hydraulic turbine**

A machine which converts the energy of an elevated water supply into mechanical energy of a rotating shaft. Most old-style waterwheels utilized the weight effect of the water directly, but all modern hydraulic turbines are a form of fluid dynamic machinery of the jet and vane type operating on the impulse or reaction principle and thus involving the conversion of pressure energy to kinetic energy. The shaft drives an electric generator, and speed must be of an acceptable synchronous value.

The impulse or Pelton unit has all available energy converted to the kinetic form in a few stationary nozzles and subsequent absorption by reversing buckets mounted on the rim of a wheel (Fig. 1). Reaction units of the Francis or the Kaplan types run full of water, submerged, with a draft tube and a continuous column of water from head race to tail race (Figs. 2 and 3). There is some fluid acceleration in a continuous ring

Fig. 1   Cross section of an impulse (Pelton) type of hydraulic-turbine installation.

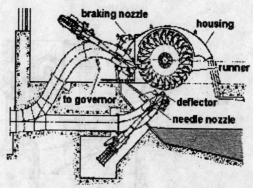

Fig. 2   Cross section of a reaction (Francis) type of hydraulic-turbine installation.
1 ft = 0.3 m.

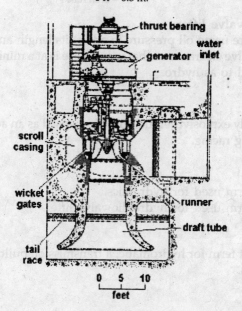

of stationary nozzles with full peripheral admission to the moving nozzles of the runner in which there is further acceleration. The draft tube produces a negative pressure in the runner with the propeller or Kaplan units acting as suction runners; the Francis inward-flow units act as pressure runners. Mixed-flow units give intermediate degrees of rotor pressure drop and fluid acceleration.

Fig. 3   Cross section of a propeller (Kaplan) type of hydraulic turbine installation.

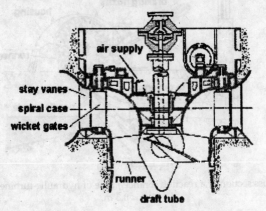

## hydraulic valve lifter

A device using oil pressure to adjust its length and maintain zero valve clearance so that valve noise is at a minimum. Also referred to as hydro.

## hydrazine

A highly explosive jet fuel sometimes used as an additive fuel for drag racing.

## hydro

1. A term used for hydraulics.
2. A term used for hydraulic-valve lifter.

## Hydro

A short term for hydromatic, a transmission built by General Motors.

## hydro-boost

A type of brake power booster that uses hydraulic pressure provided by the power-steering pump to reduce pedal effort.

## hydro cam

A camshaft especially designed to operate with hydraulic valve lifters.

## hydrocarbon (HC)

A compound containing hydrogen (H) and carbon(C), such as gasoline.

## hydrocarbon emissions

A term used for exhaust emissions or unburned hydrocarbons.

## hydrocarbon reactivity

A measure of the smog-forming potential of a hydrocarbon.

## hydrochloric acid

A corrosive acid produced when water and R-12 are mixed as within an automotive air-conditioning system.

## hydrochlorofluorocarbon

A group of refrigerants that contain the chlorine (Cl) atom and the hydrogen (H) atom, which causes the chlorine atom to dissipate more rapidly in the atmosphere.

## hypoid gears

A spiral-bevel gear that allows the pinion to be placed below the center of the ring gear in a final drive assembly.

## hypoid gear set

Two gears that transmit power at a 90 degree angle or other angles having the driving gear below the driven gear centerline to allow for lowering the drive shaft.

## hysteresis

A function in which the algorithm for computing output

changes at defined events or thresholds, such that output follows one path as input increases and another path as input decreases; Hysteresis can be formalized: (0) at initialization, select algorithm-0 (1).if event-1 occurs, switch to algorithm-1 (2) if event-2 occurs, switch to algorithm-2 ... (N) if event-n occurs, switch to algorithm-n Frequently in avionics, hysteresis prevents a test from oscillating near the transition point due to noise. Implementation is usually: (0) at initialization, set $y = 0$ (1) if $x_c + h/2 \le x$, then set $y = 1$ (2) if $x_c - h/2 < x < x_c + h/2$, then let y retain its value (3) if $x \le x_c - h/2$, then set $y = 0$.

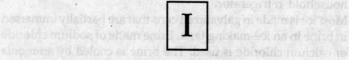

# IATA
International Air Transport Association.

# IATAN
International Airlines Travel Agency Network

# IATAN card
Photo identification issued by IATAN. Widely accepted as the only identification for travel agents. Sometimes called, erroneously, "IATA card."

# IATAN list
A list maintained by a travel agency listing those employees and independent contractors who qualify for travel benefits, as determined by IATAN.

# I-beam axle
A beam axle having an I-shaped cross section.

# I-beam rod
A connecting rod having an I-shaped cross section.

# Ice manufacture
Commercial production of manufactured artificial ice from water, or of dry ice from the solidification of carbon dioxide, by mechanical refrigeration. Of great economic importance

was the manufacture of water ice for use in refrigeration units, fishing boats, fish- and meat-packing plants, and dairies. However, there was a sharp increase in the trend toward cubing, sizing, and packaging of ice. The domestic ice market practically vanished with development of the automatic household refrigerator.

Most ice is made in galvanized cans that are partially immersed in brine in an ice-making tank. Brine made of sodium chloride or calcium chloride is used. The brine is cooled by ammonia as the refrigerant evaporates in pipe coils or brine coolers submerged in the ice tank. The ice cans are filled with raw water, or treated water if it initially contains large amounts of impurities. The water is usually precooled. Cold brine circulates around the ice cans to freeze the water. Commercial ice is frozen in 300- or 400-lb (135- or 180-kg) blocks for which the freezing time with brine at 12°F (-11°C) is 38-42 h. Freezing time depends largely on the thickness of the ice cake and the brine temperature. In large plants, cans are arranged in group frames for harvesting as many as 34 cans at a time. A traveling crane picks up a frozen group, transports and drops it into a dip tank for thawing, then moves it to a can dump where the ice cakes slide out and into a storage room. The empty cans

Typical can ice plant. 300 lb = 135 kg.

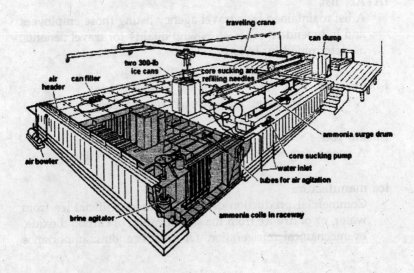

are refilled with fresh water and are returned to the ice tank by the crane.

If clear ice is required, the water in each can must be agitated with air during freezing; otherwise opaque ice is formed. Because the water must be cooled to 32°F (0°C) before freezing can start and because of system losses, about 1.6 tons (1.5 metric tons) of refrigeration is required to make 1 ton (0.9 metric ton) of ice when the raw water enters at 70°F (21°C). The manufacture of ice in slush, flake, or cube form by continuous ice-makers (Fig. 2) constitutes a large portion of the commercial market. Also, small, fully automatic, self-contained, cube and flake ice-makers are used in bars, restaurants, hotels, and hospitals.

Fig. 2   Commercial flake ice machine.

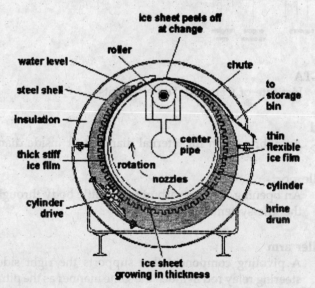

ice sheet peels off
at change

roller

water level

steel shell

insulation

thick stiff
ice film

cylinder
drive

chute

to
storage
bin

thin
flexible
ice film

cylinder

brine
drum

center
pipe

rotation

nozzles

ice sheet
growing in thickness

### ice-melting capacity
A refrigeration effect equal to the latent heat of fusion of a stated weight of ice, at 144 Btu per pound.

### Ignition system
Inductive discharge ignition system for a four-cylinder engine. The cylinder firing order is 1-3-4-2.

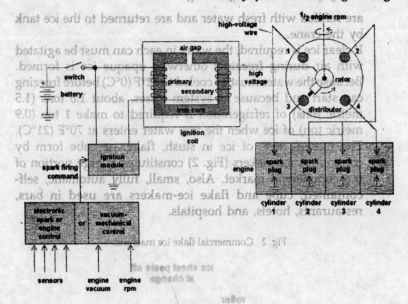

## ICTA
Institute of Certified Travel Agents.

## i.d.
An abbreviation for internal diameter or inside diameter.

## idle port
An opening into the carburetor throttle body through which the idle system discharges fuel.

## idler arm
A pivoting component that supports the right side of the steering relay rod in much the same manner as the pitman arm supports the left side.

## idler eccentric
A device used in a belt-drive system using the idler pulley as a means of tightening the belt.

## idler gear

A gear connecting two other gears in a manner so that they will turn in the same direction.

## idler pulley

A pulley that is used to adjust the belt in a belt-drive system.

## idle speed

The speed at which an engine idles in revolutions per minute (rpm), usually between 600 and 850 rpm. The idle speed is specified on the under-hood emissions decal.

## idle-speed adjustment

The idle speed on carbureted engines without computer idle-speed control is set by turning a screw that opens or closes the throttle plates. On fuel-injected engines without computer idle-speed control, idle speed is set by turning an idle-air bypass screw that allows air to bypass the throttle plates. Idle speed is not adjustable on engines with computer idle-speed control.

## idle-stop solenoid

An electromagnetic device mounted on the carburetor linkage that maintains the proper throttle opening for specified idle speed while the ignition is on, but allows the throttle to close further when the ignition is switched off, reducing the amount of air that can enter the engine and the likelihood of dieseling.

## idle system

The passages of a carburetor through which fuel is fed when the engine is idling.

## idle vent

An opening in an enclosed chamber through which air can pass under idle conditions.

## I-4

An abbreviation for an inline four-cylinder engine.

**IFS**

An abbreviation for independent front suspension.

**if you can't find 'em, grind 'em**

An admonition to a driver who misses a shift.

**ignition**

The firing of a spark plug to ignite the air/fuel mixture in the combustion chamber.

**ignition advance**

The moving forward, in time, of the ignition spark relative to the piston position.

**ignition coil**

A transformer containing a primary and secondary winding that acts to boost the battery voltage of 12 volts to as much as 30,000 volts to fire the spark plugs.

**ignition distributor**

A term used for distributor.

**ignition map**

A chart showing the precise advance and retard of the ignition on an electronic control-equipped engine.

**ignition points**

A term used for points.

**ignition reserve**

The difference between the minimum available and maximum required voltage for proper operation.

**ignition resistor**

A resistance element in series with the primary circuit to reduce the voltage supplied to the coil during engine operation.

**ignition retard**

The moving back in time of the ignition spark relative to the position of the piston.

## ignition switch

A five-position switch that is the power distribution point for most of the vehicle's primary electrical systems. The spring-loaded START position provides momentary contact and automatically moves to the RUN position when the key is released. The other switch detent positions are ACCESSORIES, LOCK, and OFF.

## ignition system

The major components, such as the battery, coil, ignition switch, distributor, high-tension wiring, and spark plugs, that provide the right spark at the right time to ignite the air/fuel mixture.

## ignition temperature

The lowest temperature at which a combustible material will ignite and continue to burn independent of the heat source.

## ignition timing

The timing of the spark, expressed in crankshaft degrees, in relation to top dead center.

## ignition timing-retard sensor

A term used for knock sensor.

## I-head

An overhead valve engine having both intake and exhaust valves directly over the piston.

## I-head engine

An overhead valve engine with the valves in the head.

## Industrial trucks

Manually propelled or powered carriers for transporting materials over level, slightly inclined, or slightly declined running surfaces. Some industrial trucks can lift and lower their loads, and others can also tier them. All trucks maintain contact with the running surface over which they operate and, except when towed by a chain conveyor, follow variable paths of travel as distinct from conveying machines or monorails.

See also: Materials-handling equipment

Running gear

The means employed to support a truck and its load and to provide rolling-friction contact with the running surface is the running gear. Factors in the selection of running gears include load capacity, operating conditions, travel surface, kind of material to be handled, protection of load and machine, economy, and, in the case of hand trucks, ease of manipulation and the reduction of operator fatigue.

Rollers, used in dollies, are of solid or tubular steel with antifriction bearings. Rigid and swivel casters are used with the dollies and with hand and powered trucks. Swivels differ from rigid casters in that they are offset wheels that swivel about their own vertical axis, thereby easing the turning of the hand truck with its load. Steel, solid rubber, semipneumatic, and other wheels fitted with plain or antifriction bearings are designed to meet specific requirements. Industrial wheels for heavier-duty and special automotive-type wheels in a wide selection of tire treads are used with powered trucks and tractors.

Hand trucks

The manually operated, two-wheel hand truck, regarded by some as old fashioned and inefficient, still plays a prominent part in the handling of materials in some of the most modern plants. The hand truck is inexpensive, requires a negligible amount of maintenance, and is convenient for handling light loads for short distances. Its light weight makes it ideally suited for applications where small quantities are handled, with a low frequency of movement, where floor loading restrictions preclude the use of the heavier powered trucks. The hand truck is also easily adapted for use in explosive atmospheres.

The key feature to the hand truck is the running gear. Care must be taken to select the type and size of wheel to suit the carrying load and operating conditions. In many cases, depending on the loads and the surface of the operating floor, inexpensive cast-iron or steel wheels may be more suitable than higher-priced pneumatic tires or plastic-rimmed wheels. Basic types of hand trucks and their distinctive features are shown in the table. Two-wheel hand trucks are classified broadly as eastern and western (Fig. 1). Multiwheel hand trucks are produced in many models, but platform types continue to be the most widely used in industry and distribution. Stakes, end-and-side gates, solid panels, and other superstructures add versatility to the basic machines. Low-lift types of hand trucks elevate their loads just sufficiently to clear the running surface (Fig. 2).

Fig. 1 Two-wheel hand trucks. (a) Eastern. (b) Western.

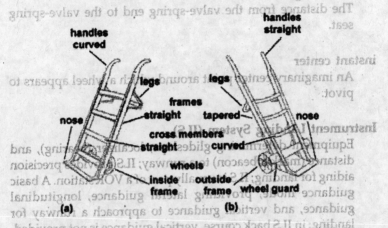

Fig. 2 Low-lift hand trucks elevate loads to clear running surface. (a) Carboy. (b) Trunnion box.

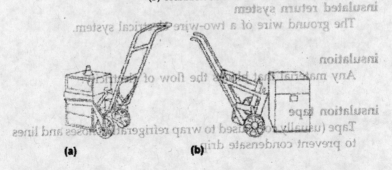

**inspection**
The process of measuring, examining, testing, gauging, or otherwise comparing the unit with the applicable requirements or specifications.

**inspection maintenance (I/M)**
The periodic and systematic inspection and maintenance of a vehicle's ignition, fuel, and emissions-control systems.

**install**
To set up an accessory part or kit for use in a vehicle.

**installed height**
The distance from the valve-spring end to the valve-spring seat.

**instant center**
An imaginary center point around which a wheel appears to pivot.

**Instrument Landing System (ILS)**
Equipment determining glideslope, localizer (bearing), and distance (marker beacon) to a runway; ILS provides precision aiding for landing; ILS is usually part of a VOR station. A basic guidance mode, providing lateral guidance, longitudinal guidance, and vertical guidance to approach a runway for landing; in ILS back course, vertical guidance is not provided.

**insulated return system**
The ground wire of a two-wire electrical system.

**insulation**
Any material that blocks the flow of electricity.

**insulation tape**
Tape (usually cork) used to wrap refrigeration hoses and lines to prevent condensate drip.

**insulator**
A material with high electrical resistance that supports or separates conductors to prevent undesired flow of current to other objects.

**insulator ribs**

In a spark plug, unevenly spaced circular ridges on the upper section of the insulator to reduce or prevent flashover of the high voltage from the terminal to the lower shell.

**Insurance Information Institute**

A public information and communications association.

**Insurance Institute for Highway Safety**

A highway and vehicle safety research organization.

**intake**

The point at which a fluid or gas enters a pipe or channel Z. The act of taking in.

**intake manifold**

1. A metal component used to duct:
2. The air/fuel mixture from the carburetor to the intake ports.
3. Air in an injected engine to the intake ports.

**intake over exhaust (IOE)**

An engine design having intake valves in the cylinder head and exhaust valves in the block.

**intake ports**

1. Passages in the cylinder head that direct air/fuel mixture from the intake manifold to the intake valves.
2. Passages in an L-head engine block that direct the air/fuel mixture from the intake manifold to the intake valves.
3. Passages in the head or block of an injected engine that direct air to the intake valves from the intake manifold.

**intake stroke**

A downward stroke of a piston that draws the air/fuel mixture into the cylinder.

**intake valve**

A valve that opens to admit the air/fuel mixture.

**integral**

Internal or built-in as a part of the whole.

**integral-type power steering**

A steering system with a built-in power assist.

**integral valve guide**

A valve guide machined into the cylinder head.

**integral valve seat**

A valve seat machined into the cylinder head.

**Integrator**

A function that integrates; Many types of integrators exist; in fact, they constitute entire books. Avionics software usually relies on rectangular, single integrators, but occassional uses trapezoidal or double integrators.

**inter-axle differential**

A third differential between the front and rear differentials that permits differences in speed between the front and rear driving axles.

## jacketed gasket

A gasket having metal grommets around bolt and water holes.

## jacking

Modifying the suspension to raise or lower one corner of an oval-track race car in order to provide better handling characteristics.

## jackrabbit start

The sudden acceleration from a standing start.

## jackshaft

A shaft found in most overhead cam engines that is used to drive the distributor, fuel pump, and oil pump.

## Jack the Bear

A top-performing driver.

## Jacob's ladder

A triangular control linkage to center the rear axle assembly found on some rear-wheel-drive race cars.

## Jake brake

A hydraulically operated compression braking system used to slow the truck by alternating the engine's exhaust valve opening time; named for its inventor, Jacobs.

**jalopy**
1. A low-budget, dirt-track racing car rebuilt from an older vehicle.
2. An old automobile.

**JAMA**
An abbreviation for Japan Automobile Manufacturers Association.

**jam nut**
A second nut tightened against a primary nut to prevent it from working loose; used on inner and outer tie-rod adjustment nuts and on many pinion-bearing adjustment nuts.

**Japan Automobile Manufacturers Association (JAMA)**
An international trade association of Japanese car, truck, motorcycle, and bus manufacturers.

**Japanese Industrial Standard (JIS)**
Japan's equivalent of the DIN in Germany or the SAE in the United States.

**jeeping**
Driving a 4WD vehicle, generally off the road.

**jeep trail**
A road or trail suitable only for a 4WD vehicle.

**Jerk**
Rate of change of acceleration, either scalar or vector, often with subscripts such as ENU or XYZ to denote the coordinate frame; time derivative of acceleration; *Symbols:* j,J; *Typical Units:* ft/s-cubed; *Dimensions:* Length / Time-cubed.

**jet car**
A race car powered by a jet aircraft engine for open course competition.

**jump**
1. To begin early rapid acceleration in a rolling-start race before the green flag.
2. To make an early, sudden start off the line in drag racing before the green light.
3. To bypass the ignition switch to start a vehicle.
4. To jump start a vehicle.
5. An obstacle that causes an off-road vehicle to become airborne.

**jumper cable**
Two heavy-duty cables used to connect two batteries, as for starting a vehicle.

**jumpers**
A term used for jumper cable or jumper wire.

**jumper wire**
A wire used to bypass electrical circuits or components for testing purposes.

**jump out**
A condition when a fully engaged gear and sliding clutch are forced out of engagement.

**jump start**
Using battery jumper cables to connect an able battery to a disabled battery to start the vehicle.

**junction block**
A device on which two or more junctions may be found.

**Junior fueler**
An old drag-racing term for a lower-class fuel dragster.

**Junior stocker**
An old drag-racing term for a lower-class fuel stocker.

**junk**

Anything that is so badly worn or deteriorated that it is of no further use.

**junk box**

1. A vehicle that has been rebuilt from well-worn parts.
2. A vehicle that is ready to be scrapped.

**junker**

A vehicle that is ready for the junk box.

**junkyard**

A vehicle salvage business that sells used parts.

kandy apple: A rich, red finish popular on kustom cars.

**K**

## kart
A small, open, four-wheeled vehicle with a single cylinder, two- or four-cycle gasoline engine.

## Kalman filter
A filter for combining multiple data sources, usually of different types, to produce an estimate better than any single source; *Compare:* averaging filter, complementary filter.

## K-car
A compact front-wheel drive vehicle introduced by Chrysler in the early 1980s.

## KD set
An abbreviation for knocked down set.

## Keenserts
A trade name for a thread-repair system using spiral inserts to repair damaged threads.

## keeper grooves
The grooved area on a valve stem to accommodate the keepers.

## keepers
Key-like, tapered-metal locking devices used to hold valve retainers in place on the valve stem.

**KE-Jetronics**
A continuous electronic fuel-injection system by Bosh that has been modified using a lambda oxygen sensor.

**kemp**
A kustom car or lead sled.

**keyboard**
An input device used to key programs and data into the computer's storage.

**keyless entry**
A system using a coded keypad that allows the operator to unlock the doors or the trunk from outside the vehicle without the use of a key.

**key-off loads**
A term used for parasitic loads.

**keystone ring**
Compression piston ring, double tapered and shaped like a keystone.

**keyway**
A groove milled or machined onto a shaft or into a bore to accept a square, half moon, or round piece of metal.

**kg**
An abbreviation for the metric kilogram.

**kickdown**
A downshift to the next lower gear in an automatic transmission when the driver applies full throttle, as in overtaking and passing another vehicle.

**kickdown pressure**
The pressure developed to downshift the transmission from a high gear to a lower gear.

## kickdown valve
A valve located in the valve body that develops kickdown pressure.

## kick out of gear
To shift to neutral.

## kickpad
The area along the inside bottom of a car door.

## kickup
A section of a chassis frame that is raised to clear the axles or suspension.

## killed
To bring to a stop, such as to kill an engine.
To overcome completely or with irresistible effect.

## kill switch
A switch used to disconnect the electrical system in an emergency.

## kilogram (kg)
A metric unit of measure for weight, as in English pounds.

## kilometer (km)
A metric measure for distance, as in English miles.

## kilo Pascal (kPa)
A metric unit of measure equal to 6.895 psi.

## kinetic energy
The energy of motion, such as that of a flywheel.

## King Kong
A hemi-engined Dodge or Plymouth stock car racer during the 1960s and 1970s.

**kingpin**
> A pin or shaft on which the steering spindle assembly rotates. The pin, mounted through the center of the trailer upper-bolster plate, that mates with the fifth wheel and locks to secure the trailer to the fifth wheel.

**kingpin angle**
> A term used for kingpin inclination.

**kingpin axis**
> The inward tilt of the steering axis from the vertical.

**kingpin inclination**
> A major factor in a vehicle's directional control and stability; the angle of a line through the center of the kingpin in relation to the true vertical centerline of the tire viewed from the front of the vehicle.

**kit car**
> A knocked-down vehicle designed to be built by the owner.

**K-Jetronic**
> A continuous fuel-injection system; a forerunner of the KE-Jetronic system.

**knee bolster**
> An energy-absorbing pad used on a passive-restraint system to cushion the forward motion of the driver during an accident by restricting leg movement.

**knock**
> A noise within an engine generally caused by detonation or preignition.

**knocked-down set (KD set)**
> A package of automotive parts, assemblies, and subassemblies packaged at one location to be assembled at another location.

## knock off
1. A counterfeit.
2. A cheap auto part packaged to represent a popular brand.

## knock-off hub
A large, single, two- or three-eared wing nut used to retain a wheel; illegal for street use.

## knock sensor
A sensor that signals the engine-control computer when detonation is detected, momentarily retarding ignition timing until detonation ceases.

## knuckle arm
The arm that extends backward from steering knuckle to provide attachment for the tie rods.

## knurl
A series of ridges formed on the outer surface of a piston or the inner surface of a valve guide to help reduce clearance and hold oil for added lubrication.

## KOEO
An abbreviation for key on engine off.

## KOER
An abbreviation for key on engine running.

## kPa
An abbreviation for the metric kiloPascal, as in the English pounds per square inch.

## kustom
A term George Barris used for custom, now in common use.

## kustom car
A custom car, specifically one built by George Barris, a noted California customizer.

**labeled**
> An identifying mark or trademark of a nationally recognized testing lab that is attached to signify that the item has been tested and meets appropriate standards.

**lag**
> 1. The incorrect operation of a shock absorber because of aeration due to the mixing of air with oils, causing the shock absorber to produce a poor ride.
> 2. To fail to keep up; to fall behind.

**lakes**
> A dry lake used for high-speed performance trials.

**lakes pipes**
> Straight exhaust pipes with no muffler.

**lakester**
> A hot rod with minimal frontal area and fully exposed wheels designed for lakes competition.

**LA Kit**
> A reconditioned crankshaft that is supplied with the appropriate bearings and an installation kit.

**LAL**
> An abbreviation for lowest achievable level.

**lambda**
1. The Greek letter L.
2. A term used by engineers to represent the air/fuel ratio.
3. A European auto maker's term for the oxygen sensor.

**landau top**
A passenger-car top partially covered with vinyl to give it a convertible-like appearance.

**landing gear**
Retractable supports for a semi-trailer to keep the trailer level when the tractor/truck is detached from it.

**land speed record (LSR)**
1. The maximum speed obtained by:
2. A wheel-driven, internal-combustion engine vehicle.
3. A thrust-driven jet or rocket engine vehicle.

**lap**
1. A complete trip around an oval track or road course.
2. To gain a full lap over the second place competitor.

**lap joint**
A joint between two overlapping members in parallel planes.

**Laplace transform**
A mathematical relationship to model a continuous function in the complex frequency domain (S-plane); Laplace transforms are commonly used by systems engineers to describe avionics systems; *Compare:* continuous-time equation, difference equation, differential equation, discrete-time equation, state-space model, Z transform; *See Also:* first-order filter, integrator, second-order filter, unit functions.

**lapping**
A valve-grinding process using a paste-like grit on the face of the valve.

**lapping compound**
A paste-like grit used for lapping valves.

**lap weld**
A welding process between two overlapping members in parallel planes.

**laser**
1. An acronym for light amplification by stimulated emissions of radiation.
2. A device that produces a concentrated, coherent light beam by stimulated electronic or molecular transitions to lower energy levels.

**Laser obstacle avoidance / terrain avoidance sensor (OA/ TA)**
A sensor that provides warnings for long, thin objects (like wires). It has at least a 20deg x 30deg FOV, which is both velocity tracked and pitch stabilized. It provides warnings (every 2.5 seconds) for long, thin obstacles (like wires) at 400 meters detection range and contour flight at 80-120 knots.

**lash**
The clearance between two parts.

**lash-pad adjusters**
Small round metal pieces of various thickness used to adjust valve clearance.

**late apex**
Getting to the inside of a turn later than usual due to a late entry into the corner.

**latent heat**
The amount of heat required to cause a change of state of a substance without changing its temperature.

**latent heat of condensation**
The quantity of heat given off while changing a substance from a vapor to a liquid.

## latent heat of evaporation
The quantity of heat required to change a liquid into a vapor without raising the temperature of the vapor above that of the original liquid. Also known as latent heat of vaporization.

## latent heat of fusion
The amount of heat that must be removed from a liquid to cause it to change to a solid without causing a change of temperature.

## latent heat of vaporization
A term used for latent heat of evaporation.

## Lateral
Related to latitude; across an aircraft left to right.

## lateral acceleration
The centrifugal force that tends to push a vehicle sideways, toward the outside of a turn.

## Lateral cue
A cue to control heading; lateral cyclic cue *See Also:* wheel cue.

## lateral cyclic
A flight control operated by moving left or right with hand in rotary-wing aircraft, primarily to control roll (heading); controls differential pitch of the rotors as they rotate from one side to the other on a rotary-wing aircraft.

## Lateral cyclic cue
A lateral flight director cue for rotary-wing aircraft, primarily to control heading, by changing roll; *Compare:* wheel cue; *Symbols:* Gamma sub 'LAT'; *Typical Units:* percent,in.

## Lateral guidance
Calculations for the lateral axis of the appropriate guidance modes. The control law lateral axis input data are: **Cross Track Deviation, Cross Track Deviation Rate, Cross Track Deviation Rate Gain, Track Angle Error, Track Angle Error Gain, Course**

Cut Limit, Path Integral Limit, Path Integral Gain. The major output from Longitudinal Guidance is the speed error for the selected longitudinal guidance mode.

**lateral link**

A suspension component used to reduce side-to-side movement of a wheel.

**lateral runout**

A tire that has excessive variations in width; the measured amount of sideways wobble on a rotating tire.

**lateral weight transfer**

The momentary shift of a vehicle weight from the inside tires to the outside tires, or outside to inside, due to cornering forces.

**Latitude**

Position on earth, north or south of the equator; *See Also:* astronomical latitude, geocentric latitude, geodetic latitude; *Symbols:* Phi; *Typical Units:* rad, deg.

**launch**

A good start off the starting line in drag racing.

**lay a patch**

The same as to lay rubber.

**lay a scratch**

The same as to lay rubber.

**lay on it**

To go fast.

**lay on the iron**

To cut to the inside of another car on a turn, forcing it away from the apron or apex and out of the groove.

**layout**

Lines scribed on a piece of material or metal as a guide in bending or forming.

**lay rubber**

To leave streaks of rubber on the pavement during rapid acceleration. Also lay a patch and lay a scratch.

**lay the crank**

A reconditioned crankshaft supplied with the appropriate bearings and an installation kit.

**LCD**

An abbreviation for liquid crystal display.

**lead**

1. An element, Pb, often used as a body filler.
2. To use lead as a body filler.
3. Short for tetraethyl lead, a compound formerly used to increase the octane rating of gasoline.

**lead**

To be out in front.

**leaded gasoline**

Gasoline to which a small amount of tetraethyl lead is added to improve engine performance and reduce detonation, a practice no longer allowed due to EPA regulations.

**leadfoot**

A person who drives faster than necessary.

**leading link**

A component of the suspension system that is attached to the chassis behind the wheel and positioned to resist fore-and-aft movement of the wheel.

**lean**

A term often used for lean mixture or lean out.

**Lean Burn**

A Chrysler electronic engine control that appeared in the mid 1970s. It maintains precise control of the spark timing to allow a very lean mixture to burn properly, reducing emissions using an analog computer.

**leaner and later**

Early calibration strategies for air/fuel mixture and ignition timing to reduce HC and CO formation.

**lean misfire**

A condition caused by a vacuum leak or open EGR valve that results in an air/fuel mixture too lean to sustain combustion, causing one or more cylinders to pass unburned fuel into the exhaust system, resulting in an increase in hydrocarbon (HC) emissions.

**lean mixture**

An air/fuel mixture with too much air.

**lean on it**

A term often used for lay on it or lay on the iron.

**lean out**

1. To increase the portion of air or decrease the portion of fuel in an air/fuel mixture.
2. To decrease the portion of nitro in a fuel mixture.

**lean roll**

To turn carburetor idle-mixture screws in enough to effect a slight rpm drop, causing a leaner mixture.

**leaver**

A drag-race driver that red lights by leaving the line too soon.

**left-hand thread**

A thread pattern on a bolt or nut that requires it to be turned to the left or counter-clockwise for tightening.

**Leg**

A segment of a flight plan; flight path between two waypoints. A single segment of an itinerary.

**lifter**

1. A part between the camshaft and push rod on an OHV engine.
2. A part between the camshaft and valve stem on an OHC engine.
3. Also known as follower.

**lifter bore**

The hole in which a valve lifter is located.

**liftgate**

The rear opening of a hatchback or liftback.

**lift it**

Get off the throttle.

**lift kit**

A suspension package designed to raise the vehicle body above the frame and tires.

**lift-throttle oversteer**

A loss of grip on the drive wheels of a rear-drive vehicle when the throttle is lifted during fast cornering causing the rear of the vehicle to swing toward the outside of the turn.

**light-duty vehicle**

Any motor vehicle rated at 8,500 pounds (3,856 kilograms) GVWR or less, having a curb weight of 6,000 pounds (2,722 kilograms) or less, and having a frontal area of 45 square feet (4.2 square meters) or less.

**light it off**

Start an engine.

**light-off, mini-oxidation catalytic converter**
A small catalyst mounted just behind the exhaust manifold that gets hot very quickly after the engine is started, so that it begins working in time to neutralize much of the extra pollution that is produced during cold running.

**lights**
The timing lights at the end of a drag strip.

**light the rugs**
To smoke the drive tires at the start of the race.

**light the weenies**
Same as light the rugs.

**light up**
To perform a burn out.

**lightweight leaf spring**
A fiber-composite spring.

**lightweight-skin spare tire**
A bias-ply, compact spare tire with a reduced tread depth to provide about 2,000 miles (3,218 kilometers) of tread life; designed for emergency use only, and driving speed limited to 50 mph.

**lime deposits**
A condition that exists in a cooling system when the lime, present in water-based coolants, comes out of solution and coats the engine's water passages.

**limited-production option (LPO)**
An item of new car equipment available for a limited market, such as a high-performance police package.

**limited-slip differential**
A differential having special friction mechanisms tending to keep both rear-axle shafts rotating at the same speed, regardless of unequal tire-to-road surface friction.

### limited-slip differential gear oil

A specially formulated gear oil required in limited-slip differentials because of the extreme pressures on the clutch cones or clutch plates and discs.

### Limiter

A filter that passes the input to the output, except that the output is limited to a minimum value and a maximum value; *Compare:* rate limiter;

### limiting valve

A term used for front-axle limiting valve.

### limits

The maximum and minimum values designated for a specific element.

### limo

Short for limousine.

### limousine

1. A chauffeur-driven formal sedan having a glass partition separating the driver from the passengers.
2. A bus or van used to carry people to and from an airport or train station.

### line-and-hose tape

A type of insulation tape.

### Linear EGR

An AC Rochester EGR system using a linear motor to move the valve's pintle in small steps, which provides precise control of recirculation.

### linear-rate coil spring

A coil spring with equal spacing between the coils, one basic shape, and constant wire diameter having a constant deflection rate regardless of load.

**line contact**
1. The contact made between the cylinder and the torsional rings, usually on one side of the ring.
2. The contact made between the valve and the valve seat.

**line job**
Beating a drag competitor from the start.

**line mechanic**
1. A mechanic who works on the repair line at a dealership.
2. A mechanic who is skilled in a particular automotive system.

**line pressure**
1. The base pressure established in a transmission by the pump and pressure regulator valve.
2. The pressure present in a line or hose.

**liner**
The synthetic, gum-rubber material bonded to the inner surface of the tire to seal it.
A sleeve used to repair a worn cylinder.
An insert used to repair a worn valve guide.
Short for streamliner.

**line ream**
To ream bearings or bushings to size after they have been installed.

**line-setting card**
A card provided by the vehicle manufacturer that lists its specifications and equipment.

**line-setting tag**
A tag provided by the vehicle manufacturer that lists its specifications and equipment.

**Linkage (mechanism)**
A set of rigid bodies, called links, joined together at pivots by means of pins or equivalent devices. A body is considered to

be rigid if, for practical purposes, the distances between points on the body do not change. Linkages are used to transmit power and information. They may be employed to make a point on the linkage follow a prescribed curve, regardless of the input motions to the linkage. They are used to produce an angular or linear displacement $f(x)$, where $f(x)$ is a given function of a displacement $x$.

If the links are bars the linkage is termed a bar linkage. In first approximations a bar may be treated as a straight line segment or a portion of a curve, and a pivot may be treated as a common point on the bars connected at the pivot. A common form of bar linkage is then one for which the bars are restricted to a given plane, such as a four-bar linkage (Fig. 1). A body pivoted to a fixed base and to one or more other links is a crank. As crank 4 in Fig. 1 rotates, link 2 (also a crank) oscillates back and forth. This four-bar linkage thus transforms a rotary motion into an oscillatory one, or vice versa. Link AB, marked 1, is fixed. Link 2 may be replaced by a slider 5 (Fig. 2). As end $D$ of crank 4 rotates, pivot $C$ describes the same curve as before. The slider moves in a fixed groove.

Fig. 1    Four-bar linkage.

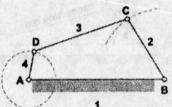

Fig. 2    Equivalent of four-bar linkage.

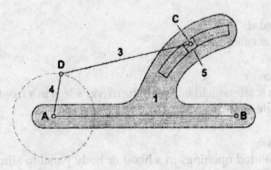

A commonly occurring variation of the four-bar linkage is the linkage used in reciprocating engines (Fig. 3). Slider C is the piston in a cylinder, link 3 is the connecting rod, and link 4 is the crank. This mechanism transforms a linear into a circular motion, or vice versa. The straight slider in line with the crank center is equivalent to a pivot at the end of an infinitely long link. Let $R$ be the length of the crank, $L$ the length of the connecting rod, while \_chars/theta/special/thgr/black/med/base/glyph.gif align=bottom> denotes the angle of the crank as shown in Fig. 3. Also, let $x$ denote the coordinate of the pivot C measured so that $x = 0$ when \_chars/theta/special/thgr/black/med/base/glyph.gif align=bottom> $= 0$. Length $L$ normally dominates radius $R$, whence the approximate relation in Eq. (1) holds.

$$x = R(1 - \cos\theta) + \frac{R^2}{2L}\sin^2\theta$$

Fig. 3  Slider crank mechanism.

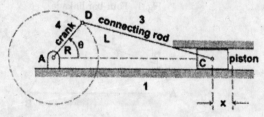

**lost foam casting**
A casting method using a model part made of styrofoam.

**loud pedal**
An accelerator.

**lover cover**
The scattershield between the driver's legs in a front-engined, single-seat drag car.

**louvers**
1. Slotted openings in a hood or body panel to admit or emit ambient air.

2. A vertical blind-type shutter to reduce or block airflow through a device, such as a radiator.

**love taps**
The bumping and shoving that often occurs when cars are running in a closely packed group in circle-track racing.

**low beam**
A headlamp intensity for use when meeting or following another vehicle.

**low end**
Low engine speed.

**low end power**
The engine horsepower output during the first 25–30% of engine rpm range.

**low fare search**
A continuous, computerized search for the lowest current available fares designed to lower the cost of trips already booked but not yet taken.

**low season**
The time of year when travel to a destination is at its lowest and prices decline.

**lower**
To reduce the ride height of a vehicle by modifying its suspension.

**lower A-arm**
The lower member of a double A-arm suspension system.

**lower control arm**
A front suspension component connected between the pivoting attachment point on the car frame and the lower ball joint, which is fastened to its outer end.

**lower end**
The crankshaft, main bearings, and connecting rod bearings assembly in an engine.

**lower entry sleeve**
A cylinder sleeve used to repair a lower entry.

**lower heating value (LHV)**
The latent heating value of water that is exhausted as steam.

**lowering block**
A device that may be used to reduce the riding height of certain vehicles.

**lower mount**
A support for the engine or transmission that is below the crankshaft centerline.

**lower radiator hose**
The radiator hose from the outlet of the radiator to the inlet of the water pump.

**lowest achievable level (LAL)**
A term used to define the lowest amount of emission permitted for any substance considered toxic or otherwise hazardous.

**lowest logical airfare**
The lowest fare that is consistent with a corporation's travel policy.

**Low Frequency Automatic Direction Finding (LF ADF)**
Equipment that determines bearing to a radio station on a low frequency band, usually the standard AM band.

**Low-pass filter (LPF)**
A filter that allows frequencies below a cutoff frequency to pass while attenuating frequencies above the cutoff frequency; *See Also:* first-order filter.

**low gear**
A speed obtained from a planetary gear set when the internal gear is held and power is applied to the sun gear, producing an increase in torque.

**low gearing**
A drive ratio that provides maximum output at a low road speed.

**low head**
A term used for low-head pressure.

**low-head pressure**
The high-side pressure that is lower than expected for a given condition.

**low-lead fuel**
A gasoline that contains less than 0.018 ounces (0.5 grams) per gallon (3.785 liters) of tetraethyl lead, no longer sold in this country due to the environmental impact.

**low-loss fitting**
A fitting designed to close automatically or manually to prevent fluid or vapor loss when used at connection points between hoses, service valves, vacuum pumps, recovery, or recycle machines.

**low maintenance battery**
A conventional, vented lead-acid battery that requires periodic maintenance.

**low-mounted coil spring suspension**
A type of suspension having a coil spring located above the lower control arm, with the top end of the spring contacting the car frame, found primarily on vehicles having a separate or stub frame.

**low pedal**
1. A condition where excessive clearance, at some point in the

s

braking system, or a low fluid level, causes almost full pedal movement for the application of the brakes.
2. The clutch-pedal position of a Model T when engaged in low gear.

**low-pressure control**
An electrical or mechanical device used to control pressure in the low side of a system.

**low-pressure cutoff switch**
An electrical switch that is activated by a predetermined low pressure to open a circuit during certain low-pressure periods.

**low-pressure line**
A hose or line used to carry low pressure vapor, liquid, or air.

**low-pressure side**
1. Usually refers to the return side of a fluid or air system having a low pressure.
2. Often referred to as suction side.

**low-pressure switch**
A switch that is actuated due to a fall in pressure.

**low-pressure vapor line**
A term used for suction line.

**low rider**
A vehicle with small wheels so that it has been lowered as much as possible.

**Low Risers**
Standard-height cylinder heads developed in the early 1960s by Ford for 406, 427, and 428 cid engines.

**low side**
A term used for suction side.

**low-side pressure**
The pressure in the low side of an air conditioning system, from the evaporator inlet to the compressor inlet, as may be noted on the low-side pressure gauge.

**low-side service valve**
A device located on the suction side of the system that allows the service technician to check low-side pressures or perform other necessary service operations.

**low-speed system**
A circuit in the carburetor that provides fuel to the air passing through it during part-throttle, low-speed operation.

**low-suction pressure**
Pressure that is lower than normal in the suction side of the system due to a malfunction of the unit.

**LPG**
An abbreviation for liquified petroleum gas.

**LPO**
An abbreviation for limited-production option.

**LPV**
An abbreviation for load-proportioning valve.

**LSR**
An abbreviation for land speed record.

**lubricant**
1. A substance, usually petroleum based, used to coat moving parts to reduce friction between them.
2. The new synthetic product poly alkaline glycol (PAG) and ESTER used with new refrigerants.
3. A term often used to identify an organic mineral-based grease or oil product.

## Lubrication

The use of lubricants to reduce friction and wear. Whenever two bodies in contact are made to slide relative to one another, a resistance to the motion is experienced. This resistance, called friction, is present in all machinery. Approximately 30% of the power of an automobile engine is consumed by friction. Friction and wear can be significantly reduced, and thus relative motion of machine parts made possible, by interposing a lubricant at the interface of the contacting surfaces; the machine elements designed to accomplish this are called bearings. Bearings can be lubricated by solids such as graphite or, more commonly, by liquids and gases.

Conventionally, lubrication has been divided into (1) fluid-film lubrication (hydrostatic, hydrodynamic, and elastohydrodynamic), where the sliding surfaces are separated by a relatively thick, continuous film of lubricant; and (2) boundary lubrication, where contact surface separation is but a few molecular layers and asperity contact is unavoidable.

### Lubricant films

When the lubricant film in a bearing is discontinuous, partial or boundary lubrication results. In this case, the coefficient of friction $f = F/N$, where F represents tangential (frictional) and N normal components of the contact force, depends on the characteristics of both the lubricant and the contacting surfaces. The coefficient of friction can be analyzed by the methods of surface chemistry and physics. When the lubricant film is continuous, such as in the case of fluid film lubrication, frictional characteristics are defined solely by the material properties of the lubricant but not of the bounding surfaces. Continuous lubricant films can be generated in either of two modes, termed hydrostatic (externally pressurized) and hydrodynamic (self-acting).

### Hydrostatic bearings

Hydrostatic films are created when a high-pressure lubricant is injected between opposing (parallel) surfaces (pad and runner), thereby separating them and preventing their coming into direct contact. Hydrostatic bearings require external pressurization. The film is 5-50 micrometers thick, depending on application. Though hydrostatic lubrication does not rely on relative motion of the surfaces, relative motion is permitted and can even be discontinuous. Figure 1 is a schematic of a hydrostatic bearing pad. To handle asymmetric loads, hydrostatic systems generally employ several evenly spaced pads. The pads are usually supplied from a common reservoir and are equipped with flow restrictors. Flow restrictors are flow control devices, such as orifices and capillaries, across which minute changes in flow rate cause large changes in pressure drop. Thus, if variation in the load vector causes even a small variation in film thickness over a particular pad, a large change in the recess pressure of that pad will result, yielding a righting moment on the runner. Hydrostatic bearings find application where relative positioning is of extreme importance; machine tools using this type of bearing can grind parts round within 5 $\mu$m, with a 2.5-$\mu$m surface finish.

Fig. 1   Hydrostatic bearing pad.

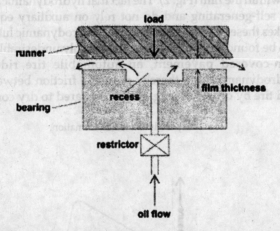

Hydrostatic bearings are also applied where a low coefficient of friction ( 10-6 to 10-4) at vanishing relative velocity is required. The 200-in. (5-m) optical telescope at Mount Palomar, which weighs 500 tons (454 metric tons), is supported on hydrostatic pads and kept synchronized with the aid of a $\frac{1}{4}$-hp (190-W) clock motor. Hydrostatic lifts are often built into the hydrodynamic bearings of a large rotating apparatus to facilitate starting and stopping, when a continuous hydrodynamic film is absent. The advantages of hydrostatic bearings are low friction, exact relative positioning of the bearing surfaces, and insensitivity to magnitude and continuity of relative motion. Among their disadvantages is the need for auxiliary equipment, the high risk of failure in the absence of a back-up system, and the high capital cost. Because of these disadvantages, hydrostatic bearings are used less frequently than are hydrodynamic bearings.

Hydrodynamic bearings

Hydrodynamic bearings are self-acting. To create and maintain a load-carrying hydrodynamic film, it is necessary only that the bearing surfaces move relative to one another and ample lubricant is available. The surfaces must be inclined to form a clearance space in the shape of a wedge, which converges in the direction of relative motion. The lubricant film is then created as the lubricant is dragged into the clearance by the relative motion. This viscous action results in a pressure build-up within the film (Fig. 2). The fact that hydrodynamic bearings are self-generating and do not rely on auxiliary equipment makes these bearings very reliable. Hydrodynamic lubrication can be found to operate even when highly undesirable; on the rain-covered pavement, an automobile tire rides on a hydrodynamic film, thereby reducing friction between road and tire by orders of magnitude compared to dry conditions.

Fig. 2  Hydrodynamic film formation.

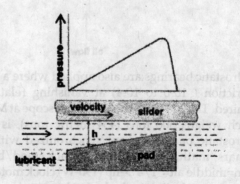

Hydrodynamic journal bearings (Fig. 3) and thrust bearings (Fig. 4) are designed to support radial and axial loads, respectively, on a rotating shaft. The film thickness (h) in these bearings is in the 10-200-$\mu$m range, and the coefficient of friction $10^{-2}$ to $10^{-3}$. Because of their relatively large contact area, the pressures generated in hydrodynamic bearings are low, in the range of 1-10 megapascals (10-100 atm). They operate with the bearing surfaces remaining rigid, although at higher speeds and loads both thermal and elastic deformations can be considerable. Hydrodynamic bearings are usually lubricated with liquids (such as mineral oil), but for light loads and high speeds, as in sophisticated navigational equipment, gas lubrication is preferred.

Fig. 3 Journal bearing.

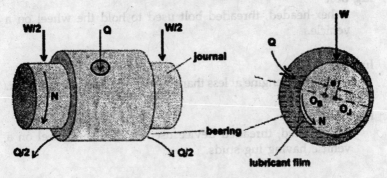

Key:

| | | |
|---|---|---|
| Q = oil flow | N = shaft rotation | $O_B$ = center of bearing |
| W = load | e = bearing eccentricity | $O_J$ = center of journal |

Fig. 4 Thrust bearing.

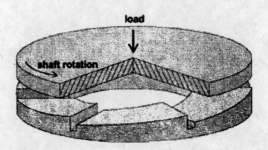

**lubrication guide book**

A specially prepared publication, detailing required lubrication services with related information for each make and model of automobile.

**lubrication interval**

Manufacturer's recommended mileage and/or time limit when periodic lubrication services should be performed as a part of a preventative maintenance program.

**lubrication system**

The oil pump, filter, hoses, lines and passages in an engine that facilitate the oiling of all moving parts.

**lug bolt**

A hex-headed, threaded bolt used to hold the wheel on a vehicle.

**lugging**

Running an engine at less than normal rpm, causing it to balk.

**lug nut**

A hex-sided, threaded device used to hold the wheel on a vehicle having lug studs.

**lug stud**

A threaded protrusion used with a lug nut to hold the wheel on a vehicle.

**ma**
    An abbreviation for milliampere.

**machinability**
    The relative ease with which materials can be shaped **by** cutting, drilling, or other chip-forming processes.

**machine**
    1. A car, usually a late-model car.
    2. A device capable of doing work.

**Machine elements**
    lementary mechanical parts used as building blocks for the construction of most devices, apparatus, and machinery. The gradual development of these building blocks, following the invention of the roller or wheel and the arm or lever in ancient times, brought about the Industrial Revolution, starting with the assembly of James Watt's engine for harnessing the force of steam and proceeding into the advanced mechanization of present automatic control.
    The most common example of a machine element is a gear, which, fundamentally, is a combination of the wheel and the lever to form a toothed wheel (see illus.). The rotation of this gear on a hub or shaft drives other gears which may rotate faster or slower, depending upon the number of teeth on the basic wheels. The material from which the gear is made establishes its strength, and the hardness of its surface

determines its resistance to wear. Knowledge of the forces on the gear makes possible the determination of its size. Changes in its shape allow modifications in its use. These applications, as in most machine elements, have developed into many standard forms, such as spur, bevel, helical, and worm gears. Each of these forms has required the development of a special technology for its production and use.

Fig.   The gear, a machine element which combines features of the wheel and the lever.

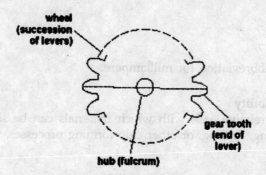

**Magneto**

A type of permanent-magnet alternating-current generator frequently used as a source of ignition energy on tractor, marine, industrial, and aviation engines. The higher cost of magneto ignition is not warranted in modern automobiles, where storage batteries are required for other electrically operated equipment. Hand-operated magneto generators were once widely used for signaling from local battery telephone sets. See also: Generator

Modern induction-type magnetos consist of a permanent-magnet rotor and stationary low- and high-tension windings, also called the primary and secondary windings. The illustration shows two induction-type magnetos in a dual-ignition circuit for a nine-cylinder aircraft engine. The two magnetos are identical, but only magneto no. 1 is shown schematically. The ignition system may receive energy from either or both magnetos, according to the position of the switch.

Fig. Multipolar aviation magneto in dual-ignition circuit for nine-cylinder radial engine.

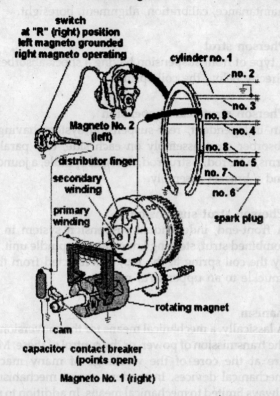

switch
at "R" (right) position
left magneto grounded
right magneto operating

cylinder no. 1

no. 2

no. 3

Magneto No. 2
(left)

no. 9

no. 4

distributor finger

no. 8

no. 5

secondary
winding

no. 7

no. 6

primary
winding

spark plug

rotating magnet

cam

capacitor  contact breaker
(points open)

Magneto No. 1 (right)

## Magnetic heading

Heading of the aircraft relative to magnetic north; A Magnetic Heading Sensor provides this heading data. *Symbols:* psi sub M; *Typical Units:* rad, deg.

## Magnetic variation (MVAR, MAGVAR)

Difference between true north and magnetic north, varying with position; magnetic variation drifts with time; *Symbols:* nu; *Typical Units:* rad, deg.

## MAGVAR

Magnetic variation.

**maintenance**

Indicates device is in a maintenance mode; *Values:* non-maintanance, calibration, alignment, boresight.

**MacPherson strut**

A type of front suspension having a shock absorber mounted directly below the coil spring.

**MacPherson strut rear suspension**

An independent, rear-suspension system having a shock-absorber strut assembly on each side, two parallel control arms, a tie rod, a strut rod, a forged spindle, a jounce bumper, and a bracket assembly.

**MacPherson strut suspension**

A front-end, independent suspension system in which the combined strut, steering knuckle, and spindle unit, supported by the coil spring at the top, is connected from the steering knuckle to an upper-strut mount.

**Mechanism**

A lassically, a mechanical means for the conversion of motion, the transmission of power, or the control of these. Mechanisms are at the core of the workings of many machines and mechanical devices. In modern usage, mechanisms are not always limited to mechanical means. In addition to mechanical elements, they may include pneumatic, hydraulic, electrical, and electronic elements. In this article, the discussion of mechanism is limited to its classical meaning. Mechanisms are found in internal combustion engines; compressors; locomotives; agricultural, earth-moving, excavating, mining, packaging, textile, and other machinery; machine tools; printing presses; engraving machines; transmissions; ordnance equipment; washing machines; lawn mowers; sewing machines; projectors; pinspotters; toys; pianos; ski bindings; artificial limbs; door locks; nutcrackers; counters; microswitches; speedometers; and innumerable other devices.
Components
Most mechanisms consist of combinations of a relatively small number of basic components. Of these, the most important are

cams, gears, links, belts, chains, and logical mechanical elements.

## Cams and cam followers

A cam is a specially shaped part designed to impart a prescribed law of motion to a contacting part called the follower. In Fig. 1 the cam is in the form of a disk, the shape of which governs the motion of the follower. Followers may be translating (Fig. 1a and b) or swinging (Fig. 1c ) and may be in sliding (Fig. 1a) or rolling (Fig. 1b and c ) contact with the cam. The law of motion is the relation between cam rotation and follower displacement. Contact between cam and follower is often (but not necessarily) maintained by a return spring. See also: Cam mechanism

Fig. 1 Cam-follower configurations. (a) Disk cam with flat-faced translating follower. (b) Disk cam with translating roller follower. (c) Disk cam with swinging roller follower.

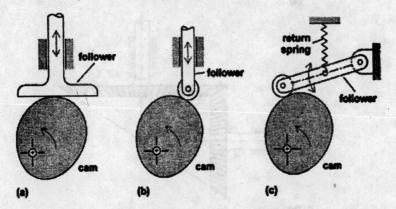

## Gears

Gears are toothed wheels that provide a positive connection between rotating shafts. The most familiar are spur gears, which are used to connect parallel shafts. The teeth of straight spur gears (Fig. 2a) may be imagined mounted on right circular cylinders. When the shaft axes are intersecting, bevel gears can be used. The teeth of the straight bevel gears (Fig. 2b ) may be imagined mounted on right circular cones. Gear teeth are so shaped that the angular-velocity ratio of the connected shafts is constant. Other forms of gearing include helical (these may be spur gears or crossed helical gears), worm, and hypoid.

The latter two, as well as crossed helical gears, are used to connect shafts with nonparallel, nonintersecting axes. See also: Gear

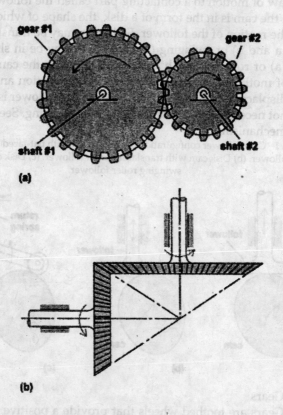

Fig. 2   Gear configurations. (a) Spur gears. (b) Bevel gears.

### Links

For practical purposes, a link may be defined as a rigid body which is connected to other rigid bodies by joints. The most common joints (Fig. 3) are the pin joint (symbolized by R), the sliding joint (P), the cylindrical joint (C), the ball joint (S), and the screw joint (H). The tooth connection between gears and the contact between cam and follower are also usually regarded as joints. Typical link configurations are shown in Fig. 4. See also: Linkage (mechanism)

Fig. 3 Common joints, including joint symbols and degree of freedom f of relative motion at joint. (a) Pin joint. (b) Sliding joint. (c) Cylindrical joint. (d) Ball joint. (e) Screw joint.

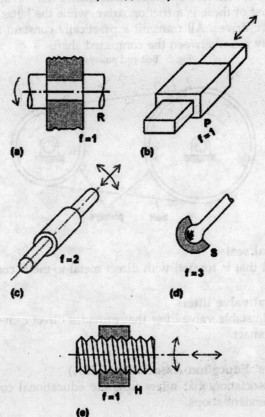

Fig. 4 Typical links. (a) Crank. (b) Slotted link. (c) Slider with provision for pin connection. (d) Triangular link.

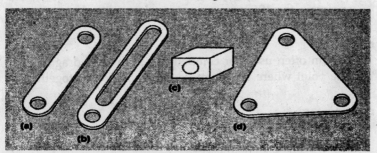

Belts and chains

These flexible connectors include pulleys and flat belts (Fig. 5), timing belts and sprockets, and chain belts and sprockets. The first of these is a friction drive, while the latter two are positive drives. All transmit a practically constant angular-velocity ratio between the connected shafts.

Fig. 5   Belt and pulleys.

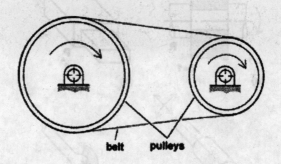

belt      pulleys

**mechanical seal**

A seal that is formed with direct metal-to-metal contact.

**mechanical valve lifters**

An adjustable valve lifter that provides direct cam-to-push-rod contact.

**Mechanics' Education Association (MEA)**

An association that offers upgrade educational courses to independent shops.

**medium riser**

Standard-height cylinder heads offered for the Ford 427 cid engine in the 1960s.

**meet**

A term often used for competition, such as in drag meet. The point where two or more pieces are joined together.

**meeting fare**

Special fare negotiated with an airline for passengers traveling to attend a specific meeting or convention.

## M85

A fuel blend of 85% methanol and 15% gasoline.

## mega-agency

A very large travel agency with nationwide operations. There are currently about seven such agencies in the United States.

## MEK

An abbreviation for methyl ethyl ketone.

## melt

To destroy or damage by overheating.

## melt down

A description among drivers of what happens to pistons when they seize in an engine due to preignition or too lean a mixture.

## melting capacity

A term used for ice-melting capacity.

## melting range

The temperature range between solidus and liquidus.

## melting point

The temperature at which a solid becomes a liquid.

## melting time

1. The time required for an overcurrent to sever a fuse element.
2. The time required for a solid to become a liquid.

## MEMA

An abbreviation of Motor and Equipment Manufacturers Association.

## member

1. An essential part of a machine or an assembly.
2. A person that belongs to a club or a group.

**memory chip**
> A semiconductor device that stores information in the form of electrical charges.

**memory seat**
> A power-seat feature which allows the driver to program different seat positions that can be recalled at the push of a button.

**memory steer**
> An occurrence when steering does not return to the straight-ahead position after a turn, and attempts to continue in the original turn direction caused by a binding condition in the steering column or in the steering-shaft universal joints.

**meniscus**
> The top of a column of liquid in a tube.

**MEP**
> An abbreviation for mean effective pressure.

**mercury**
> 1. An element (Hg).
> 2. A term used to designate a vacuum on the English scale, such as inches of mercury or in-Hg.

**meshing**
> The engaging or mating of the teeth of two gears.

**metal conditioner**
> A chemical used to remove light rust from a metal before surfacing or painting.

**metal filament**
> The electrical conductor that glows when heated, as in an incandescent lamp.

**metal inert gas (MIG)**
> A gas used to shield a weld to prevent oxidation.

**metri-pack connector**
A connector similar to the weather-pack connector, but without the seal on the cover half.

**mica**
An insulating material used to separate the commutator bars of a generator or starter motor.

**Mickey Thompson Entertainment Group (MTEG)**
An organization to promote stadium races for off-road vehicles.

**microchip**
A tiny silicon chip with thousands of electronic components and circuit patterns etched onto its surface.

**microetch test**
A test in which the specimen is prepared with a polished finish, etched, and examined under high magnification.

**microfinish**
A machine process to finish a surface of a part to reduce friction.

**micron**
A metric unit of linear measure equal to one-millionth of a meter.

**microprocessor**
The basic electronic arithmetic, logic, and control computer elements required for processing. Widely used as the control devices for microcomputers; very useful and extremely important to the automotive industry.

**microprocessor control unit (MCU)**
A device referred to as an electronic control unit or ECM. The black box that controls various electrical and mechanical functions of a vehicle.

**mid-engined**

A chassis layout whereby the engine is behind the driver, but in front of the rear wheels.

**midget**

A small, oval-track racing car.

**midnight auto parts**

Parts that were stolen. Also known as midnight auto supply.

**midnight auto supply**

Same as midnight auto parts.

**mid-office system**

The management information (or MIS) portion of a travel agency's computer system, as distinct from the CRS (front office) and accounting functions (back office).

**midpositioned**

The position of a stem-type service valve where all fluid passages are interconnected.

**midseated**

An incorrect term used for midpositioned.

**MIG**

An acronym for metal inert gas.

**MIG welding**

A term used for metal inert gas welding.

**mil**

Short for millimeter.

**mild steel**

A steel alloy with a low carbon content.

**Mission processor (MP)**
A general purpose computer to host avionics software. *Synonyms:* mission computer.

**Mitsubishi Jet Valve**
A tiny third valve that admits nothing but air to churn up the air/fuel charge and promote lean running and a complete burn.

**mixing**
1. To blend or combine.
2. To use parts, such as tires, of two or more sizes or types.

**mixing chamber**
That part of an apparatus in which a fuel gas, and oxygen or air are mixed.

**mixture adjustment**
To adjust the portions of a mixture, such as air and fuel.

**MK**
An abbreviation for master kit.

**MKT**
An engine parts kit that contains all of the parts found in an MK plus the timing gears.

**MMC**
An abbreviation for metal matrix composite.

**Mobile Air Conditioning Society (MACS)**
A nonprofit organization founded in 1981 for the dissemination and distribution of comprehensive technical information, training, and communications to its members consisting of automotive air-conditioning shops, installers, distributors, suppliers, and manufacturers in the United States and Canada.

**mode**
1. A term generally used to describe a particular set of operating characteristics.

2. A selection of one of several alternatives, such as guidance mode (VOR, TACAN, or Waypoint), or navigation mode (INS, Doppler, or dead reckoning)

**model year**
The year of vehicle manufacture, as designated by the manufacturer; not consistent with the calendar year.

**modem**
A device, which enables one computer to call another, needed to get on-line.

**modesty panel**
The panel below the bumpers that conceals the chassis components. Also known as modesty skirt.

**modesty skirt**
Same as modesty panel.

**modified American plan**
A hotel rate that includes two meals daily, usually breakfast and dinner.

**modification**
To alter or change from the original.

**modified**
A vehicle that has been reworked for high-performance operation.

**Modified Everest**
A standard model for computing earth data.

**modified MacPherson strut**
A type of MacPherson strut suspension that uses shock struts with coil springs mounted between the lower arms and spring pockets in the cross member, to absorb minor road vibrations by the chassis rather than fed back to the driver through the steering system.

**modified strut**
A strut suspension where the coil spring is not part of the assembly and is independently located between the lower control arm and the frame.

**Moding cursor**
A symbol on a display, moved by an operator much like arrow keys for menu selection, to select one of several options.

**modular wheel**
A wheel made of different sections that are bolted or riveted together.

**modulated vacuum**
A vacuum signal regulated to a particular level.

**modulator**
1. A device that varies the frequency amplitude and phase of electromagnetic waves.
2. A device that regulates hydraulic line pressure in a transmission to meet varying load conditions.

**module**
A semi-conductor control for an electronic-ignition system.

**modulus of elasticity**
The point at which a material has been bent too far to snap back into shape.

**moisture**
Humidity, dampness, wetness, or small droplets of water.

**moisture ejector**
A valve mounted to the bottom or side of the supply and service reservoirs that collects water and expels it every time the air pressure fluctuates.

**mold**
1. A hollow form into which molten metal is poured to form

a part.
2. A fungus.
3. To form or shape an object.

## molded

To rejoin body panels using a filler material to conceal the seam.

## molded connector

A male or female electrical connector usually having one to four wires that are molded into a one-piece component.

## molded curved-radiator hose

A term used for preformed radiator hose.

## molded hose

A section of hose permanently formed to fit a particular application.

## molecular sieve

A drying agent.

## molecule

The smallest particle a substance can be divided and still remain that substance.

## moly

Short for molybdenum.

## molybdenum

An element (Mo) used in some steel alloys to add hardness and strength.

## molybdenum disulfate

A combination of molybdenum (Mo) and sulfur (S) sometimes added to oil and grease to improve their lubricating qualities.

## Monorail

distinctive type of materials-handling machine that provides an overhead, normally horizontal, fixed path of travel in the form of a trackage system and individually propelled hand or powered trolleys which carry their loads suspended freely with an intermittent motion. Because monorails operate over fixed paths rather than over limited areas, they differ from overhead-traveling cranes, and they should not be confused with such overhead conveyors as cableways.

Relatively simple but adequately efficient monorail systems for specialized applications have flat steel bars or galvanized pipes for trackage. However, standard I beams or other similar shapes are used more and more frequently, with the wheels of the trolley bearing directly upon the lower flange of the beam. The latter type are used more for heavy-load service. Garment manufacturers and cleaning establishments use the simple pipe-rail system for hanging garments on hangers or wheel-equipped trolleys. Switches, crossovers, and other components make setups flexible (see illus.). These systems can be arranged to run onto freight elevators, along loading platforms, and directly into carriers.

Fig. Typical parts of overhead monorails. (a) Slide (glider) type. (b) I-beam track. (c) Powered trolley.

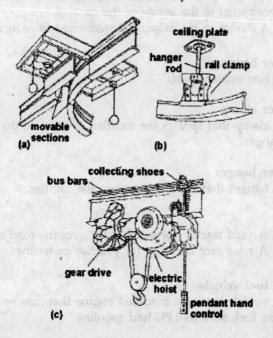

**mud and snow tire**
1. An all-season tire.
2. A term used for snow-and-mud tire.

**mud bogging**
Racing an off-road vehicle through a 100–200 foot (30–61 meter) mud hole.

**mud flap**
A flap hanging down behind a tire to prevent the tire from throwing debris against the lower panel of the vehicle or into the path of a following vehicle.

**mud plug**
A cap installed in the center of a wheel to keep out mud and other debris.

**muffler**
1. A hollow, tubular device used in the lines of some air conditioners to minimize the compressor noise or surges transmitted to the inside of the car.
2. A device in the exhaust system used to reduce noise.

**muffler bearing**
A non-existent part.

**muffler clamp**
A clamp that secures the muffler, or pipe, to the bracket or hanger.

**muffler hanger**
A hanger that is used to secure the muffler.

**mule**
1. A yard tractor not suitable for over-the-road service.
2. A road race car used for practice or testing.

**multi-fuel vehicle**
A vehicle having a modified engine that runs on more than one fuel, such as LPG and gasoline.

**Multi-mode radar (MMR)**

A Multi-Mode Radar is used for Terrain Following (TF) and Terrain Avoidance (TA), Ground Mapping (GM) and Air-to Ground Ranging (AGR). The TF mode supplies commands which are processed and displayed as climb/dive commands on the Flight Director display and E-squared video used by the operators in anticipating near term TF commands. When in TA or GM modes, the operator is provided with a Plan Position Indicator (PPI) display. The AGR mode allows the operators to determine the range to a designated target, which can be used for position updates.

**multi-access system**

A CRS that can directly access the computers of several airlines or other travel suppliers.

**multi-leaved spring**

A flat suspension spring having more than one leaf.

**multiple disc**

A clutch with several driving and driven discs.

**multiple-disc clutch**

A clutch having a large drum-shaped housing that can be a separate casting or a part of the transmission housing.

**multiple-leaf spring**

Leaf springs having a series of flat, steel leaves of varying lengths clamped together with a center bolt extending through them to maintain their position.

**multiple pass**

A term that applies to a recovery/recycle unit that removes refrigerant from an air-conditioning system and circulates it through the recovery/recycle unit to remove contaminants before it is pumped into the recovery cylinder.

**multiple-strand chain**

An assembly made up of two or more rows of roller links

joined into a single structure by pins extending transversely through all rows.

## multiple-viscosity oil

An engine oil that has a low viscosity when cold and a high viscosity when hot.

## multiple-wire hard-shell connector

A connector, usually having a removable, hard-plastic shell, that holds the connecting terminals of separate wires.

## multi-point fuel injection

A type of fuel-injection system that has a separate fuel injector for each of the engine's cylinders to deliver better performance and lower emissions than throttle-body injection (TBI) systems.

## multi-point injection

A term used for multi-port fuel injection.

## multi-purpose vehicle

A term used for sports vehicle.

## multi-valve head

A cylinder-head design having more than one exhaust and/ or intake valve per cylinder.

## multi-viscosity oil

An oil having a low viscosity when cold and a high viscosity when hot.

## Muncie

A popular four-speed manual transmission built by General Motors in Muncie, Indiana.

## Muroc

An early, dry-lake site in the Mojave Desert, now known as Rogers dry lake; it is a space shuttle landing site at Edwards Air Force Base.

**muscle car**
A high-performance car with a big-block engine in a light-weight chassis on heavy-duty suspension with a two-door body.

**mushroomed valve stem**
A valve stem that is worn so much that its end has spread and metal is hanging over the valve guide.

**mushroom lifter**
A valve lifter having a foot diameter larger than the body diameter.

**mutual induction**
A condition whereby a voltage is generated in a secondary coil due to the application of voltage in an adjacent primary coil, such as the coil used in a conventional ignition system.

**MVMA**
An abbreviation for Motor Vehicle Manufacturers Association.

## NAAA
An abbreviation for National Auto Auction Association.

## naturally aspirated
An engine that uses atmospheric pressure to force the air into the cylinders.

## Navigation
A system, usually software, in which the primary purpose is to generate position relative to a coordinate frame, usually fixed earth frame, such as latitude and longitude or UTM.

## Navigation aid
A device or process to help with navigation, such as a VOR station or a position update.

## Navigation reference point (NRP)
A point, usually fixed in earth coordinates but possibly moving; Also, a basic guidance mode, providing lateral guidance to an NRP, either by course or by direct (operator selectable); *Synonyms:* point.

## NC
An abbreviation for normally closed, usually expressed nc. Sometimes used to indicate no connection.

**NDRA**
An abbreviation for the Nostalgia Drag Racing Association.

**NDT**
An abbreviation for non-destructive test.

**near side**
The side of a vehicle closest to the curb.

**necking**
A narrowing area of the exhaust pipe due to a buildup of exhaust by-products.

**necking knob**
A knob attached to the steering wheel that permits rapid one-hand steering.

**needle and seat**
A metering assembly to admit fuel into the carburetor.

**needle bearing**
A bearing that contains needle-like rollers.

**needle valve**
The small, tapered male part of a needle and seat.

**negative**
1. One of the two poles of a magnet.
2. One of the two poles of a battery, representing ground.

**negative back-pressure EGR valve**
An exhaust-gas-recirculation valve having a normally closed bleed hole which opens when back pressure drops, reducing vacuum above the diaphragm and cutting the recirculation flow.

**negative camber**
The inward vertical tilt of the wheels on a vehicle.

**negative offset**
>A wheel rim that has been placed inward from the center of its mounting flange.

**negative pole**
>The negative terminal on a battery. Also known as negative post.

**negative terminal**
>The side of a battery or electrical device nearest ground potential, often identified by a minus (-) sign.

**neoclassic**
>The modern design of a car to resemble a classic of the late 1920s and early 1930s.

**neoprene**
>A type of synthetic rubber that is resistant to heat, light, oil, and oxidation.

**nerf bars**
>Small, tubular bumpers at the front and rear of an oval-track race car.

**net amount**
>The amount due the supplier after commissions have been deducted.

**net fare**
>The wholesale price that is marked up for sale to the customer.

**net horsepower**
>The maximum engine horsepower as measured on a dynamometer.

**net torque**
>The maximum engine torque as measured on a dyno.

## Newton's laws of gravity

1. Every mass in the universe exerts an attractive influence on every other mass.

2. For two objects, the force of gravitation acting between them is directly proportional to the product of their masses, and inversely proportional to the square of the distance between their centers of mass.

## Newton's laws of motion: There are three laws

1. A body in motion remains in motion, and a body at rest remains at rest, unless some outside force acts on it.

2. A body's acceleration is directly proportional to the force applied to it, and the body moves in a straight line away from the force.

3. For every action, there is an equal and opposite reaction.

## N-heptane

A hydrocarbon with an octane number of 0.

## NHRA

An abbreviation for the National Hot Rod Association.

## NHTSA

An abbreviation for the National Highway Traffic Safety Administration.

## nickel

An element, Ni, used in alloys and electroplating.

## Nikasil

A trade name of a popular coating applied to the walls of cylinder sleeves to reduce friction and promote sealing at high temperatures.

## nitride

A compound containing electronegative nitrogen and an electropositive element or metal.

**nitrile seal**
> Seal made by mixing butadiene and acrylonitrile.

**nitro**
> A short term used for nitromethane.

**nitrogen**
> A colorless, odorless, tasteless gas that makes up 78% of the atmosphere and is part of all living tissues.

**nitrogen oxide**
> Any chemical compound of nitrogen and oxygen (NOX) as a by-product of combustion that forms smog in the presence of sunlight.

**nitromethane**
> A highly combustible liquid that is the main ingredient in drag-racing fuels.

**nitrous**
> A term used for nitrous oxide.

**nitrous oxide**
> A non-flammable, non-explosive gas (N2O) used as an oxidizing agent with gasoline or methanol to increase the rate and efficiency of combustion thereby increasing the horsepower.

**Nitrous Oxide Systems (NOS)**
> A popular manufacturer of nitrous oxide injection systems.

**NO**
> An acronym for normally open, usually given as no.

**noble metals**
> A rare and expensive group of metals that resist corrosion such as gold (Au), iridium (Ir), platinum (Pt), palladium (Pd), ruthenium (Ru), and rhodium (Rh), some of which may be found in catalytic converters.

**nodular cast iron**
Cast iron used to make engine blocks that is treated, while molten, with an alloy that causes the formation of graphite in very small lumps.

**no good (NG)**
Not fit for service.

**Noise**
Part of received data that is undesired, consisting of random sinusoidal terms added to a signal; *Compare:* offset, signal.

**no-load test**
A starting-motor test to determine the rpm and current draw of a starter motor. A mechanical tachometer is placed on the drive end of the armature shaft and the motor is then connected to a proper power source. An ammeter, attached to the power means, determines current required.

**Nomex**
A popular trade name for a fabric that is used in race drivers' apparel.

**nominal rating**
The lowest rating of a system or device.

**nominal size**
A designation used for general identification, such as the inside diameter of a tube.

**nonconductor**
1. A material that does not conduct electricity.
2. A material that is resistant to the conduction of heat.

**noncorrosive flux**
A soldering paste, usually composed of resin-based materials, that does not chemically attack the base metal.

**non-destructive test (NDT)**
A method of testing without causing damage.

**NOS**

1. An abbreviation for Nitrous Oxide Systems.
2. An abbreviation for new old stock.

**nose**

1. Front end of a vehicle.
2. The uppermost part of a camshaft lobe.
3. The front of a semi-trailer.

**NOX**

Oxides of nitrogen, not to be confused with nitrous oxide (N2O).

**NOX control system**

A device or system used to reduce the oxides of nitrogen (NOX) produced by an engine.

**nozzle**

The orifice or jet through which fuel passes when it is discharged into a carburetor.

**NSRA**

An abbreviation for the National Street Rod Association.

**number of cylinders**

The total number of cylinders (1, 2, 4, 6, or 8) contained in an engine.

**numeric tire rating**

An alpha-numeric group molded into the tire sidewall indicating tire application, aspect ratio, and rim size.

**nut**

A fastener having internal threads used on a bolt to secure two or more pieces together.

# O

**OASIS**
An acronym for On-Line Automotive Service Information System.

**observed horsepower**
The brake output of an engine as observed on a dynamometer.

**offside**
The side of a vehicle away from the curb.

**off the line**
A good start from the starting line in a drag race.

**off-the-road vehicle (ORV)**
A term used for off-road vehicle.

**ogee**
An S-shaped curve.

**OHC**
An abbreviation for overhead cam or overhead camshaft.

**ohm**
A metric unit of electrical resistance.

**ohmmeter**

An analog or digital instrument used to measure electrical resistance in ohms.

**Ohm's law**

The law that states that the direct current through an electric circuit is proportional to the voltage applied; given by the equation $I = E/R$, where I is current, E is electromotive force, and R is resistance.

**OHV**

1. An abbreviation for off-highway vehicle.
2. An abbreviation for overhead valve.

**oil**

1. A diesel fuel.
2. A liquid lubricant used to reduce friction between moving parts.

**oil/air separator**

A device used to prevent the aeration of oil.

**oil bath filter**

An engine air filter that channels the air through an oil bath that traps dust and debris.

**oil bleed line**

An external line that usually bypasses a metering device to ensure positive oil return to the compressor at all times.

**oil bleed passage**

Internal orifice that bypasses a metering device to ensure a positive oil return to the compressor.

**oil burner**

1. A diesel.
2. An older car or truck that uses excessive oil, generally evident by a smoking exhaust.

A device for converting fuel oil from a liquid state into a combustible mixture. A number of different types of oil burners are in use for domestic heating. These include sleeve burners, natural-draft pot burners, forced-draft pot burners, rotary wall flame burners, and air-atomizing and pressure-atomizing gun burners. The most common and modern type that handles 80% of the burners used to heat United States homes is the pressure-atomizing-gun-type burner (Fig. 1).

Fig. 1  Oil burner of the pressure-atomizing type.

**oil canning**

A sheet-metal panel popping from convex to concave and/ or vice versa.

**oil clearance**

The small space between the main bearing and crankshaft journal, usually 0.001 to 0.003 inch (0.025 to 0.076 mm), for lubricating oil to circulate.

**oil control ring**

The bottom piston ring that scrapes the oil from the cylinder wall.

**oil cooled piston**

A piston that is cooled by a jet of oil sprayed under the dome of some diesel- and endurance-race engines.

**oil cooler**
1. A device used to cool oil or automatic transmission fluid.
2. A device used to cool race-car manual transmission and final-drive lubricants.

**oil dilution**
The thinning of oil in the crankcase, usually caused by gasoline seepage past the piston rings from the combustion chamber.

**oil dipper**
A small scoop located at the bottom of the connecting rod in early, low-performance engines to dip into the oil to lubricate the rod bearings and crankshaft.

**oil filter**
A component, located near the oil pump, that removes abrasive particles from the motor oil by a straining process as the oil circulates through the lubrication system.

**oil-fouled plug**
A wet, oily deposit on a spark plug that may be caused by oil leaking past worn piston rings.

**onboard diagnostics (OBD)**
A special, standardized diagnostic software and hardware system used to detect performance problems that adversely affect emissions and engine performance.

**onboard fire-extinguisher system**
A fire-extinguishing system permanently installed in the driver's compartment of a vehicle; required by most race-sanctioning bodies.

**one off**
A custom-built vehicle with no plans for mass production.

**one-piece oil ring**
An oil ring having the expander and rails combined in a single part.

### one-way clutch
A friction or ratcheting device that permits motion in only one direction.

### one-way roller clutch
A term used for one-way clutch or overrunning clutch.

### one-wire system
An electrical system using body and/or chassis metal as a ground circuit.

### On-Line Automotive Service Information System (OASIS)
A computerized information system for service technicians.

### online connection
A change of planes that does not involve a change of airlines.

### on-line service
A service that packages information and is a vehicle to the internet. This includes America Online.

### on-road
Refers to paved or smooth-graded surface terrain on which a tractor/trailer will operate; generally considered to be part of the public highway system.

### on the bubble
The last position on the grid subject to be bumped if another driver achieves a better qualifying speed.

### on the cam
The operation of an engine at its most efficient rpm.

### on the grid
A starting position for a race. Also known as on the line.

### on the line
Same as on the grid.

**on the piano**
A term used when something is misplaced.

**on the wood**
An accelerator pedal pressed to the floor.

**oodle**
To operate an engine at idle speed.

**open-chamber head**
A cylinder head in which the cylinders have no quench area.

**open circuit**
A circuit in which there is a break in continuity.

**open course**
That part of a race track that extends beyond the finish line into a shut-off area.

**open-end spring**
A coil spring having its end loops apart from the spring coils.

**open loop**
In engines with a computer and oxygen-sensor control system, a mode of operation during which the computer ignores the signal from the oxygen sensor, typically before the engine reaches normal operating temperature.

**open skies**
Referring to an agreement between two countries allowing unrestricted air services between them.

**open structural member**
A flat body panel having an open access from the rear.

**open system**
A crankcase, emission-control system having no tube from the crankcase to the air cleaner; drawing air through the oil filter cap only.

**open the tap**
Increase the speed.

**open ticket**
A valid ticket that does not specify flight numbers, dates, or times. The holder of the ticket makes arrangements at a later date.

**Operations**
How well is equipment operating; *Values:* operational (all function and data is available), degraded (equipment has partially failed with some function or data unavailable and some available), failed (equipment has failed with no function or data available).

**operational control valve**
A device used to control the flow of compressed air through the brake system.

**operational specifications**
Specifications used to show how the vehicle operates, such as acceleration, tire inflation, and other general information.

**operational test**
A term used for performance test.

**opposed engine**
An engine with cylinder banks at 180 degrees, such as the Volkswagen flat four.

**opposite lock**
Turning the steering wheel in the opposite direction of a turn to control or correct oversteer.

**optical horn**
A Chrysler term for a flash to pass dimmer switch feature.

**organic brake lining**
Brake linings that are made of a carbon-based compound combined with non-organic magnesium silicate and/or glass

and synthetic fibers, replacing asbestos which has been determined to be hazardous to health and the environment.

**organic friction material**
A friction material having organic binders substantially formulated with nonmetallic fibers.

**Orientation**
Direction in reference to a coordinate frame.

**Orifice Spark Advance Control (OSAC)**
A Chrysler emissions control system which slows vacuum advance of ignition timing by means of an orifice in a component mounted on the air cleaner.

**Orifice Spark Advance Control Valve (OSAC Valve)**
A device used on some older Chrysler engines to limit oxides of nitrogen formation by delaying the vacuum signal to the distributor advance during idle and part-throttle operation.

**orifice tube**
A term used for expansion tube or fixed-orfice tube.

**O-ring**
A round ring having a square or round cross section used as a seal, such as at the end of a hydraulic line.

**ORV**
An abbreviation for off-road vehicle.

**OS**
An abbreviation for oversize.

**OSAC Valve**
An abbreviation for Orifice Spark Advance Control Valve.

**oscillating**
A device moving back and forth or to and fro, like a clock pendulum.

### oscillating fifth wheel
A term used for fully oscillating fifth wheel.

### oscillation
The rotational movement, either in a fore and aft or side-to-side direction around a pivot point, such as in a fifth wheel design in which such articulation is permitted.

### oscillation damper
A shock absorber may be considered a damper that controls energy stored in the springs under load.

### oscilloscope
An instrument that produces a visible image of one or more rapidly varying electrical quantities with respect to time or with another electrical quality.

### overhaul and maintenance specifications
Specifications used to service vehicle components such as an engine, differential, or transmission.

### overhead cam (OHC)
A term used for overhead camshaft or overhead camshaft engines.

### overhead camshaft
A camshaft mounted in the cylinder head.

### overhead camshaft engine
An engine in which the camshaft is mounted over the cylinder head.

### overhead position
The position in which welding is performed from the underside of the joint.

### overhead valve (OHV)
An I-head arrangement where the valves are located over the piston in the cylinder head.

**overhead-valve engine**
An engine in which the valves are mounted in the cylinder head over the combustion chamber.

**overheat**
To become excessively hot.

**overinflation**
The condition of a tire that is inflated to more than the recommended pressure, decreasing the contact area, increasing the rolling diameter, and stiffening the tire resulting in excessive wear at the center of the tread.

**overlap**
The interval of valve timing when the intake valve starts to open before the exhaust valve is fully closed.

**overlay cam**
A camshaft having a hard face material welded to the nose and flank of the lobes to help decrease wear and increase lift.

**overlubrication**
Term referring to the application of lubricant amounts in excess of factory recommendations that may overload or damage grease seals.

**overpull**
The pulling of a body member beyond its specifications with the expectation that it will snap back to its intended shape when the pulling effort is discontinued.

**overrev**
To run an engine at excessive rpm.

**overrunning clutch**
A device used when two members are to run freely relative to each other in one direction, but are to lock in the other direction.

**overrunning-clutch drive**

An overrunning clutch used for the engagement and disengagement of a starting motor.

**oversize (OS)**

A part that is larger than the original to make up for wear and machining.

**oversize valve stem**

A valve having a stem diameter that is larger than the stem diameter of the original valve. It is used to fit a worn valve guide that is reamed oversize.

**overspray**

1. A paint spray mist that drifts onto a surface where it is not wanted.
The overlap of new paint over old paint.

**oversquare**

A cylinder with a bore greater than its stroke.

**overstaging**

Staging a drag racer ahead of the usual staging position.

**oversteer**

A condition in cornering when the rear wheels of a race car tend to break loose and slide outward.

**oxidation**

The combination of a substance with oxygen forming an oxide, such as rust.

**oxidation catalyst**

A two-way catalytic converter which promotes the oxidation of HC and CO in an engine's exhaust stream, as distinguished from a three-way or reduction catalyst.

**oxidation inhibitor**

An additive to reduce chemicals in gasoline that react to oxygen.

**oxide**
> A compound formed when a substance combines with oxygen.

**oxides of nitrogen (NOX)**
> Harmful, gaseous emissions of an engine composed of compounds of nitrogen and varying amounts of oxygen which are formed at the highest temperatures of combustion.

**oxidize**
> To form an oxide.

**oxidizer**
> 1. A material that causes oxidation.
> 2. An additive that increases the oxygen content of an air/fuel mixture.

**oxidizing agent**
> The same as oxidizer.

**oxidizing flame**
> An oxyfuel gas flame in which there is an excess of oxygen, resulting in metal vaporization.

**oxyacetylene welding**
> An oxyfuel gas welding process that uses acetylene as the fuel gas.

**oxyfuel gas welding**
> A group of welding processes, with or without a filler metal, that produces a merger of work pieces by heating them with an oxyfuel gas flame.

**oxygen**
> A colorless, gaseous, tasteless, element (O) that makes up 21% of the atmosphere.

**oxygen cutting**
> The process of cutting metal at a high temperature with the chemical reaction of oxygen.

**oxygenerator**
>A term used for oxidizer.

**oxygen sensor**
>A device found in the exhaust manifold, which generates a small voltage dependent on the amount of oxygen present in the exhaust stream, used as a signal to the engine-control computer to determine the amount of fuel necessary to maintain a proper air/fuel ratio.

## pace car

A vehicle used in closed-course racing, usually a convertible passenger car, to lead the field up to speed for a rolling start. Also used to lead the field when a caution flag is displayed.

## pace lap

The last lap just before the start of a closed-course race, as the pace car leads the field up to speed.

## P&G check

The measurement of an engine's specifications, such as displacement, to determine the legality of competition using instruments provided by the P&G Manufacturing Company which allow such checks without the disassembly of the engine.

## panel beater

A body shop worker.

## panel cutter

Special snips used to cut through body sheet metal, designed to leave a clean, straight edge that can be easily welded.

## panel nut

A thin nut used to hold parts or fittings to a firewall or bulkhead.

**panel truck**
An enclosed light truck or van having no windows in the cargo area.

**panhard rod**
A rod that is attached to the vehicle frame at one end and to the axle at the other end to prevent the chassis from moving side to side relative to the axle; used on a beam axle or de Dion axle type rear suspension.

**paper**
Sheets of fibrous absorbent materials made from organic fibers that will swallow up liquids and may well disintegrate under such action if the liquid is a solvent for the binder.

**parade lap**
A lap or laps in closed-course racing before the pace lap to give the drivers an opportunity to warm up their tires and engines and to give the fans a chance for a good look at the cars at a slow speed.

**parallel circuit**
An electric circuit having two or more paths that the current flows through at the same time. The current is divided with more of it flowing through the path of least resistance.

**parallel-joint type**
A drive shaft installation whereby all companion flanges and/ or yokes in the drive line are parallel with each other with the working angles of the joints of a given shaft being equal and opposite.

**parallel linkage**
A steering linkage having equal-length tie rods.

**parallelogram linkage**
A steering linkage system having a short idler arm mounted on the right side in such a manner that it is parallel to the pitman arm.

## parasitic drag
Any interference of the aerodynamic efficiency of a vehicle body such as may be caused by outside mirrors, door handles, antenna, and windshield wiper arms and blades.

## parasitic load
An electrical load that is present when the ignition switch is in the OFF position.

## parent metal
The original metal in a body panel to which another metal panel has been added.

## park contacts
Electrical contacts, inside a windshield-wiper motor assembly, to provide current to the motor after the control switch has been turned to the OFF or PARK position, allowing continued motor operation until reaching the park position.

## parking brake
A mechanically applied brake system, usually to the rear wheels or drive shaft, to prevent a parked vehicle's movement.

## parking-brake cable
A cable or cables that transmit brake-actuating force in the parking-brake system.

## parking-brake equalizer
A device used to equalize the pull between the parking brake actuator and two rear wheels.

## parking-brake system
A brake system, intended to hold a vehicle stationary, in which one or more brakes may be held in the applied position without continued application of force to the control.

## particle
A very small piece of dirt, metal, or other debris which can be contained in oil, air, or fuel that can be removed with a filter.

**particulate**
   1. A solid matter, mainly soot from burned carbon, in an internal combustion engine's exhaust.
   2. A form of solid air pollution such as microscopic solid or liquid matter that floats in the air.

**particulate emissions**
   Solid particles, such as carbon and lead, found in vehicle exhaust; soot. A problem, especially in diesels.

**particulate trap**
   An emissions control device in the exhaust system of a diesel engine which is used to capture particulate before they can enter the atmosphere.

**partition coefficient**
   The ratio of the solubility of a chemical in water as compared to its solubility in oil.

**parting edge**
   The excess flash material that is found around the edge of a part that has been cast in a two-piece mold.

**part number (PN)**
   The alphanumeric designating of a part as listed in a catalog or parts list.

**parts changer**
   One who, without proper diagnostic skills, randomly changes parts until the remedy to a problem is found.

**parts chaser**
   1. A vehicle used for errands.
   2. A person who runs errands, especially for buying parts.

**parts counterman**
   One very knowledgeable in part numbers, and/or determining requirements who generally works in a parts-supply wholesale or retail outlet.

**parts distribution**
A wholesale, discount, or retail establishment that sells parts to the trade or do-it-yourselfer.

**parts manager**
One responsible for ensuring that the in-house stock of parts is adequate so the customer's parts are readily available to the service technician when needed.

**parts per million (ppm)**
1. A unit used to measure the amount of contamination in a substance, such as moisture in refrigerant.
2. A measurement of the emissions of a motor vehicle given as the number of parts of a particular chemical within one million parts of exhaust gas.

**parts requisition**
A form that is used to order parts.

**parts specialist**
One who sells automotive engine and vehicle parts.

**parts washer**
A machine that is used to clean parts.

**pass**
To run down a drag strip.

**passages**
A term often used for coolant passages or water jacket.

**passenger car**
A four-wheeled, motor-driven vehicle that carries ten passengers or less, intended for use on streets and highways.

**passenger facility charge**
A fee imposed by a facility owner, as an airport, on those using the facility; typically added to the cost of the ticket.

**payload**
The weight of the cargo that may be carried by a truck, determined by subtracting the curb weight of the vehicle and 150 pounds (68 kg) for each passenger from the gross vehicle-weight rating.

**PBEA**
An abbreviation for Paint, Body, and Equipment Association.

**PC seals**
Valve stem seals made by Perfect Circle that have Teflon inserts to wipe the stems clean.

**PCV**
An abbreviation for positive crankcase ventilation.

**PCV hose**
A Neoprene- or synthetic-rubber hose that is connected to one or both ends of a PCV valve.

**PCV valve**
A vacuum-controlled metering device that regulates the flow of crankcase fumes in the positive crankcase ventilation system by allowing more flow at high speed than at low speed, and acts as a system shutoff in case of engine backfire to prevent an explosion in the crankcase.

**PDI**
An abbreviation for predelivery inspection.

**peak**
Maximum, as in peak horsepower, meaning maximum horsepower.

**peaked**
A body panel having raised beading for a styling effect.

**peak out**
The engine speed at which maximum horsepower is developed.

**pearlescent paint**
> A color paint with fine mica particles blended into the pigment.

**Pedal**
> A flight control operated by pushing with feet, primarily to control yaw via the rudder in fixed-wing aircraft or thrust to tail rotor in rotary-wing aircraft; pedals are automatically controlled in modern aircraft;

**pedal clearance**
> The amount of downward brake-pedal movement, 1/4 inch (6.35 mm) or so, before the pushrod contacts the piston.

**pedal to the metal**
> The accelerator pedal pressed all the way to the floor.

**peel**
> To leave streaks of rubber on the pavement during hard acceleration.

**peel rubber**
> A term used for lay rubber; the same as to peel.

**peel test**
> A destructive method of testing that mechanically separates a lap joint by peeling it.

**peen**
> 1. To shape metal by pounding it.
> 2. The ball-shaped end of a hammer head.

**peg**
> 1. A pin at the top end of a speedometer or tachometer to prevent instrument damage.
> 2. The highest possible reading on a speedometer.

**PEL**
> An abbreviation for permissible exposure limit.

### pellet-bed catalytic converter

A General Motors catalytic converter design having a stainless steel shell and a bed of catalyst-coated ceramic pellets that can be replaced using special vibrator/aspirator equipment.

### pellet thermostat

An engine-coolant thermostat having a wax pellet as a power element, which grows when heated and shrinks when cooled, connected through a piston to a valve.

### penalty fare

Fare subject to a deduction or other fee should the passenger change the itinerary or cancel.

### PERA

An abbreviation for Production Engine Remanufactures Association.

### percent

The ratio of one material to another in a mixture as in a fuel mixture.

### percent of grade

A value that is determined by dividing the height of a hill by its length, often used to determine the power requirements of trucks or for determining maximum pay load.

### percolation

A condition in which the fuel-bowl vent fails to open when the engine is turned off and internal pressure forces raw fuel through the main jets into the manifold.

### performance chart

A chart that has been produced from a dynamometer showing the horsepower, torque, and fuel consumption of an engine at various speeds.

### performance test

1. Readings of the temperature and pressure, under controlled

conditions, to determine if an air-conditioning system is operating at full efficiency.

2. A test to determine if a system or sub-system is performing at maximum efficiency.

## Period

Time of a periodic process; 1/f where f is the sampling frequency; *Symbols:* T; *Typical Units:* s; *Dimensions:* Time.

## Periodic'

A process that executes at a fixed rate; *Compare:* aperiodic.

## Periodic built-in-test (PBIT)

Selftests running internal to a device as part of normal operation; *Compare:* initiated built-in-test.

## perimeter frame

A conventional chassis frame design that is similar in construction to a ladder frame, having full-length side rails that support the body at its greatest width, providing optimum protection to passengers in the event of a side impact.

## permanent magnet

A piece of ferrous material, such as steel, that retains its magnetic properties without the use of an electric current.

## permanent strainer

A device generally of a Y-configuration having an accessible cylindrical strainer element used in horizontal and vertical lines. The element, retained by a plug end which may be plain or fitted with a valve, can be opened for blow-through cleaning.

## Permatex

A tradename for a brand of engine and transmission sealants.

## permissible exposure limit (PEL)

The maximum length of time a person should be exposed to a hazard or hazardous material established by OSHA and expressed as a time-weighted average limit or ceiling exposure limit.

## Personnel Locating System (PLS)

A basic guidance mode, providing lateral guidance to a PLS transmitter from range and bearing inputs. Equipment that determines range and bearing to a personnel with a PLS transmitter; Provides range and bearing to locate ground personnel. Coded continuous or periodic interrogations of the portable ground radios are used to provide the information.

## petcock

A small faucet-like valve used for draining liquids, such as that found at the bottom of some radiators.

## petroleum

The crude oil from which gasoline, lubricant, and other such products are manufactured.

## phaeton

A four or five passenger, two- or four-door, open-body style that was most popular in the 1920s and 1930s.

## pH level

A measure of the acidity or alkalinity of a solution on a scale where pH0 is most acid, pH14 is most alkaline, and pH7 is neutral.

## phosgene gas

A highly toxic gas, carbonyl chloride ($CCOCl_2$). Until recently, it was believed that phosgene gas was produced when CFC refrigerants, such as R-12, came into contact with heated metal or an open flame. It is now known that little or none of this gas is produced in this manner.

## phosphor bronze

A hard, tough alloy of copper (Cu), lead (Pb), tin (Sn), and phosphorus (P) low in friction and resistant to wear.

**phosphoric acid**
A colorless and odorless acid (H3PO4) used to remove rust from steel and cast iron.

**photochemical smog**
A noxious, unhealthy gaseous compound in the atmosphere, formed by the interaction of various chemicals such as the pollutants hydrocarbons (HC) and oxides of nitrogen (NOX) in the presence of sunlight.

**photovoltaic diode**
A device having a junction of two dissimilar metals that produces an electrical signal proportional to the amount of light that strikes it.

**physical hazards**
Any personal hazards, such as excessive noise, temperature, pressure, and rotating equipment.

**physical properties**
Properties that pertain to the physics of a material, such as melting point, density, electrical and thermal conductivity, specific heat, and coefficient of thermal expansion.

**pickup**
Vehicle acceleration.
A term used for pickup truck.

**pickup coil**
An engine-speed sensor in an electronic ignition system.

**pickup truck**
A type of vehicle having an open cargo bed behind an enclosed cab.

**positive back-pressure EGR valve**
A common type of exhaust gas recirculation valve which uses exhaust system backpressure to sense engine load, thus more accurately metering the amount of exhaust recycled.

**positive camber**
 The outward tilt of a wheel on a vehicle.

**positive crankcase ventilation (PCV)**
 An engine emissions-control system, operating on engine vacuum, that picks up crankcase gases and meters them into the intake stream to be burned.

**positive displacement pump**
 An engine-driven air or liquid pump that displaces the same amount of air or liquid, per revolution, regardless of engine speed.

**positive offset**
 A wheel rim placed outward of the center of the mounting flange.

**positive pole**
 1. The positive terminal of an electrical device.
 2. The north pole of a magnet.

**positive post**
 The positive terminal of a battery.

**positive terminal**
 The terminal to which electrons flow in a complete electrical circuit, often identified by the symbol +.

**Positive Traction**
 A limited-slip differential by Buick.

**positive wiping seal**
 A seal that maintains constant contact with a stem or shaft to wipe off excess oil.

**Posi-Traction**
 A limited-slip differential by Chevrolet.

**post ignition**

Ignition that occurs after the engine-ignition system is shut off, due to carbon buildup in the combustion chamber.

**post start**

The time from a cold start to the warm up of an engine.

**pot**

1. A carburetor.
2. An abbreviation for potentiometer.

**potential energy**

Energy of a body or system with respect to the position of the body or the arrangement of the particles of the system.

**potentiometer (pot)**

A three-wire variable resistor that acts as a voltage divider to produce a continuously variable output signal proportional to a mechanical position.

**pounds-feet**

An English measure of torque. One pound (lb) raised one foot (ft) is equal to one pounds-feet (lb-ft).

**pounds-inch**

An English measure of torque; the energy required to raise one pound, one inch.

**pounds per horsepower**

The weight of the vehicle divided by its horsepower, a measure of the vehicle's performance.

**pounds per square inch (psi)**

An English measure for pressure or stress.

**pounds per square inch, absolute (psia)**

An English measure for pressure or stress taken from absolute pressure.

**pounds per square inch, gauge (psig)**
An English measure for pressure or stress taken from atmospheric pressure.

**poured bearings**
Bearings that are formed by first pouring molten babbitt material into the bearing cavity, allowing it to cool, then boring it to a specific size.

**pour on the coal**
To accelerate rapidly.

**pour point**
The lowest temperature at which a fluid will flow freely.

**powder puff race**
An auto-racing event strictly for women drivers.

**power**
1. A measure of work being done.
2. The rate at which work is being done.

**power brakes**
A system utilizing energy from the vehicle's engine to reduce the amount of brake-pedal pressure that must be exerted by the driver to stop the car.

**power break**
In an automatic transmission-equipped drag racer, the act of holding the brake pedal firmly while revving the engine, then simultaneously releasing the brake while flooring the accelerator to get the quickest possible start.

**power cable**
Cable used to supply electrical power (current).

**power control module**
A module or computer used in an electronic transmission to aid in control of the shift solenoids.

**power cylinder**
> 1. A shell containing the power-brake operating parts.
> 2. Linkage-type steering component attached between the frame and the steering relay rod.

**power flow**
> The flow of power from the input shaft through one or more sets of gears, or through an automatic transmission to the output shaft.

**power hop**
> The tendency of an axle housing to rotate slightly with the wheels then snap back during hard acceleration.

**power mirror**
> Outside mirrors, having reversible permanent-magnet motors, that are electrically positioned from the inside of the driver's compartment.

**power on/off watchdog circuit**
> Supplies a reset voltage to the microprocessor in the event that pulsating output signals from the microprocessor are interrupted.

**power oversteer**
> The loss of traction of the rear wheels while cornering and accelerating, causing the rear of the vehicle to swing toward the outside of the turn.

**power piston**
> A component acted on by pressurized fluid to assist wheel turning on integral or linkage-type power-steering systems.

**power section**
> The section of a gas-turbine engine containing the power turbine rotors which, through reduction gears, turn the wheels of the vehicle.

## power servo

A servo unit used in automatic temperature control which is operated by a vacuum or an electric signal.

## power shift

The rapid forced shifting of a manual transmission without releasing the clutch or accelerator.

## power tools

Tools that use compressed air (pneumatics), electricity, or hydraulic pressure to generate and multiply the force required to accomplish the work.

## power-to-weight ratio

The relationship of a vehicle's horsepower to its weight as given in horsepower per pound.

## power train

A combination of the engine, transmission, and final drive.

## power valve

A valve in the carburetor that opens during acceleration to increase fuel flow.

## pre-cat converter

A term used for light-off, mini-oxidation catalytic converter.

## Precision

Measure of exactness, possibly expressed in number of digits, for example, computed to the nearest millimeter; *Compare:* accuracy.

## precision insert bearing

Bearings that may be installed in an engine without having to be bored, reamed, honed, or ground.

## precombustion chamber

A second combustion chamber placed directly off the main combustion chamber, used to ignite a rich mixture of air and fuel which then ignites a lean mixture in the main combustion chamber.

**predelivery inspection (PDI)**
The process of inspecting, adjusting, and fine tuning a new car prior to delivery to the customer.

**preformed radiator hose**
A large-diameter hose connecting the radiator to the engine cooling system that is molded in the proper shape to fit on a certain engine.

**preheater**
A glow plug that is used to heat the precombustion chamber of a diesel engine before it is started.

**preheating**
Heating the weld area of a metal before welding, to avoid thermal shock and stress.

**pre-ignition**
The ignition of the air/fuel mixture in the combustion chamber by means other than the spark; usually caused by hot spots in the combustion chamber due to sharp edges, carbon accumulation, or spark plugs with a heat range that is too hot.

**preload**
1. The transfer of weight from one side of a vehicle to the other to compensate for the lateral weight transfer that occurs when cornering.
2. The pressure applied to a part during assembly or installation.

**prelube**
To apply lubricant to the parts of a rebuilt engine before starting it up.

**progressive linkage**
A carburetor linkage system used on multiple carburetors to progressively open the secondary circuits.

**progressive-rate spring**
A spring used in a vehicle that stiffens under load.

**Prometheus**
　　An abbreviation for Program for European Traffic with Highest Efficiency and Unprecedented Safety.

**prony brake**
　　A machine for testing the power of an engine while running against a friction brake.

**proof loading**
　　Subjecting chain to a tensile loading of some predetermined percentage of the chain's rated strength.

**propane**
　　A combustible, liquefied petroleum gas (C3H8) that becomes a liquid when compressed.

**propane enrichment**
　　A service procedure used to set idle mixture where a metered amount of propane gas is added to the intake stream and a resulting rpm increase is observed.

**propeller shaft**
　　A term used for drive shaft.
　　A hollow, steel shaft that connects the transmission output shaft to the differential drive pinion yoke through universal joints at each shaft end.

**property class**
　　A number stamped on the end of a metric bolt to indicate the hardness of the bolt.

**proportioning valve**
　　A valve in the brake hydraulic system that reduces pressure to the rear wheels to achieve better brake balance.

**pro stock**
　　A category for compact, passenger drag-racing cars with a big block V-8 engine having a maximum of 500 cubic inches (8.2 liters).

### pro street
A compact passenger car with a modified V-8 engine and rear drive built for street use.

### protective atmosphere
A gas or vacuum envelope surrounding the work pieces, used to prevent or reduce the formation of oxides and other detrimental surface substances, and to facilitate their removal.

### protective tube
A shock absorber component used to keep dirt and road dust away from the seals and piston rod.

### protest
1. To object to a rule or conditions prior to the competition.
2. To accuse a competitor of a rules violation after a race competition.

### proto
An abbreviation for prototype.

### protocol
The format in which data transfer takes place.

### proton
A positively-charged particle in the nucleus of an atom.

### prototype (proto)
1. An individually built test version of a new design of a car or system.
2. An individually built vehicle in sports-car racing when an insufficient number of vehicles have been manufactured to be placed in a category.

### put on the trailer
To decisively defeat a racing competitor.

### putter
A custom car that is not intended for high performance.

**put to the wood**
A term for applying full throttle.

**putty**
Body filler.

**PVC valve**
A valve used in positive crankcase ventilation systems to meter blowby into the intake stream.

**PVS**
An abbreviation for ported-vacuum switch.

**pyroconductivity**
Electric conductivity that develops with changing temperature, and notably upon fusion in solids that are practically nonconductive at atmospheric temperatures.

**pyrolysis**
The decomposition of a compound due to its exposure to high heat.

**pyrolytic oven**
An oven used to remove grease, oil, and rust from the surfaces of engine parts.

**pyrometer**
An instrument used to measure high temperature.

**pyrophoric**
A substance having the quality of spontaneous ignition when exposed to air.

**Q-jet**
   A Rochester Quadrajet four-barrel carburetor.

**Q-ship**
   An innocent looking vehicle with outstanding performance.

**quad**
   1. A four-barrel carburetor.
   2. Four headlamps, two on either side of the vehicle.
   3. A four-wheel drive vehicle.

**quad carburetor**
   A four-barrel carburetor.

**quad-4**
   A high-performance, four-cylinder engine developed by
   General Motors.

**quadrant**
   1. A device used to indicate the position of the gear selector
   of an automatic transmission.
   2. One quarter of a circle.

**Quadra-Trac**
   A full-time, four-wheel drive system.

**quad ring**

A rubber or plastic sealing ring with **square sides.**

**quad valve head**

A cylinder head with four valves, two exhaust and two intake, per cylinder.

**qualify**

To earn a starting position in a race.

**quarter**

A term used for a quarter-mile drag strip.

**quarter elliptic spring**

One half of a semi-elliptic spring having one end attached to the chassis frame and the other attached to the axle.

**quarter mile**

1. A distance of 1,320 feet (402 meters).
2. The standard distance for a drag strip.

**quarter-mile drag strip**

The most popular standard distance for a competitive drag-racing strip.

**quarter panel**

A term used for the metal work for either the front or rear corner of a vehicle body.

**quarter race cam**

A camshaft that has been reground to provide better than standard performance.

**quarter-speed cam**

A camshaft that rotates once for each four revolutions of the crankshaft.

**quartz-halogen**

A type of high output lamp containing a gaseous halogen; used for headlights, driving lights, or fog lights.

**quartz-iodine**

A lamp containing gaseous iodine (I).

**Quaternion**

A system of representing attitude by measuring angle of aircraft center line with respect to three orthoginal axes plus rotation about centerline; quaternions are used over Euler angles (pitch, roll, yaw) when pitch can approach 90deg because of a singularity on Euler angles at 90deg; discrete-time computations using quaternions can run more slowly than those with Euler angles while producing results of the same accuracy *See Also:* Euler parameters.

**Quattro**

A full-time, four-wheel drive system by Audi.

**quench**

To suddenly cool a heated metal or alloy by dousing it with water or oil.

**quench area**

Any internal portion of a combustion chamber which causes combustion to cease because of the temperature drop in the air/fuel charge where it meets this area.

**quick change**

Any system or sub system that is designed for ease and speed for changing or replacing.

**quick charger**

A battery charger that is designed to charge or boost a battery in a short time.

**quick coupler**

A coupler that allows hoses to be quickly connected and/or disconnected. Most shop air hoses, for example, are equipped with quick couplers.

**R**

### race

1. That element of a one-way roller clutch providing the cylindrical surface through which the rollers and cam transmit torque.
2. A groove, edge, or track on which a rolling or sliding part moves.

### race for the pink

To race for actual ownership of the competitor's vehicle.

### racer

1. A competition driver.
2. A competition vehicle.

### Radar altitude

Height with respect to the terrain below (distance above closest dirt); *Synonyms:* above ground level; *Symbols:* h sub r; *Typical Units:* ft; *Dimensions:* Length.

### Radar altitude select (RALT SEL)

A basic guidance mode, providing vertical guidance to an operator selected radar altitude.

### Radial error probability (REP)

A probability that a percentage of one-dimension measurements will lie on a radial (line) of given length, with

the origin centered at truth or mean of the **measurements;**
used to specify test cases for measurement errors of **sensors**
of one dimension, such as vertical velocity; *Compare:* circular
error probability, spherical error probability.

**radial motion**
A motion extended to either, or both, extremes of a radius.

**radial ply**
A term used for radial ply belted tire.

**radial ply belted tire**
A tire having the ply cords placed at right angles to the beads,
plus belts under the tread section providing the least tread
distortion while moving, thereby minimizing tread wear and
rolling friction.

**radial runout**
Variations in tire diameter; the measured amount of out-of-
roundness on rotating tires.

**radial tire waddle**
A term used for tire waddle.

**radiation**
A natural process by which energy is transmitted.

**radiation dose**
The amount of energy per unit of mass of material deposited
at each point of an object undergoing radiation.

**radiator**
A heat exchanger used to remove heat from the coolant in the
cooling system containing a vertical- or horizontal-finned
tubing section connected between two tanks.

**radiator cap**
A term used for radiator pressure cap.

## radiator core

The center of the radiator, made of tubes and fins, used to transfer heat from the coolant to the air.

## radiator fan

A term used for fan.

## radiator hose

An oil- and ozone-resistant synthetic-rubber hose that connects the radiator to the thermostat outlet housing and water pump inlet housing.

## radiator hose clamp

A term used for hose clamp.

## radiator pressure cap

A cap that seals in pressure from hot expanding coolant until a predetermined limit is reached, then the valve opens, allowing excess pressure to escape, generally to a coolant-recovery tank.

## radiator shutter system

An engine temperature-control system that controls the amount of air flowing through the radiator by use of a shutter system.

## Radio navigation

Navigation relative to radio station, providing, for example, of relative bearing, range, lateral deviation, and glideslope; Examples include VOR, TACAN, and PLS. Radio navigation differs from other navigation in that the transmitter signals often dropout for a long period of time, like minutes. This can occur because of natural obstructions, or because the transmitter was shut down intentionally. In hostile territory, a PLS can locate a downed pilot, who would be foolhardy to be continuously transmitting, but would transmit infrequently with small bursts of data. The Radio- Navigation system accommodates this phenomenon by simulating range and bearing to the fixed site when it is not transmitting. After reacquiring a mobile transmitter, the mobile station's position is re-determined. The navigation component supports wash-out filters on output data.

**radius**
>A line extending from the center of a circle to its boundary.

**radius arms**
>Longitudinal suspension arms used to position a beam axle.

**radiused**
>1. A procedure that is used to reduce the radius diameter at the area the valve stem meets the valve head.
>2. A valve type that is ground with a radial grinder to aid in air flow around the valve.
>3. Wheelwells that have been cut to a circular shape.

**radius ride**
>A condition where the crankshaft rides on the edge of the bearing.

**rally**
>A sports-car driving contest for driver performance as opposed to vehicle performance.

**RAM**
>An acronym for random access memory.

**ram air**
>Air forced through the radiator and condenser coils by the movement of the vehicle or the action of the fan.

**ram air cleaner**
>An air cleaner for high-performance cars that opens an air scoop on the hood to provide a ram effect when the throttle is wide open.

**ram induction**
>An intake manifold designed to cause a resonant effect at a specific predetermined engine speed.

**ram tubes**
>Short, tuned, tubular stacks on the top of carburetors.

**ramp**

The sloping section of a camshaft lobe which raises the lifter.

**ramp angle**

An angle formed by lines adjacent to the static-loaded radius of the front and rear wheels intersecting at the point of the lowest ground clearance under the middle of the vehicle.

**ram tuning**

The tuning of an intake manifold to ensure that the passages are of sufficient length to cause a resonant effect at a specific predetermined engine speed.

**Ranco control**

A tradename often used for a thermostat.

**R&D**

An abbreviation for research and development.

**random access memory (RAM)**

A computer memory into which the user can enter information and instructions (write), and from which the user can call up data (read).

**random intermittent welds**

Welds on one or both sides of a joint in which the weld increments are made without regard to spacing.

**Range (rng)**

Standard aviation term *Synonyms:* distance; *Symbols:* r; *Typical Units:* ft,nmi - method of measurement dependent on use; *Dimensions:* Length.

**R&R**

An abbreviation for remove and replace.

**range shift cylinder**

Located in the auxiliary section of the transmission, this component, when directed by air pressure via low and high ports, shifts between high and low range of gears.

### range shift lever

Located on the shift knob, this lever allows the driver to select low- or high-gear range.

### raster pattern

Also known as stacked pattern.

### rat

A Chevrolet big block V-8 engine.

### Ratchet

A wheel, usually toothed, operating with a catch or a pawl so as to rotate in a single direction (see illus.). A ratchet and pawl mechanism locks a machine such as a hoisting winch so that it does not slip. The locking action may serve to produce rotation in a desired direction and to disengage in the undesired direction as in a drill brace. A further adaptation is to drive the catch in a to-and-fro motion against the ratchet to produce intermittent circular motion. The catch or pawl may be of various shapes such as an eccentrically mounted disk or ball bearing. Gravity, a spring, or centrifugal force (with the catch mounted internal to the ratchet) are commonly used to hold the pawl against the ratchet. A ratchet and pawl provides an arresting action, whereas an escapement provides an arresting action followed by a self-initiated momentary release. In high-

Fig.   Toothed ratchet is driven by catch when arm moves to left; pawl holds ratchet during return stroke of catch. In roller ratchet, rollers become wedged between driver and follower when driver turns faster than follower in direction of arrow.

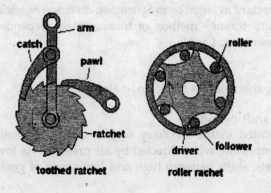

toothed ratchet                    roller rachet

speed machines, the abrupt action of a toothed ratchet produces severe shock. In such situations, a continuously variable yet directionally sensitive action is achieved by wedging rollers or specially shaped sprags between the input and output members.

**rate desk**
The office of an airline that calculates fares for travel agents and passengers.

**Rate limiter**
A filter that passes the input as the output, except that rate of change of the output is limited to a maximum absolute value; *Compare:* limiter.

**ratio**
1. The relative amounts of two or more substances in a mixture.
2. The comparison of two numbers as in teeth on gears.

**ratio valve**
A device used on the front or steering axle of a heavy-duty vehicle to limit the brake application pressure to the actuators during normal service braking.

**rat motor**
A Chevrolet big block V–8.

**Ravigneaux gear train**
A planetary gear train with two sun gears, three long and three short planetary pinions, planetary carrier, and ring gear.

**Raw**
Data taken directly from the sensor; *Compare:* derived, estimated, filtered, measured, selected, smoothed.

**RC engine**
A shortened term for rotary combustion engine.

**RCRA**
An abbreviation for Resource Conservation and Recovery Act.

**reaction time**
1. The amount of time required to physically apply the brakes of a vehicle after mentally being aware of the necessity to do so.
2. The amount of time required from the moment the Christmas tree light turns green until the vehicle trips the starting-line timing light.

**rebound**
The outward extension of the springs and shocks in a vehicle suspension system.

**rebound clip**
Metal clamps placed at three or four intervals around multi-leaved springs to prevent the leaves from becoming separated on rebound.

**rebound travel**
The downward movement of a wheel from its normal position when the spring and shock are expanding, as the sudden drop of a wheel into a depression and a weight transfer away from the wheel.

**rebound valve**
A calibrated piston valve mounted on the shock piston that provides variable resistance to fluid flow during rebound.

**recall**
A notice issued by the vehicle manufacturer that a certain make and model vehicle should be returned to the dealer for a correction of a suspected or known problem.

**Reference acceleration (REFACC)**
A guidance control law parameter, generated by the longitudinal guidance modes; *Typical Units:* ft/s-squared, g; *Dimensions:* Length / Time-squared.

### Reference acceleration gain (KLA)
A guidance control law parameter, generated by the longitudinal guidance modes; *Typical Units:* s; *Dimensions:* Time.

### refrigerant
The chemical compound used in a refrigeration system to produce the desired cooling effect.

### refrigerant-containment device
A device introduced on some car lines to guard against high pressure resulting in refrigerant loss by controlling the compressor and/or condenser fan motor.

### refrigerant lines
Specially designed vapor-barrier hoses reinforced with woven nylon mesh and fabric capable of withstanding the high temperatures and pressures of the system.

### refrigerant recovery
The act of recovering refrigerant.

### refrigerant recycle
The act of recycling refrigerant.

### Refrigerant CFC-12 (R-12)
The refrigerant, dichlorodifluoromethane (CCl2F2), used in automotive air conditioners, as well as other air-conditioning and refrigeration systems.

### Refrigerant HCFC-22 (R-22)
A refrigerant, monochlorodifluoromethane (CHC1F2), used in some early automotive applications but not to be used for today's automotive air conditioners because of high pressures.

### Refrigerant HFC-134a (R-134a)
The refrigerant of choice, tetrafluoroethane (CH2FCF3), to be used in automotive air conditioners as R-12 is being phased out.

### refrigeration
To use an apparatus to cool; keep cool; or keep chilled under controlled conditions by natural or mechanical means, as an aid to ensure personal safety and comfort.

### refrigeration cycle
The complete cycle of the refrigerant back to the starting point, evidenced by temperature and pressure changes.

### refrigeration lubricant
A mineral oil or synthetic oil-like lubricant, such as PAG and ESTER, that is formulated for specific use and application in designated refrigeration systems.

### refrigeration oil
A highly refined (specially formulated), non-foaming organic mineral oil free from all contaminants, such as sulfur, moisture, and tars, used to lubricate the air-conditioner compressor.

### refrigeration tape
A term used for insulation tape or duct tape.

### regeneration system
A system in a gas turbine that converts some of the heat, usually wasted, into usable power.

### regenerator
A device placed on a gas turbine to take the heat of exhaust and put it into the intake of the engine.

### regional carrier
An airline that serves only one clearly defined area of the country.

### regional offices and distributorships
Offices owned and operated by the automobile company, and considered to be the link between the manufacturer and the dealerships.

**register**

A high-speed device used in a central processing unit for temporary storage of small amounts of data or intermittent results during processing.

**regular-duty coil spring**

A coil spring supplied to handle average loads to which the vehicle is subjected, having a small wire diameter as compared to a heavy-duty spring.

**roll out**

The distance a race car travels in a drag-racing event at the beginning of a run before the front tires clear the stage beam and start the clock.

**rollover**

An accident in which the vehicle rolls over and over or turns upside down.

**roll steer**

The direction and amount that the rear axle may cause the vehicle to steer as it moves through its travel when the body rolls during cornering requiring the driver to oversteer or understeer to compensate for the problem.

**roll stiffness**

The resistance, measured in pounds per inch of spring travel, of a suspension system to the rolling of the vehicle's mass.

**rolly**

A term used for roller cam.

**RON**

An acronym for research octane number.

**R-134a**

A trade term for refrigerant HFC-134a.

## Rolling contact

ontact between bodies such that the relative velocity of the two contacting surfaces at the point of contact is zero. Common applications of rolling contact are the friction gearing of phonograph turntables, speed changers, and wheels on roadways. Rolling contact mechanisms are, generally speaking, a special variety of cam mechanisms. An understanding of rolling contact is essential in the study of antifriction bearings. The concepts are also useful in the study of the behavior of toothed gearing.

Pure rolling contact can exist between two cylinders rotating about their centers, with either external or internal contact. Two friction disks (Fig. 1) have external rolling contact if no slipping occurs between them. The rotational speeds of the disks are then inversely proportional to their radii.

Fig. 1    Rolling friction disks.

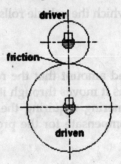

Fig. 2    Pure rolling between bodies in contac

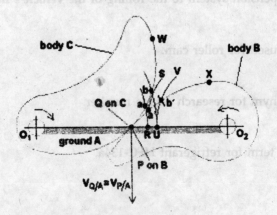

The general case of pure rolling between contacting bodies is illustrated in Fig. 2. Particle Q on body C and particle P on body B coincide at the moment. The velocities of these particles relative to ground frame A must be the same if there is to be no slip. It can be shown, using the theory of kinematics of mechanisms, that for two bodies to have rolling contact at an instant the point of contact must lie on the line joining the two centers of rotation.

## rookie
A race-car driver in competition for the first season in an event or series of events.

## room night
One hotel room occupied for one night; a statistical unit of occupancy.

## room temperature vulcanizing (RTV)
The trade name for a rubber-like sealing compound.

## Root mean square (RMS)
A statistical measure of data; the root of the mean of the square; for variables with mean of zero, the standard deviation is equal to the rms; *Compare:* root sum square.

## root bead
A weld bead that extends into, or includes part or all of the joint root.

## roots supercharger
A mechanically driven, positive-displacement blower with hourglass-shaped rotors.

## rope seal
A type of seal used on crankshafts shaped much like a small, thin rope.

## Root sum square (RSS)
A statistical measure of data; the root of the sum of the square;

for a vector, its length is equal to the rss of its scalar elements;
*Compare:* root mean square.

### rosette weld

A term used for plug weld.

### rosin

A sticky substance applied to the rear tires of drag-race cars
for better traction off the line.

### rotary

The turning motion around an axis.

### rotary engine

1. A form of radial engine used in early aircraft, outmoded
by the end of World War I.
2. An engine with a three-sided rotor in a slightly hourglass-
shaped oval chamber.
**Cat-and-mouse engines**
Intake-compression-power-exhaust cycle of the Tschudi engine.

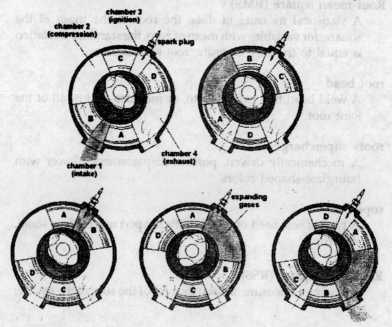

Eccentric-rotor engines
Operation and basic components of the Wankel engine.

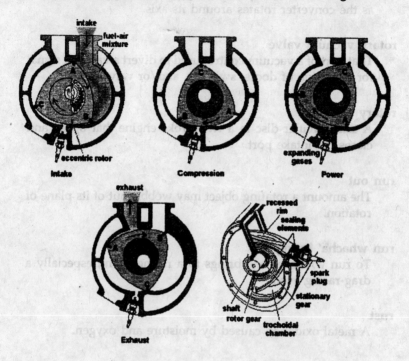

rotary combustion engine (RC engine)
A four-cycle engine having a revolving triangular-shaped rotor to transfer power thrust via eccentric(s) to the output shaft.

rotary diesel
A rotary combustion engine operating on diesel principles in which the fuel injected into the combustion chamber at the end of the compression phase is ignited by the heat produced during compression, rather than by the spark from a plug.

rotary flow
Torque converter oil flow associated with the coupling stage of operation.

**rotary oil flow**
> A condition caused by the centrifugal force applied to the oil as the converter rotates around its axis.

**rotary vacuum valve**
> That part of a vacuum control used to divert a vacuum signal for operation of doors, switches, and/or valves.

**rotary valve**
> A semi-circular disc in a two-stroke engine that opens and closes the intake port.

**run out**
> The amount a rotating object may wobble out of its plane of rotation.

**run whacha' brung**
> To run whatever one brings to a racing event, especially a drag-racing event.

**rust**
> A metal oxidation caused by moisture and oxygen.

**rust converter**
> A liquid that can be painted over that is sprayed on bare metal to eliminate light rust and prevent other rust from forming.

**rust inhibitor**
> A chemical added to the coolant in a radiator to reduce the build-up of rust.

# S

## saddlebag

Air chambers or openings in the left- and right-front corners of the car body between the kickpads and the exterior of the car. The evaporator is sometimes located in the right saddlebag.

## Safety valve

A relief valve set to open at a pressure safely below the bursting pressure of a container, such as a boiler or compressed air receiver. Typically, a disk is held against a seat by a spring; excessive pressure forces the disk open (see illus.). Construction is such that when the valve opens slightly, the opening force builds up to open it fully and to hold the valve open until the pressure drops a predetermined amount, such as 2-4% of the

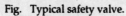
Fig.   Typical safety valve.

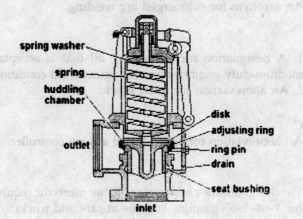

opening pressure. This differential or blow-down pressure and the initial relieving pressure are adjustable. Adjustments must be set by licensed operators, and settings must be tamperproof. The ASME Boiler Construction Code gives typical requirements for safety valves.

**saturated drier**
A drier, accumulator-drier, or receiver-drier having a saturated desiccant.

**saturated point**
The point at which matter must change states at any given temperature and pressure.

**saturated temperature**
The boiling point of a substance at a particular pressure.

**saturated vapor**
A term that indicates that the space holds as much vapor as possible and no further vaporization is possible at that particular temperature.

**sauce**
Racing fuel.

**SAW**
An acronym for submerged arc welding.

**SB**
1. A designation for lubricating oil that is acceptable for medium-duty engines operated under mild conditions.
2. An abbreviation for small block.

**SBEC**
An abbreviation for single-board engine controller.

**SC**
The designation for lubricating oil that meets the requirements for 1964–1967 gasoline engines in cars and trucks.

**scattered**

An engine that has literally blown apart.

**scattershield**

A reinforced housing around the clutch and flywheel to protect the driver from flying parts.

**scavenge pump**

An oil pump that returns oil to the sump in a dry-sump system.

**scavenger**

A powerful car that is difficult to beat in a race.

**scavenger deposits**

White or yellow carbon deposits that normally occur when certain fuels are burned.

**scavenging**

The forced removal of exhaust gases from a cylinder during the overlap period.

**SCCA**

An abbreviation for Sports Car Club of America.

**schematic**

A map-like drawing of the electrical system that gives the colors and shows the terminal points; used to trace the circuit for troubleshooting.

**Schrader valve**

A spring-loaded valve, similar to a tire valve, located inside the service-valve fitting and some control devices to hold vapor or fluid in the system. It requires special adapters for access to the system.

**scoop**

An opening in the hood or body panel used to take in ambient air for cooling or ventilation.

**scope**
A term used for oscilloscope.

**score**
A scratch or small dent in the finished surface of a vehicle.

**SCORE**
An acronym for Short Course Off-Road Enterprises.

**SCORE International**
The actual name for SCORE.

**scoring**
The grooves worn into the friction surface of a brake drum or rotor which may be machined away; if the depth exceedsspecified limits, the drum or rotor must be replaced.

**SCR**
An abbreviation for silicone controlled rectifier.

**scraper ring**
The second ring from the top of a piston used to scrape oil from the cylinder wall.

**scrap yard**
1. A firm selling used parts.
2. A firm that accepts scrap metal for recycling.

**scratch**
1. To spin the drive wheels, usually enough to leave a mark on the road surface.
2. A mark on the finish of a body surface made by a scribe or other sharp object.
3. To make a mark on a finished surface using a sharp object, such as a key.

**scratch built**
A vehicle built from the ground up, generally of an original design.

**screamer**

A vehicle with spectacular performance.

**screw**

The final drive gear.

**screw it on**

To rapidly accelerate.

**screw it on the meter**

To install an engine on a dynamometer.

**Screening**

A mechanical method of separating a mixture of solid particles into fractions by size. The mixture to be separated, called the feed, is passed over a screen surface containing openings of definite size. Particles smaller than the openings fall through the screen and are collected as undersize. Particles larger than the openings slide off the screen and are caught as oversize. A single screen separates the feed into only two fractions. Two or more screens may be operated in series to give additional fractions. Screening occasionally is done wet, but most commonly it is done dry.

Industrial screens may be constructed of metal bars, perforated or slotted metal plates, woven wire cloth, or bolting cloth. The openings are usually square but may be circular or rectangular. In rectangular openings the separation is controlled by the smaller dimension.

When the opening in a screen is larger than 1 in. (2.5 cm), the actual opening size in inches is specified. When the opening is 1 in. or less, the screen size is designated as the number of openings per linear inch; that is, a 20-mesh screen has 20 openings per inch. The actual size of an opening is less than that corresponding to the mesh number by the thickness of the metal between openings. Mesh sizes range from about 4 in. (10 cm) to 400-mesh, but screens finer than 100- or 150-mesh are seldom used industrially. Particles smaller than this are usually separated by other methods. See also: Mechanical classification; Sedimentation (industry)

Testing sieves are used to measure the size distribution of mixtures of particles and to specify the performance of commercial screens and other equipment. They are made of woven wire screening. Mesh and wire size of each screen are standardized. The usual range is from 1- to 200-mesh. In use, a set of standard screens is arranged serially in a stack, with the finest mesh on the bottom and the coarsest on top. An analysis is conducted by placing a weighed sample on the top screen and shaking the stack mechanically for a definite time. Particles passing the bottom screen are caught in a pan. The particles remaining on each screen are removed and weighed, and the weights of the individual increments are converted to percentages of the total sample.

**Fig.  Types of screens. (a) Trommel. (b) Gyratory.**

In most screens the particles are pulled through the openings by gravity only. Large particles are heavy enough to pass through the openings easily, but intermediate and smaller particles are too light to pass through the screen unaided. Most screens are agitated to speed the particles through the openings. Common methods are to revolve a cylindrical screen about an axis slightly inclined to the horizontal or to shake, gyrate, or vibrate a flat screen.

Two effects tend to restrict the fall of small particles through a screen: blinding of the screen by wedging of particles into the openings and sticking of individual particles to each other and to the screen. The motion of the screen reduces blinding, and sometimes positive means are provided to drive wedged particles back through the openings. Sticking is severe if the particles are damp, and may be reduced by drying the feed. Two common screens are shown in the illustration. The trommel, a revolving screen, is a combination of four screens in series. This unit gives five products. The gyrating screen uses bouncing balls under the sizing screens to dislodge particles caught in the meshes. The balls are supported on coarse screens which offer no resistance to the materials passing the sizing screens. This screen gives four products.

Fig.   Types of screens. (a) Trommel. (b) Gyratory.

## screw-thread pitch gauge
A thin material with V-shaped notches that, when matched with a thread of a bolt or nut, indicates the number of threads per inch or millimeter, as well as the thread pitch.

## scribe
A sharp, pointed steel tool with a hardened end for marking lines on metal in laying out work.

## SCRS
An abbreviation for the Society of Collision Repair Specialists.

## scrub
A term used for tire scrub.

**scrub radius**

The distance between the centerline of the ball joints and the centerline of the tire at the point when the tire contacts the road surface.

**scuff**

A surface that has been roughened by scraping.

**scuff in**

To run a new set of racing tires long enough to bring them up to temperature, and wear the manufacturer's protective coating off the tread area. Also known as scuff off.

**SD**

The designation for a lubricating oil developed for use in 1968–1971 cars and some trucks.

**Sewing machine**

mechanism that stitches cloth, leather, book pages, and other material by means of a double-pointed needle or an eye-pointed needle. In ordinary two-threaded machines, a lock stitch is formed (see illus.). An eye-pointed reciprocating needle

Fig.   Modern sewing machine.

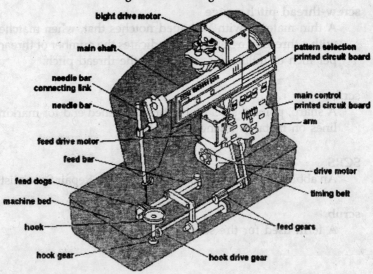

carries an upper thread through the layers of fabric, forming a loop beneath the material. A shuttle carrying a bobbin of under thread passes through the loop. Alternatively, a rotary hook takes the loop of upper thread and passes it around the bobbin of under thread. The needle withdraws, and a thread take-up lever pulls the stitch tight. The machine carries out these necessary motions and also feeds the material past the needle intermittently between each pass of the needle. A presser foot held against the material with a yielding spring adjusts itself automatically to variations in thickness of material and allows the operator to turn the material as it feeds through the machine. A cluster of cams, any one of which can be selected to guide the needle arm, makes possible a variety of stitch patterns.

## shim

1. A thin metal spacer used to align the clearance of a part.
2. A slotted strip of metal used to adjust the front-end alignment on many vehicles.

## shimmy

A harsh, side-to-side vibration of the steering wheel usually due to front wheel imbalance.

## shim stock

Thin metal, usually in a roll, that can be easily cut to be used as a shim.

## shock

A term used for shock absorber.

## shock absorber

A hydraulic device used at each wheel of the suspension system to help control the up, down, and rolling motion of a car body by dampening the oscillations or jounce of the springs when the car goes over bumps, thereby contributing to vehicle safety and passenger comfort. Also referred to as shock.

Effectively a spring, a dashpot, or a combination of the two, arranged to minimize the acceleration of the mass of a mechanism or portion thereof with respect to its frame or support.

Fig. 1  Spring-type shock absorber.

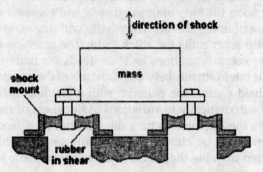

Fig. 2  Dashpot-type shock absorber.

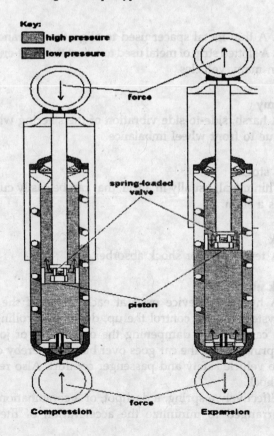

The spring type of shock absorber (Fig. 1) is generally used to protect delicate mechanisms, such as instruments, from direct impact or instantaneously applied loads. Such springs are often made of rubber or similar elastic material. Their design in relation to the natural frequency of the supported system and the forcing frequency of the applied load is most important.

The dashpot type of shock absorber is best illustrated by the direct-acting shock absorber in an automotive spring suspension system (Fig. 2). Here the device is used to dampen and control a spring movement. The energy of the mass in motion is converted to heat by forcing a fluid through a restriction, and the heat is dissipated by radiation and conduction from the shock absorber. See also: Automotive suspension; Vibration damping

**shock-absorber function**

A typical shock absorber has three functions to dampen the effect of spring oscillation in order to control the ride stabilization of a vehicle, to control body sway, and to reduce the tendency of a tire tread to lift off the road surface (a problem often caused by static unbalance).

**shock-absorber lag**

The incorrect operation of a shock absorber because of aeration due to the mixing of air with oils, causing the shock absorber to produce a poor ride.

**shock-absorber ratio**

A rating of shock-absorber extension control compared to the amount of compression control, varying from 50/50 to 80/20.

**shock-absorber strut assembly**

In a MacPherson strut, the independent rear-suspension system that includes a rubber isolated top mount, upper and lower spring seat, coil spring insulator, and coil spring.

**shock compression**

The shock absorber in its shortened position, which occurs when the wheel moves upward.

**shock fluid**
Specially formulated hydraulic fluid used inside of shock absorbers.

**shock foaming**
The mixing of air and shock fluid, due to rapid movement of fluid between the chambers, causing the shock absorber to develop a lag because the piston is moving through an air pocket that offers up resistance. A gas-filled shock absorber is designed to reduce oil foaming.

**shock hydraulic principles**
Fluid is forced through orifices and/or valves at a controlled rate to provide the desired dampening effect.

**shock mounting position**
The direction and/or angle at which a shock absorber is mounted vertical, horizontal, or slanted inward at the top.

**shock mounts**
The rubber isolating bushing or grommets attached to the upper shock-mounting piston rod and the lower mounting cylinder tube in which the piston operates.

**shoe hold-down spring**
A coiled compression spring that applies pressure to hold the brake shoes against the backing plate.

**shoe retracting spring**
A coiled tension spring that pulls the shoes away from the brake drum after the pedal is released, forcing the brake fluid back into the master cylinder.

**shortest operated mileage**
Under the mileage system of computing fares, the shortest distance between two points on an itinerary, omitting any intermediate connections.

**sorbead**
   A desiccant.

**sorted out**
   Corrected, such as a problem that has been corrected.

**soup**
   1. A special racing-fuel mixture.
   2. To increase the output of an engine.

**Southern California Timing Association (SCTA)**
   A sanctioning body concerned with the annual Bonneville speed trials.

**south pole**
   The pole or end at which magnetic lines of force enter a magnet.

**S-plane**
   Continuous complex frequency plane; S-plane is used in control systems engineering in the design of control laws *See Also:* Laplace transform.

**space frame**
   A light-weight race car frame constructed of small-diameter metal tubing that is welded together in such a manner as to provide high rigidity.

**spacer**
   A device, such as a shim or washer, that is used to increase the space between two mating surfaces or parts.

**space-saver spare tire**
   1. A deflated, compact spare tire that must be inflated to 35 psi (241 kPa) with a vehicle-battery powered air compressor or a can of compressed air.
   2. An inflated spare tire which is smaller and narrower than those on the vehicle that is to be used in an emergency only.

**spalling**

A condition where chips, flakes, or scales of metal break off a part due to fatigue rather than by wear.

**span**

The width of an air foil.

**spanner**

The British term for wrench.

**spare**

1. Not in regular use or immediately needed.
2. Extra or reserve.
3. A term used for spare tire.

**spare tire**

A full-size replacement tire or a compact space-saver tire, generally for emergency service, but available for use when needed.

**spark advance**

The moving ahead of the ignition spark in relation to the piston position.

**spark advance curve**

The rate at which ignition timing advances as plotted on a graph; the line rises from some initial amount of advance and levels off at the maximum advance.

**spark decel valve**

A vacuum valve, located in the line between the distributor and carburetor, to advance the spark during deceleration, to reduce emissions.

**spark delay valve (SDV)**

A vacuum valve acting like a restrictor, used in the vacuum line between the distributor and carburetor, to delay vacuum-timing advance under certain driving conditions to reduce NOX (oxides of nitrogen) emissions.

**spark duration**
The time a spark is established across the gap of a spark plug.

**spark ignition (SI)**
An engine-operating system where the air/fuel mixture is ignited by an electrical spark.

**spark knock**
A term used for detonation or ping.

**spark line**
The line on an oscilloscope that indicates the voltage required to fire the spark plug and the number of degrees the distributor turns while the spark exists.

**spark plug**
An ignition component threaded into the cylinder head that contains two electrodes extending into the cylinder that form a gap across which high-voltage electricity arcs to ignite the compressed air-fuel mixture.

**sprocket**
A sheet-like disk with teeth around its outer perimeter that mesh with a belt or chain.

**sprocket pitch**
The dimension between the centers where the rollers would be bedded against the bottoms of adjacent tooth spaces.

**sprocket-pitch diameter**
The pitch diameter of a sprocket used in a synchronous belt drive that coincides with the belt pitch line and is always greater than the sprocket outside diameter.

**sprung weight**
The mass of the vehicle that is supported by the springs, including the body, engine, and transmission.

## spun bearing
Any bearing on the crankshaft that has seized on the journal and turned in the housing bore.

## spur gear
A transmission or differential gear having teeth cut straight across its face, parallel to the rotational axis.

## spyder
1. A light, two-person, horse-drawn carriage.
2. A light, two-person sports roadster.

## square engine
An engine in which the bore and stroke dimensions are the same.

## squash area
A term used for quench area.

## squat
The tendency of the rear end of a vehicle to press down on its springs during hard acceleration.

## squeak
A high-pitched noise of short duration.

## squeal
A continuous high-pitched noise.

## squeegee
1. A flexible rubber block used to apply glazing putty and light coats of body filler.
2. A metal-backed rubber blade having a handle used to clean windshields.

## squirrel
A driver that cannot handle a vehicle very well.

**squirrelly**

Poor handling.

**squirt hole**

1. A hole in the side of a connecting rod in an OHV engine which squirts oil toward the camshaft.

2. A hole in the pin end of a connecting rod to squirt oil to the underside of a piston for cooling.

**squirt racing**

A term used for drag racing.

**squish**

The action where some compressed air/fuel mixture is pushed out of a decreasing space between the piston and cylinder head of the combustion chambers in some engines.

**starboard**

A nautical term for the right-hand direction or side of a ship.

**State data**

Data that defines aircraft parameters, such as position, velocity, attitude; Some standard terms for state data include: Groundspeed vector, wind speed vector, true airspeed vector, true bearing, true track, ground track angle, relative bearing, sideslip angle, drift angle, true heading, magnetic variation, grivation. earthspeed vector, vertical velocity, air mass flight path angle, earth-referenced flight path angle, angle of attack, pitch, radar altitude, barometric altitude, earth radius, glideslope, gravity vector, lift vector, lateral acceleration vector, bank angle.

**State-space model**

A mathematical relationship of a system in time using state variables, inputs, outputs, and constants; The state-space model is composed of n state variables ($x$ sub 1 , $x$ sub 2 , ..., $x$ sub n), m input variables ($u$ sub 1 , $u$ sub 2 , ..., $u$ sub m), k output variables ($y$ sub 1 , $y$ sub 2 , ..., $y$ sub k), and four constants a, b, c, and d. Alternatively, a state-space model can be expressed with matrices. *Compare:* continuous-time equation, difference equation, differential equation, discrete-time equation, Laplace transform, Z transform.

## Static pressure

A measure of barometric pressure as if the sensor were not moving with respect to the air; *Compare:* total pressure; *Symbols:* p sub s; *Typical Units:* psi,lbf/in-squared; *Dimensions:* Mass / Time-squared * Length.

## Station

A structure on the ground, perhaps containing VOR or TACAN.

## Status

An indicator of how well a system or subsystem is working.

## Status indicator

An binary indicator of a particular aspect of a device; status indicators are independent of each other; status indicators listed in this dictionary are derived from existing programs. *See Also:* off, warning, operations, communications, useability, initialization, test, maintenance, unknown.

## Status words ·

Data words reported by devices to indicate status; Each bit is defined on a device-by-device basis. The number of words vary from device to device. Status words are used by maintenance personnel and maintenance software. Present, past, and test status words are reported.

## steam holes

Passages designed to permit the flow of steam in an engine cooling system in hot spot areas where steam is expected to collect.

## Steam jet ejector

steam-actuated device for pumping compressible fluids,

usually from subatmospheric suction pressure to atmospheric discharge pressure. A steam jet ejector is most frequently used for maintaining vacuum in process equipment in which evaporation or condensation takes place. Because of its simplicity, compactness, reliability, and generally low first cost, it is often preferred to a mechanical vacuum pump for removing air from condensers serving steam turbines, especially for marine service. See also: Vacuum pump

Principle

Compression of the pumped fluid is accomplished in one or more stages, depending upon the total compression required. Each stage consists of a converging-diverging steam nozzle, a suction chamber, and a venturi-shaped diffuser. Steam is supplied to the nozzle at pressures in the range 100-250 lb/in.2 gage (0.7-1.7 megapascals). A portion of the enthalpy of the steam is converted to kinetic energy by expanding it through the nozzle at substantially constant entropy to ejector suction pressure, where it reaches velocities of 3000-4500 ft/s (900-1400 m/s). The air or gas, with its vapor of saturation, which is to be pumped and compressed is entrained, primarily by friction in the high-velocity steam jet. The impulse of the steam produces a change in the momentum of the air or gas vapor mixture as it mixes with the motive steam and travels into the converging section of the diffuser. In the throat or most restricted area of the diffuser, the energy transfer is completed and the final mixture of gases and vapor enters the diverging section of the diffuser, where its velocity is progressively reduced. Here a portion of the kinetic energy of the mixture is reconverted to pressure with a corresponding increase in enthalpy. Thus the air or gas is compressed to a higher pressure than its entrance pressure to the ejector. The compression ratios selected for each stage of a steam jet ejector usually vary from about 4 to 7. See also: Diffuser

Application

Two or more stages may be arranged in series, depending upon the total compression ratio required (Fig. 1). Two or more sets of series stages may be arranged in parallel to accommodate variations in capacity.

Fig. 1 Typical multistage steam jet ejector with contact barometric condensers;
first and second stages condensing and third stage noncondensing.

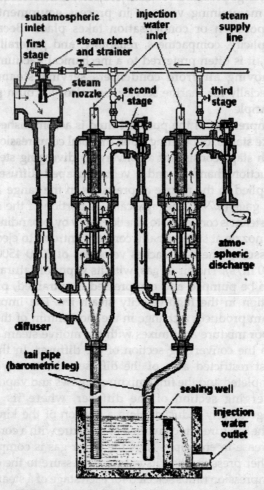

## Steam temperature control

Means for regulating the operation of a steam-generating unit
to produce steam at the required temperature. The temperature
of steam is affected by the change in the relative heat absorption
as load varies, by changes in ash or slag deposits on the heat-
absorbing surface, by changes in fuel, by changes in the
proportioning of fuel and combustion air, or by changes in
feedwater temperature. Low steam temperature lowers the

efficiency of the thermal cycle. However, high steam temperature, which increases thermal efficiency, is restricted by the strength and durability of materials used in superheaters. Control of steam temperature is, therefore, a matter of primary concern in the design of modern steam-generating units.

Steam temperature can be controlled by one or more of several methods (see illus.). These include (1) the damper control of gases to the superheater, to the reheater, or to both, thus changing the heat input; (2) the recirculation of low-temperature flue gas to the furnace, thus changing the relative amounts of heat absorbed in the furnace and in the superheater, reheater, or both; (3) the selective use of burners at different elevations in the furnace or the use of tilting burners, thus

Fig. Methods of controlling steam temperature. (a) Bypass dampers. (b) Tilting burners. (c) Spray attemperation. (d) Gas recirculation.

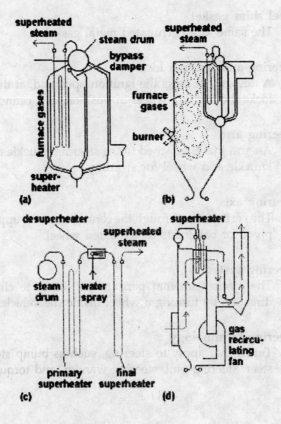

changing the location of the combustion zone with respect to the furnace heat-absorbing surface; (4) the attemperation, or controlled cooling, of the steam by the injection of spray water or by the passage of a portion of the steam through a heat exchanger submerged in the boiler water; (5) the control of the firing rate in divided furnaces; and (6) the control of the firing rate relative to the pumping rate of the feedwater to forced-flow once-through boilers. Generally, these various controls are adjusted automatically.

**steam rollers**
Huge drag-racing slicks.

**steelies**
Wheels made of a ferrous material.

**steel shim gasket**
The same as a corrugated metal gasket.

**steering-and-ignition lock**
A device that locks the ignition open and, at the same time, locks the steering wheel in position so it cannot be turned.

**steering arm**
An arm that is attached to the steering knuckle that turns the knuckle and wheel for steering.

**steering axis**
The vertical line through the centerline of the upper and lower pivot- or ball-joints on a steered wheel.

**steering system**
The mechanism that permits the driver to change vehicle direction by turning a wheel inside the vehicle.

**steering terminology**
Terms that apply to steering, such as bump steer, memory steer, steering pull, steering wander, and torque steer.

**steering wander**
> The tendency of the steering to pull to the right or left when the vehicle is driven straight ahead on a smooth road surface that may be caused by improper caster adjustment.

**steering wheel**
> The wheel, located at the top of the steering shaft, which the driver uses to steer the vehicle.

**steering wheel centering**
> The procedure of turning both tie-rod couplings equally in the proper direction to correctly position the steering-wheel spokes, and placing the steering gears on their high (center) position.

**Stellite**
> A tradename for a very hard alloy made from cobalt (Co), chromium (Cr), and tungsten (W) used for valve-seat inserts.

**stemming**
> A condition where the valve radius section has corroded to the extent that it has a smaller diameter than the stem.

**stem-type service valve**
> A service valve requiring a special wrench be affixed to a stem for opening and closing.

**step**
> 1. The raised portion of a chassis providing added clearance over the axle.
> 2. A term used for stepped flywheel.
> 3. A raised portion on one part so another part can be joined to it.

**stepless transmission**
> A transmission without gears that goes from low gear to overdrive without meshing gears.

**stepped flywheel**
> A flywheel having a ledge to which a pressure plate is attached.

**stepped resistor**
1. A resistor having two or more fixed-resistance values.
2. A resistor assembly having a switch that is wired in series to increase/decrease the circuit resistance thereby controlling an electrical motor speed.

**step ratio**
A transmission with steps or gear ratios, such as four steps for a four-speed transmission.

**Step side**
The tradename of a popular pickup truck by Chevrolet.

**stethoscope**
A medical-type listening device used to detect and isolate noises within an engine while it is running.

**stick**
1. A camshaft.
2. A term used for stick shift.

**stick shift**
A manual transmission.

**stiffness**
A measure of the dynamic elongation of a belt under tension.

**stinger**
A slightly conical pipe used as an exhaust resonator to which individual headers feed, such as at the top of a high-performance Volkswagen Beetle engine.

**Stirling engine**
A type of internal-combustion engine where the piston is moved by changes in pressure of the alternately heated and cooled working gas.

**straightaway**
A straight stretch in a closed race course such as the front and back straightaway at Indy.

**straight cut gear**
A term used for spur gear.

**straightedge**
A metal bar used to check the engine block deck and cylinder head for warpage.

**straight eight**
An inline, eight-cylinder engine.

**straight flexible hose**
A term used for flexible hose.

**straight four**
An inline, four-cylinder engine.

**straight in**
Hitting the wall nose first in closed-course racing.

**straight in damage**
1. Damage caused by one vehicle hitting another vehicle directly or straight on.
2. Damage caused by hitting the wall nose first in closed-course racing.

**Straight-line mechanism**
A mechanism that produces a straight-line (or nearly so) output motion from an input element that rotates, oscillates, or moves in a straight line. Common machine elements, such as linkages, gears, and cams, are often used in ingenious ways to produce the required controlled motion. The more elegant designs use the properties of special points on one of the links of a four-bar linkage.
Linkages
Four-bar linkages that generate approximate straight lines are not new. In 1784 James Watt applied the concept to the vertical-cylinder beam engine. Prior to the use of this linkage, the piston of the steam engine was guided with a chain attached to a centrally pivoted circular sector of a "walking beam."

Other similar applications used the properties of slider cranks and inverted slider cranks to generate the required approximate straight-line output motion. Examples of some of the classical mechanisms.

By selecting the appropriate link lengths, the designer can easily develop a mechanism with a high-quality approximate straight line. Contemporary kinematicians have contributed to more comprehensive studies of the properties of the mechanisms that generate approximate straight lines. The work not only describes the various classical mechanisms, but also provides design information on the quality (the amount of deviation from a straight line) and the length of the straight-line output. Subsequently design data were provided on those mechanisms that have a controlled velocity ratio (output velocity/input velocity) along the generated straight-line path.

**Fig. 1**   Geared straight-line mechanisms. (a) Cardan circle pair; small-gear diameter = 0.5 large-gear diameter. (b) Standard gear; gear diameter 2 = 0.5 gear diameter 1; gear diameters 3 and 4 are arbitrary.

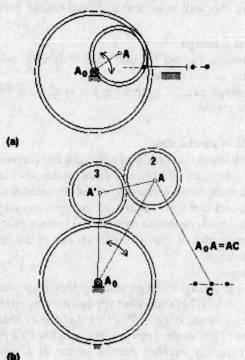

(a)

$A_0 A = AC$

(b)

## Gears

Gears can also be used to generate straight-line motions. The most common combination would be a rack-and-pinion gear; other combinations are the Cardan circle pairs (Fig. 1a). The unique property of this mechanism is that a point on the pitch circle of the smaller gear moves in a straight line with simple harmonic motion as the smaller gear rotates within the larger one. A number of Cardan pairs can also be combined to produce paths with special output velocity and acceleration specifications. Also, standard gears can be combined to achieve the same result (Fig. 1b). Although the mechanism is more complex, its main advantages are that the internal gear is eliminated and the stroke is considerably increased.

## Cams

Cam mechanisms are generally not classified as straight-line motion generators, but translating followers easily fall into the classical definition. Cam mechanisms have kinematic instantaneously equivalent linkage representations (Fig. 2). However, there is no single equivalent mechanism that can represent the cam motion for the full operational mode. Cam mechanisms have an intrinsic property not possessed by the linkage or gear combinations. As higher-order properties

**Fig. 2** Translating follower cam mechanism with an instantaneously equivalent slider-crank representation.

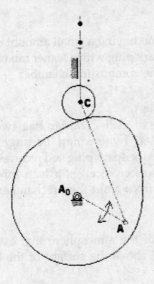

(velocity and acceleration) are assigned to the straight-line portion of the generated path, fewer four-bar linkages are available to a designer. Cam mechanisms are not as restricted by the limitations, and the designer can select the velocity or acceleration properties for the particular application. See also: Cam mechanism

**straightness**

A condition where all elements of a surface or an axis are in a straight line.

**straight six**

An in-line, six-cylinder engine.

**Strapdown inertial sensor**

Accelerometers mounted to a platform fixed to the aircraft; *Compare:* gimbaled inertial sensor.

**stranded wire**

A conductor made up of several small wires twisted together.

**stratified**

To layer or to have in layers.

**stratified charge**

A type of combustion having a small amount of rich air/fuel mixture near the spark plug with a leaner mixture throughout the remainder of the combustion chamber.

**stratified-charge engine**

An engine in which each cylinder has two combustion chambers connected by a small passage; the smaller prechamber contains the spark plug and receives a rich mixture while the main chamber receives a lean mixture which is ignited by a flame front from the prechamber.

**stratosphere**

An upper portion of the atmosphere that extends 10 to 30 miles (16 to 48 km) above the surface of the Earth.

## stratospheric ozone layer

A layer extending from 6 to 15 miles (9.7 to 24.1 km) above Earth's surface, protecting the Earth from ultraviolet (UV) rays from the sun.

## streamliner

1. A specific class vehicle with a fully enclosed body, including the wheels, for dry-lakes racing.
2. A racing car with an aerodynamically enclosed body.

## swash plate

1. An angular plate attached to the bottom of the four pistons on a Stirling engine. As the pistons move downward, the swash plate is turned.
2. A mechanical system that is used for pumping, having an angled plate attached to a center shaft, and pistons that are attached to the plate along the axis of the shaft. As the shaft rotates, the pistons move in and out of a cylinder, producing suction and pressure.
3. A device to control the pitch of rotors; on rotary-wing aircraft, the swashplate is controlled by a collective and a cyclic.

## swash-plate compressor

A compressor in which the pistons are driven by an offset (swash) plate affixed to the main shaft, such as the six-cylinder air-conditioning compressor.

## sway bar

A bar on the suspension system that connects the two sides together. It is designed so that during cornering, forces on one wheel are shared by the other.

## sway-bar link

A connector from the lower control arm to the sway bar.

## sweeping

A term used for purge.

**swing attachment**
A leaf-spring shackle.

**swing axle**
A drive system used with independent rear suspension systems.

**swing pedals**
Pedals that are suspended from beneath the dash, such as clutch, brake, and accelerator.

**swirl**
A cylinder-head design that causes the air/fuel mixture to enter the combustion chamber at a high rate of speed, increasing its atomization.

**switch**
An electrical device that controls the on and off of a subsystem or system.

**swivel foot**
A valve-adjusting screw having a ball that swivels when it contacts the valve stem.

**symmetrical**
Corresponding in size, form, and relative position on opposite sides of a line, plane, point, or axis.

**symmetrical camshaft lobes**
Camshaft lobes having identical opening and closing ramps.

**symmetrical rear-leaf spring**
A term used for rear-leaf spring.

**Synchro**
The trade name for an all-wheel drive system by Volkswagen.

**synchromesh**
A type of manual transmission where the synchronizer is used

to bring a selected gear up or down to the speed of the main shaft.

**synchromesh transmission**
A transmission having a synchronizer.

**synchronize**
To cause two or more events to operate at the same time and/ or the same speed.

**synchronizer**
A device used in a manual transmission to bring a selected gear up or down to the speed of the main shaft.

**synchronous belt**
A belt having cogs or teeth that mesh in mating cogs or teeth of a pulley.

**synfuel**
A term for synthetic fuel.

**synthetic fuel**
A fuel made by liquefying coal or by extracting oil from shale or tar sands.

**synthetic oil**
1. A type of engine lubricant consisting of highly polymerized chemicals.
2. A non-mineral based lubricant for use in automotive air conditioners.

**System**
Applied to measurements, means the best value that the system can determine.

**system-dependent recovery system**
Refrigerant recovery system that relies on system components, such as the compressor, to remove the refrigerant from the system.

**system pressure**

The average pressure in a system, such as the fuel-injection system.

**system protection valves**

A device that is used to protect the brake system against accidental loss of air pressure, buildup of extreme pressure, or backflow and reverse air flow in a truck braking system.

# TAC

An abbreviation for thermostatically controlled air cleaner.

# TACAN Point-to-Point (TCNP)

A basic guidance mode, providing lateral guidance to a point relative to a TACAN station by specified range and bearing.

# throttle-body injection system (TBI)

A fuel-injection system that resembles a carburetor and has fuel injectors located in a common throttle body. It provides many of the advantages of fuel injection, such as easier starting and lower emissions, without the cost and complexity of a multiport-injection system.

# Throttle cue

A longitudinal flight director cue for fixed-wing aircraft, primarily to control speed, by changing power; *Compare:* longitudinal cyclic cue; *Symbols:* Gamma sub LONG; *Typical Units:* percent,in.

# throttle cut-out relay

A term used for wide-open-throttle cut-out relay.

# throttle position sensor

A variable three-wire resistor-type electrical sensor which sends a signal to the electronic control unit relative to the throttle position.

**throttle return check**
> A .dashpot.

**throttle solenoid positioner**
> An electric device that holds the throttle plate in the hot-idle position and closes it when the ignition switch is turned off.

**throttle valve**
> A flap valve that controls the amount of air admitted into the induction system.

**throttling valve**
> A term used for throttle valve, suction throttling valve, or evaporator pressure regulator.

**through fare**
> Fare to a foreign destination reached via a gateway city.

**through passenger**
> Any passenger that is not disembarking at a particular stop.

**through service**
> An airline flight which makes a stop but does not require a change of planes.

**throw**
> 1. A connecting rod journal on a crankshaft.
> 2. The number of output circuits on a switch.

**throw a rod**
> A loose connecting-rod bearing.
> A broken connecting rod that has been forced through the block or oil pan.

**throwaway**
> An element of a travel product or package that is purchased but not used.

**throwout bearing**
The clutch-release bearing.

**Thrust**
Force, created by engines and rotors, acting in the direction of the engine; *Symbols: T; Typical Units:* lbf,kip; *Dimensions:* Mass * Length / Time-squared.

**thrust bearing**
A bearing or a part of the main bearing that limits end-to-end movement of the crankshaft.

**thrust load**
Load placed on a part that is parallel with the center of the axis.

**thrust plate**
A retainer that positions the camshaft in an OHV engine and limits its end-to-end movement.

**thrust surface**
The area of a crank or block that absorbs end-to-end thrust pressure.

**thrust washer**
A washer that is capable of supporting a thrust load.

**thumbnail grooves**
Small grooves in a thrust bearing that provide a path for lubrication to the thrust surfaces.

**tie rod**
The linkage between the idler arm or pitman arm and the steering arm.

**tie-rod coupling**
A threaded sleeve between the tie rod and the tie-rod end providing lengthwise adjustment to set front-wheel toe in.

**tip the can**
: To increase the ratio of nitro in a racing-fuel mixture.

**tire**
: An air-filled or solid covering for a wheel, normally of rubber. A device made of rubber, fabric and other materials that, when filled with fluid or gas under pressure and mounted on a wheel, cushions and sustains the imposed load. Tires contribute to the ride and steering quality of a vehicle and play a significant role in vehicle safety. Tires must be designed to carry the weight of the vehicle, transfer braking and driving torque to the road, and withstand side thrust over varying speeds and conditions.

**tire aspect ratio**
: A term used for aspect ratio. Also known as series number.

**tire balancing**
: The procedure of using special equipment for identifying the lighter portions of a tire and adding weights until opposite tire sections weigh the same.

**tire bead**
: A term used for bead.

**tire black**
: A black liquid dressing used to refresh the appearance of tires.

**tire carcass**
: The plies that make up the underbody of the tire.

**tire casing**
: Layers of cord called plies on which the rubber tread is applied.

**tire chain**
: Specialty chains which may be placed over the tires to improve traction when driving on ice or snow; typically used in emergency situations such as driving on snow-covered or ice-covered mountain roads.

## tire coding

Information required by federal legislation to be placed on all tires, such as manufacturer and tire name, size designation, maximum load-carrying characteristics, limit, and range, a ten-digit Department of Transportation serial number indicating where and when it was made, and the letter A, B, or C, indicating conformity to a uniform tire quality grading system.

## tire conicity

A condition where the plies and/or belts are not level across the tire tread and are somewhat cone shaped. This causes a pull to one side as the car is driven straight ahead if the tires are on the front of the vehicle.

## tire construction

A typical, modern, tire-construction design has two wire beads, bead filler, liner, steel reinforcement in the sidewall, sidewall with hard side compound, rayon carcass plies, steel belts, jointless belt cover, hard under-tread compound, and hard high-grip tread compound.

## tire contact area

The footprint, patch, or patch area of the tire that is in contact with the road surface when the tire is supporting the vehicle weight.

## tire deflection

The difference between the free diameter and the rolling diameter of the tire.

## tire design

The three basic tire construction designs are based on the arrangement of the body plies bias, belted radial, and belted bias. A bias-ply tire is constructed with the plies arranged on a bias crossing each other. A belted radial-ply tire is constructed with plies that run at right angles to the circumference of the tire. A belted bias-ply tire is constructed with reinforcing belts beneath the tread section.

**tongue weight**
> The load applied to the hitch by the trailer tongue, equal to about 10–15 percent of the trailer gross weight.

**ton of refrigeration**
> The effect of melting one ton of ice in 24 hours equal to 12,000 Btu per hour.

**tooling**
> A set of required standard or special tools needed to produce a particular part, including jigs, fixtures, gauges, and cutting tools, but excluding machine tools.

**tooth**
> A projection on a gear rim or synchronous belt that meshes or engages with another component.

**tooth cracks**
> In a synchronous belt drive, tooth cracks and eventual tooth separation can be caused by under tensioning, over tensioning, or using a backside idler with too small a diameter or as a result of an under-designed belt drive.

**tooth form**
> The shape of the working surface of a sprocket tooth from the bottom of the seating curve up through the working faces to the tip of the tooth.

**tooth separation**
> A tooth crack.

**topcoat**
> Usually the final paint film applied to a surface.

**top dead center (TDC)**
> The piston position at the top of its stroke.

**top eliminator (TE)**
> The overall winner in a series of drag races.

**top end**
> 1. High engine rpm; a point that horsepower is the greatest.
> 2. The far end of a quarter-mile drag strip.

**top-end power**
> The engine output at high speed.

**top fuel**
> The hottest category in drag racing having cars capable of a quarter mile in less than five seconds, and a top speed of over 300 mph (482.7 km/h).

**top inch**
> The first downward inch of a piston stroke where most wear occurs.

**top loader**
> A Ford four-speed transmission of the mid 1960s to early 1970s.

**top-mount battery**
> A battery having terminals located at the top of the case.

**top ring**
> The top ring of a piston.

**top time (TT)**
> The speed at which a vehicle passes through the traps at the end of a quarter mile.

**top U-bolt plate**
> A plate located on the top of the spring and held in place when the U-bolts are tightened, clamping the spring and axle together.

**torching**
> 1. The cutting or burning of a valve face caused by excessive detonation.
> 2. To flame-cut metal.

## Torque converter

A device for changing the torque-speed ratio or mechanical advantage between an input shaft and an output shaft. A pair of gears is a mechanical torque converter. A hydraulic torque converter, with which this article deals, is an automatically and continuously variable torque converter, in contrast to a gear shift, whose torque ratio is changed in steps by an external control.

### Converter characteristics

A mechanical torque converter transmits power with only incidental losses; thus, the power, which is the product of torque T and rotational speed N, at input I is substantially equal to the power at output O of a mechanical torque converter, or TINI = kTONO, where k is the efficiency of the gear train. This equal-power characteristic is in contrast to that of a fluid coupling in which input and output torques are equal during steady-state operations.

In a hydraulic torque converter, efficiency depends intimately on the angles at which the fluid enters and leaves the blades of the several parts. Because these angles change appreciably over the operating range, k varies, being by definition zero when the output is stalled, although output torque at stall may be three times engine torque for a single-stage converter and five times engine torque for a three-stage converter. Depending on its input absorption characteristics, the hydraulic torque converter tends to pull down the engine speed toward the speed at which the engine develops maximum torque when the load pulls down the converter output speed toward stall. Converter power efficiency is highest (80-90%) at a design speed, usually 40-80% of maximum engine speed, and falls toward zero as shaft speed approaches engine speed. Because of this characteristic, the mode of operation may be modified to change from torque conversion to simple fluid coupling or to direct mechanical drive at high speed.

### Hydraulic action

These characteristics are achieved by the exchange of momentum between the solid parts of the converter and the fluid (Fig. 1). A vaned impeller on the input shaft pumps the fluid near the axis of rotation to the outer rim. Fluid momentum increases because of the greater radius and the influence of the vanes. The high-energy fluid leaves the impeller and impinges on the blades of a turbine, giving up its energy to drive the turbine, which is connected to the output shaft. The fluid discharges from the turbine into a bladed reactor. The reactor blades are fixed to the frame; they deflect the fluid flow and redirect it into the impeller. This change in flow direction produced by the stationary reactor is equivalent to an increasing change in momentum which adds to the momentum imparted by the impeller to give a torque increase at the output of the converter.

Fig. 1 Elementary hydraulic torque converter.

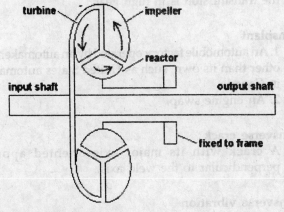

**transistorized ignition**

An ignition system having conventional breaker points with transistor regulation of voltage.

**transitional spring coil**

Coils that become inactive when compressed to their maximum load-carrying capacity.

**transmission**

A gearing device of a vehicle that provides variable ratios between the engine output and the differential input.

**transmission controlled spark (TCS)**

An emissions-control system to prevent distributor vacuum advance at normal operating temperature until the transmission has shifted into high gear by using a transmission-mounted electric switch controlling a solenoid-actuated vacuum valve.

**transmission oil cooler**
Heat exchanger located in the radiator outlet end section through which transmission fluid flows for cooling purposes on most automatic transmission cars.

**transmission-regulated spark system (TRS)**
A system that allows distributor vacuum advance only when the transmission is in high gear.

**transplant**
1. An automobile factory operated by an automaker in a country other than its own, such as United States automaker's plants in Canada.
2. An engine swap.

**transverse crack**
A crack with its major axis oriented approximately perpendicular to the weld axis.

**transverse vibration**
A vibration caused by an unbalanced drive line.

**traps**
1. The measured section at the end of a drag strip.
2. The fastest part of an oval track or road racing course.

**trash box**
1. An engine built from junk parts.
2. A car built from junk parts.

**travel**
1. A term used for rebound travel.
2. To move or go from one place to another.

**travel advisory**
A formal warning, issued by the united States Department of

State, advising caution in traveling to specific countries due to political unrest, natural disaster, or other cause.

**travel-sensitive strut**

A strut with the capability to adjust its firmness in relation to the amount of piston travel within.

**travel trailer**

A trailer with living accommodations.

**traverse engine**

An engine mounted sideways in a vehicle, such as in most front- drive vehicles.

**traverse leaf spring**

A leaf spring mounted sideways, such as in the Model T, or Corvette.

**tread**

That portion of a tire that comes into contact with the surface of the road and is designed to allow the air flow to cool the tire and to channel water during wet weather.

**Truck**

A motor vehicle carrying its load on its own wheels and primarily designed for the transportation of goods or cargo. A truck is similar to a passenger car in many basic aspects, but truck construction is usually heavier throughout with strengthened chassis and suspension, and lower transmission and drive-axle ratios to cope with hilly terrain. Other common truck characteristics include cargo-carrying features such as rear doors or tailgate, and a flat floor. However, there are many different kinds of trucks, often specially designed with unique features for performing a particular job. See also: Automobile; Automotive electrical system; Bus

Types

A truck is rated by its gross vehicle weight (gvw), which is the combined weight of the vehicle and load. Trucks are classified as light-, medium-, or heavy-duty according to gross

vehicle weight as follows:
- Light-duty trucks
  - Class 1:  0-6000 lb (0-2700 kg)
  - Class 2:  6001-10,000 lb (2700-4500 kg)
  - Class 3:  10,001-14,000 lb (4500-6300 kg)
- Medium-duty trucks
  - Class 4:  14,001-16,000 lb (6300-7200 kg)
  - Class 5:  16,001-19,500 lb (7200-8775 kg)
  - Class 6:  19,501-26,000 lb (8775-11,700 kg)
  - Class 7:  26,001-33,000 lb (11,700-14,850 kg)
- Heavy-duty trucks
  - Class 8:  33,001 lb up (14,850 kg up)

Although a variety of models and designs are available in each category, there are two basic types of vehicles, the straight truck and the truck tractor.

The straight truck has the engine and body mounted on the same chassis. The chassis includes the engine, frame, and other essential structural and mechanical parts but not the body. The body is the structure or fixture especially provided to contain or support the goods or cargo to be transported. The truck tractor is essentially a power unit that is the control and pulling vehicle for truck trailers such as full trailers or semitrailers. A full trailer has a front axle and one or more rear axles and is constructed so that all its own weight and that of its load rests on its own wheels. A semitrailer has one or more axles at the rear, and is constructed so that the front end and a substantial part of its own weight and that of its load rests upon another vehicle. A retractable mechanism mounted at the front end of the semitrailer is lowered to support it when the pulling vehicle is disconnected. A full trailer may be drawn by a truck, or behind a semitrailer.

The truck or truck tractor may have a single driving axle at the rear for lighter loads, relatively short distances, and tight maneuvering. For heavier hauling, two rear axles (a tandem axle) or more may be used. In a tandem axle, the drive may be through one or both axles. When additional traction is needed, the vehicle may have all-wheel drive, in which the front axle as well as the rear axle is powered.

Truck tractor

A truck tractor is a vehicle of short wheelbase for hauling

semitrailers. It carries a swiveling mount, known as the fifth wheel, above the rear axle to support the front end of the semitrailer. If the tractor has two axles, the drive is through the rear axle. However, a three-axle tractor (one front and two rear) may drive through only one rear axle with one trailing, or through both rear axles.

The tractor-semitrailer combination permits the use of longer bodies with greater carrying capacity and better maneuverability than is possible with a straight truck. The forward positioning of the cab, the short wheelbase of the tractor, and the multiplicity of axles provide maximum payloads and operating economy in the face of restriction on overall length imposed by some states, and regulations limiting the weight carried on a single axle.

Cab and body

The cab is the part of the truck or tractor that encloses the driver and vehicle operating controls. It may be an integral part of the body, as in a van; or it may be a separate compartment alongside the engine, behind the engine, or over

Fig. Two-axle cab-over-engine truck tractor with fifth wheel mounted.

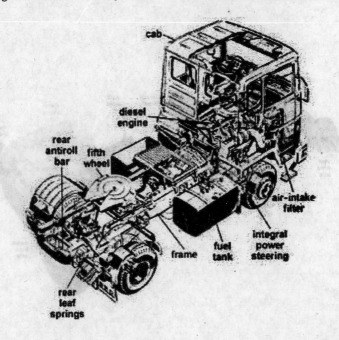

the engine. With the cab-over-engine design, the cab may be in fixed position or it may tilt forward for access to the engine. A cab with an interior or adjacent sleeping space is known as a sleeper or sleeper cab.

At highway speeds, half the fuel burned in the engine is used to overcome the air resistance or aerodynamic drag of the cab, body, and trailer. Streamlined designs, for example, contoured windshields, hoods, fenders, and bumpers and devices such as air deflectors, reduce drag. This improves fuel economy and lowers the vehicle operating cost. See also: Streamlining

**Frame**

The truck frame (Fig.) supports the load, power train, and steering mechanism while maintaining alignment of the components of the body and chassis. The load-bearing ability of a truck is determined by the strength of the frame, which is designed to handle the loads encountered in its load-rating category.

**Power train**

Power train for an on-highway truck or truck tractor, with a nondriving front axle and a tandem axle at the rear. Both rear axles are driven.

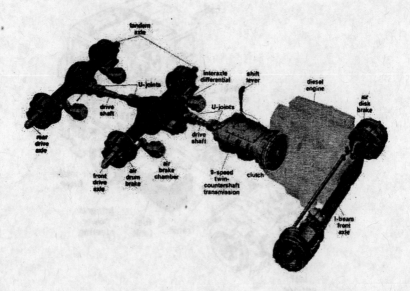

# Turbine

A machine for generating rotary mechanical power from the energy in a stream of fluid. The energy, originally in the form of head or pressure energy, is converted to velocity energy by passing through a system of stationary and moving blades in the turbine. Changes in the magnitude and direction of the fluid velocity are made to cause tangential forces on the rotating blades, producing mechanical power via the turning rotor. The fluids most commonly used in turbines are steam, hot air or combustion products, and water. Steam raised in fossil fuel-fired boilers or nuclear reactor systems is widely used in turbines for electrical power generation, ship propulsion, and mechanical drives. The combustion gas turbine has these applications in addition to important uses in aircraft propulsion. Water turbines are used for electrical power generation. Collectively, turbines drive over 95% of the electrical generating capacity in the world. See also: Gas turbine; Hydraulic turbine; Steam turbine; Turbine propulsion; Turbojet

Turbines effect the conversion of fluid to mechanical energy through the principles of impulse, reaction, or a mixture of the two. Illustration a shows the impulse principle. High-pressure fluid at low velocity in the boiler is expanded through the stationary nozzle to low pressure and high velocity. The blades of the turning rotor reduce the velocity of the fluid jet at constant pressure, converting kinetic energy (velocity) to mechanical energy. See also: Impulse turbine

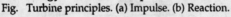

Fig. Turbine principles. (a) Impulse. (b) Reaction.

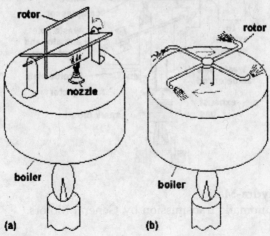

rotor

rotor

nozzle

boiler

boiler

(a)                    (b)

## turbocharger

A turbine-type supercharger driven by exhaust gases.

A n air compressor or supercharger on an internal combustion piston engine that is driven by the engine exhaust gas to increase or boost the amount of fuel that can be burned in the cylinder, thereby increasing engine power and performance. On an aircraft piston engine, the turbocharger allows the engine to retain its sea-level power rating at higher altitudes despite a decrease in atmospheric pressure. Construction and operation The turbocharger is a turbine-powered centrifugal supercharger. It consists of a radial-flow compressor and turbine mounted on a common shaft (see illus.). The turbine uses the energy in the exhaust gas to drive the compressor, which draws in outside air, precompresses it, and supplies it to the cylinders at a pressure above atmospheric pressure. Turbocharger speed, which may be upward of 130,000 revolutions/min, is not dependent upon engine speed, but is determined by the power balance between the turbine and the compressor.

**Fig.** Typical turbocharger installation on a fuel-injected spark-ignition engine, using a waste gate to limit boost pressure. Charge-air cooler is not shown.

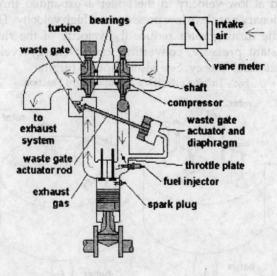

## Turbo Hydra-Matic

An automatic transmission by General Motors.

**Turbo Hydro**
A term used for Turbo Hydra-Matic.

**turbo intercooler**
A term used for intercooler.

**turbo lag**
The short delay in engine response when a driver punches the throttle in a turbocharged vehicle.

**turbosupercharger**
A term used for turbocharger.

**turbulence**
A violent disturbance such as the rapid swirling motion of the air/fuel mixture entering a combustion chamber.

**turkey pan**
Flanges that are installed as deflectors in an engine to reduce oil splash in the lifter areas.

**turn**
1. To change directions.
2. A specific speed, as in to turn 90 mph.

**turning circle**
A term used for turning diameter.

**turning diameter**
The diameter of a circle a vehicle would make if the steering were locked.

**turning torque**
Amount of torque required to keep a shaft or gear rotating.

**Twin-Grip**
A limited-slip differential by AMC.

**twin I-beam**
A front suspension using two I-beams, each attached to the

chassis at the end opposite the wheel, and a coil spring at the wheel end.

### twin-plug head

A cylinder head having provisions for two spark plugs per cylinder.

### twin-plug ignition system

An ignition system having two distributors, two coils, and two plugs per cylinder.

### twin torsion bar

A suspension system having two torsion bars, one placed above the other.

### two-bolt main

An engine block in which the mains are held in place with two bolts each.

### two-piece drive shaft

A type of drive shaft having two sections requiring a center support bearing mounted on the vehicle frame and universal joints at both ends and in the center.

### two-piece piston

A piston having a removable skirt.

### two-piece valve

A valve having a head and stem made of two different materials.

### two-plane manifold

An intake manifold with two plenums.

### two plus two

1. A term used for club coupe.
2. A four or five passenger two-door auto body with limited rear-seat space.

### two speed axle assembly

A heavy-duty, vehicle-axle arrangement having two different output ratios from the differential that are controlled from the cab or the truck.

### two-stroke cycle

An engine in which the four events, intake, compression, combustion, and exhaust, take place in two strokes of the piston.

### two-way catalyst

A catalytic converter that oxidizes hydrocarbons and carbon monoxide, but has little effect on oxides of nitrogen.

## U-bolt
U-shaped bolts to fit around the rear-axle housing for clamping the leaf spring to the housing.

## UHF/VHF Automatic Direction Finding (U/V ADF)
An Automatic Direction Finder that determines relative bearing to a transmitter to which it is tuned, in either the UHF band or VHF band.

## U-joint
A short term for universal joint.

## ultraviolet
An invisible spectrum with wavelengths shorter than visible light but longer than X-rays.

## ultraviolet light
A light source used in non-destructive testing for cracks in metal parts.

## umbrella seal
An umbrella-shaped valve stem seal used to direct oil away from the stem and guide.

## unburned hydrocarbons
HC is a major pollutant in exhaust gases as a result of the partially unburned fuel after combustion.

## undercarriage
The chassis of a vehicle.

## undercharge
An air-conditioning system that is short of refrigerant, resulting in improper cooling.

## under-dash unit
A term used for hang on unit such as for a CB radio or other aftermarket accessory.

## underfill
A depression on the weld face or root surface extending below the adjacent surface of the base metal.

## under-hood lubrication services
The work performed under the hood during a chassis lubrication such as lubricating the distributor, manifold heat-control valve, upper suspension, hood hinges and latch, checking the fluid level in the engine crankcase, brake master cylinder, radiator, battery, and power steering reservoir, plus inspecting belts and safety-related items.

## underinflation
A condition with respect to tire inflation that decreases the rolling diameter and increases the contact area, which results in excessive sidewall flexing and tread wear causing excessive heat buildup, ultimately leading to severe tire damage.

## undersize (US)
A part of item that is smaller than that specified.

## underslung suspension
A suspension system in which the spring is positioned under the axle.

## understaging
A vehicle placed at the beginning of a drag race, behind the normal starting point.

**understeer**

A condition where the front of the vehicle tends to break out and slide toward the outside of a turn.

**undertread compound**

A blend of synthetic rubbers used in the material under the tire tread.

**under-vehicle lubrication services**

Work performed under the vehicle during a chassis lubrication such as changing oil and filter, checking or changing transmission fluid, and gear oil or differential gear oil, lubricating the suspension and steering system, universal joints, clutch and/or transmission linkage, front-wheel bearings, and inspection of safety-related items.

**UNEP**

An abbreviation for United Nations Environment Program.

**unequal A-arms**

A suspension system where one arm is larger than the other.

**unequal length control-arm suspension**

Front suspension-control arms of unequal length to compensate for jounce and rebound.

**unfair advantage**

Not really unfair, the term given for that extra margin realized by a racing team with careful planning and attention to detail.

**unglued**

An engine or transmission that has blown and is destroyed.

**unibody**

A short term for unit body.

**unicast**

A component or part cast as a single unit.

**unicast rotor**
Type of rotor used on many late-model cars having the rotor and hub cast as one integral component, often from gray iron rather than cast iron.

**uniform pitch spring**
A valve spring having uniformly spaced coils.

**uniform tire quality grading**
Information required by the Department of Transportation to be molded into the sidewall of each tire to provide information relating to tread wear, traction, and temperature ratings.

**unit**
1. One.
2. An assembly or device that can perform its function without outside interference or assistance.

**unit body**
A form of vehicle construction that includes the chassis, frame, and body in one unit.

**unit cable**
A cable having pairs of cables placed into groups (units) of a given quantity, then these groups form the core.

**unit distributor**
A breakerless ignition distributor used by General Motors containing the ignition coil, magnetic pickup coil, and timer core.

**Unit functions**
A collection of functions used as standard test cases in control systems engineering; The primary unit functions of interest in avionics are the unit impulse, the unit step, and the unit ramp. *Symbols:* u sub k ( t ).

**Unit impulse**
A function used as a standard test case in control systems

engineering; a spike of "area" one at time t = 0; *Synonyms:* impulse; *See Also:* unit functions; *Symbols:* u sub <0> ( t ), delta ( t ).

## Unit ramp

A function used as a standard test case in control systems engineering; a line of slope 1 starting at zero at time t = 0; *Synonyms:* ramp; *See Also:* unit functions; *Symbols:* u sub < -2> ( t ).

## Unit step

A function used as a standard test case in control systems engineering; a step from zero to one at time t = 0; *Synonyms:* step; *See Also:* unit functions; *Symbols:* u sub< -1>( t ), u( t ).

## United Nations Environment Program (UNEP)

A program or agreement mandating the scheduled phaseout of CFC refrigerants.

## Unitless

No units, such as ratios; a quantity with standard units of 1; a quantity with primary units of 1; *Synonyms:* dimensionless.

## Units

A standard quantity, such as ft or mi; *Synonyms:* dimension.

## United States Auto Club (USAC)

A sanctioning body for oval-track racing, such as the Indianapolis 500.

## United States Customary System (USC measurements, USCS)

The type of measuring system used in the United States, such as gallon, inch, mile, and pounds.

## unitized construction

A type of vehicle construction whereby the frame and body parts are welded together to form a single assembly.

## Unloader

A power device for removing bulk materials from railway freight cars or highway trucks. Especially in the case of railway cars, the car structure may aid the unloading, as in the hopper-bottom dumper; here the unloader may be a vibrator which improves flow of the bulk material into a storage bin or to a conveyor. Thus an unloader is the transitional device between interplant transportation means and intraplant materials-handling facilities. See also: Materials-handling equipment; Transportation engineering

Basically, design considerations for an unloader are similar to those for a device for removing bulk from a storage bin or warehouse with low headroom and limited access. A special

Fig.   Unloader. (a) Power scoop. (b) Rocker. (c) Tilter.

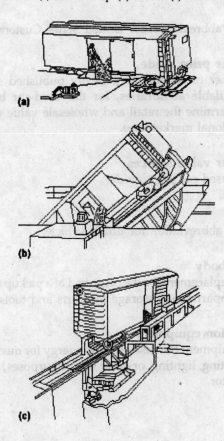

consideration is the possible need for an elevating platform to bring the car or truck floor to the level of the unloading dock and to maintain the alignment as material is removed and the vehicular springs expand. Unloading may then be accomplished by portable belt, drag-chain, flight, or similar conveyor (illus. a).

## URL
Universal Resource Locator or Web site address.

## USC measurements
1. A term used for United States Customary System.
2. The standard English system of measurement.

## USCS
An abbreviation for United States Customary System.

## used-car price guide
Either of several periodically published sources, generally available at libraries, for the used-car buyer or seller to determine the retail and wholesale value of a vehicle in the regional marketplace.

## used-car value sources
A used-car price guide.

## ute
An abbreviation for utility vehicle.

## utility body
A replacement for the cargo bed of a pickup truck that includes compartmental storage for parts and tools.

## utilization equipment
Equipment that uses electric energy for mechanical, chemical, heating, lighting, or other useful purposes, such as an electric motor.

**U-tube**
 A term used for manomometer.

**UV**
 An abbreviation for ultraviolet.

**UV light**
 That portion of the light spectrum beyond violet.

## V

**vacuum**
An enclosed space from which all air has been removed, having an absolute atmospheric pressure of near zero.

**vacuum advance**
The principle-advancing ignition timing by using the vacuum generated by the engine, accomplished through the use of a mechanism attached to the distributor which moves the breaker point or pickup coil plate when it receives vacuum.

**vacuum-advance control**
An emissions-control system component that allows vacuum advance only during certain modes of engine operation.

**vacuum-advance solenoid**
An electrically operated two-position valve that provides or prevents a vacuum signal to the distributor vacuum-advance unit.

**vacuum amplifier**
A term used for venturi vacuum amplifier.

**vacuum booster**
A power-brake actuating mechanism that uses vacuum on one side of a diaphragm as a power source to amplify braking force.

**vacuum reserve tank**
A container used to store and provide reserve engine vacuum.

**vacuum secondaries**
The secondary bores of a four-barrel carburetor that are opened by a vacuum.

**vacuum selector valve**
A vacuum valve that controls the vacuum motors, which, in turn, operate the airflow-control doors.

**vacuum-suspended power brake**
A type of power brake in which both sides of the piston are subject to a vacuum.

**vacuum switch**
An electrical switch controlled by a vacuum.

**vacuum tank**
A term used for vacuum canister, vacuum chamber, or vacuum reserve tank.

**vacuum tap**
A point at which a vacuum can be released from an enclosure.

**vacuum test**
A test to determine the presence of a vacuum.

**validity list**
A list of valid bulletins supplied by the manufacturer.

**value guides**
A used-car price guide.

**value added tax (VAT)**
A form of taxation in which taxes are added cumulatively as a product changes hands. A common tax in Europe, which, upon application, can often be refunded to foreign visitors

after their visit.

## value season

1. Shoulder season. 2. Low season. 3. Any period during which lower rates or fares are offered.

## valve

A circular-stemmed device used to control the flow of air/fuel mixture in and the flow of burned gasses out of the engine. A flow-control device. This article deals with valves for fluids, liquids, and gases. Valves are used to regulate the flow of fluids in piping systems and machinery. In machinery the flow phenomenon is frequently of a pulsating or intermittent character and the valve, with its associated gear, contributes a timing feature. For electrical valves See also: Electron tube Pipe valves

The valves commonly used in piping systems are gate valves (Fig. 1), usually operated closed or wide open and seldom used for throttling; globe valves (Fig. 2), frequently fitted with a renewable disk and adaptable to throttling operations; check valves (Fig. 3), for automatically limiting flow in a piping system to a single direction; and plug cocks (Fig. 4), for

Fig. 1 Gate valves with disk gates shown in color. (a) Rising threaded stem shows when valve is open. (b) Nonrising stem valve requires less overhead.

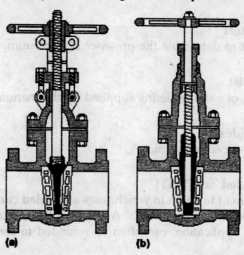

**(a)**                    **(b)**

operation in the open or closed position by turning the plug through 90° and with a shearing action to clear foreign matter from the seat.

Fig. 2   Globe valves with (a) gasket in disk and (b) ground metal-faced disk.

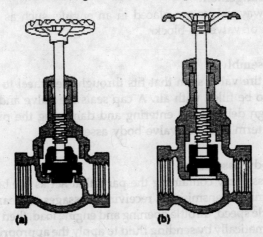

Fig. 3   Various types of straightway check valves. (a) Swing. (b) Ball. (c) Vertical.

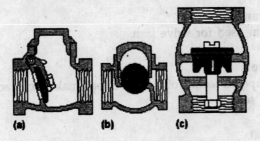

Fig. 4   Plug valve in (a) closed and (b) open positions.

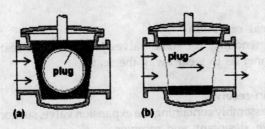

**valve angle**
The angle at which the valve face is machined.

**valve arrangement**
The way valves are placed in an engine, such as valves-in-head or valves-in-block.

**valve assembly**
1. A tire valve stem that fits through the wheel to allow the tire to be filled with air. A cap seals the valve and prevents foreign debris from entering and damaging the pin.
2. A term used for valve body assembly.

**valve body assembly**
An assembly containing the parts that act as the brain of an automatic transmission, receiving messages on gear selected, vehicle speed, throttle opening and engine load, then operating automatically by sending fluid to apply the appropriate bands and/or clutches.

**valve clearance**
A term used for valve lash.

**valve face**
The tapered section of the valve head making contact with the valve seat.

**valve float**
1. A valve that does not close completely.
2. A valve that does not close at the proper time.

**valve-seat recession**
The tendency for some valves to contact the seat in such a manner as to wear away the seat.

**valves-in-receiver**
An assembly containing the expansion valve, suction throttling valve, desiccant, and receiver.

**valve spool**
A spool-shaped valve such as that in a power-steering unit.

**valve spring**
A small coil spring that closes the valve and keeps the lifter in contact with the camshaft.

**valve-spring retainer**
A device on the valve stem that holds the spring in place.

**valve-spring retainer lock**
A device on the valve stem that locks the valve-spring retainer in place.

**valve-spring seat**
The area in the cylinder where the fixed end of the valve spring is attached.

**valve stem**
A device mounted in the rim or inner tube to provide a method of increasing or decreasing air pressure inside a tire. The long, slim, round part of a valve.

**valve-stem groove**
That part of the valve stem used to position the keepers and locate the valve retainer.

**valve-stud boss**
The boss in the cylinder head that supports and holds the rocker-arm stud.

**valve temperature**
The operational temperature of a valve that may reach 1,400°F (760°C) at the head and be as low as 100°F (37.8°C) at the stem.

**valve timing**
The actual opening and closing of the valves in relationship to the number of degrees of crankshaft rotation.

**valvetrain**
The many parts making up the valve assembly and its operating mechanism.

**van**
A box-shaped, light truck with a forward cab.

**van conversion**
A van that has been customized as a camping vehicle or for some other specific use.

**vane**
A flat, extended surface such as that on an impeller of a pump.

**vane pump**
A pump having small vanes in an elliptically shaped housing.

**vanes**
The scientifically designed and positioned fins that direct or redirect fluid flow inside the torque converter.

**vapor/fuel separator**
A term used for vapor/liquid separator.

**vaporization**
The process of turning a liquid, such as gasoline, into a vapor which is often accomplished after the atomized fuel leaves the carburetor.

**vapor lines**
Lines used to carry gas or vapor.

**velocity**
1. Rate of change of location, either scalar or vector, often with subscripts such as ENU or XYZ to denote the coordinate frame; time derivative of position; time integral of acceleration; *Symbols:* v,V; *Typical Units:* kt,ft/s; *Dimensions:* Length / Time.
2. The rate of motion in a particular direction.

## Velocity east

Aircraft velocity in true east direction; *Symbols:* V sub E; *Typical Units:* kt, ft/s; *Dimensions:* Length / Time.

## Velocity error scale factor (KVSF)

A guidance control law parameter, generated by the longitudinal guidance modes.

## Velocity north

Aircraft velocity in true north direction; *Symbols:* V sub N; *Typical Units:* kt,ft/s; *Dimensions:* Length / Time.

## velocity stacks

The short tubes attached to carburetors that are tuned to a resonate frequency that forces more air into the carburetors. Also referred to as stacks.

## Velvetouch

A brand of sintered-metal brake linings.

## V-engine

An engine having two banks or rows of cylinders set at an angle to form a V.

## vent

A controlled opening through which air or other vapors can escape.

## ventilated rotor

A disc-brake rotor whose friction surfaces are separated by cooling fins having open, ventilated passages between each face for heat dissipation.

## ventilate the block

To throw a rod through the block.

## ventilation

To circulate fresh air through a space or system.

**venturi**
1. A narrow area in a pipe through which a liquid or a gas is permitted to flow.
2. The constriction of the air passageway between the choke and throttle plates in a carburetor, so as air flows past this constriction, its velocity increases and a partial vacuum is produced, thereby promoting a flow of gas from the main gas nozzle.

**venturi principle**
The condition of a gas or liquid flowing through a pipe and the pipe diameter is narrow in one place, the flow speeds up in the narrow area, causing a lower pressure in the narrow area, which may be defined as a venturi.

**venturi vacuum amplifier**
An exhaust-gas recirculation system having a device that uses the weak venturi vacuum signal to regulate the application of strong manifold vacuum to the EGR valve, usually including a reservoir that supplies sufficient vacuum when the engine is producing too little for proper operation.

**'vert**
A term used for convertible.

**Vertical**
Reference to earth radial, for example, vertical velocity is velocity along earth radial; *See Also:* East-North-Vertical.

**vertical acceleration**
Aircraft acceleration in earth vertical direction; *Symbols:* A sub V; *Typical Units:* ft/s-squared,g; *Dimensions:* Length / Time-squared.

**vintage car**
A historic car; one built before 1925.

**viscose friction**
Friction between moving parts, such as in a compressor, resulting from using an oil that is too heavy or thick.

**viscosity**
The resistance of a fluid to flowing.

**viscosity grade**
The numerical rating of a fluid's resistance to flow.

**viscosity index**
A number to indicate the change in viscosity of an oil when heated.

**viscosity rating**
A numerical indicator of the viscosity of an engine oil established by the American Petroleum Institute.

**viscous**
1. Thick.
2. Tendency to resist flowing.

**viscous coupling**
A coupling device having input and output shafts fitted with thin, alternating discs in a closed chamber filled with fluid.

**viscous damper**
A type of crankshaft harmonic balancer that contains a liquid to control engine vibration.

**viscous-drive fan clutch**
A belt-driven, water-pump mounted, liquid-filled or thermostatically controlled cooling fan clutch that drives the fan fast at high temperatures and slow at low temperatures.

**voice synthesizer**
A computer-controlled phoneme generator capable of reproducing the phonemes used for basic speech, putting them into the right combination to create words and sentences.

**voice warning system**
A warning system that uses a voice synthesizer to alert the driver of monitored conditions.

**voiture omnibus**
A French term for carriage for all, loosely translated to bus.

**volatile**
Evaporating rapidly.

**volatile memory**
Memory that does not retain data when power is interrupted to the computer.

**volatile organic compound (VOC)**
A term that relates to chemicals that are negligibly photochemically reactive.

**volatility**
The measure of how rapidly a liquid evaporates.

**Volksrod**
A Volkswagen hot rod.

**volt**
A unit of measure of electrical force required to produce a current of one ampere through a resistance of one ohm.

**voltage**
A specific quantity of electrical force.

**voltage drop**
A reduction of voltage in an electrical circuit.

**voltage-generating sensor**
A device having a junction of dissimilar metals that provide a small voltage output.

**voltage potential**
The electrical pressure at a particular point.

**voltage regulator**
An electrical device to control the output of a generator or alternator.

Dictionary of Mechanical Engineering 459

**voltmeter**
An instrument used to read the pressure behind the flow of electrons.

**volumetric efficiency (VE)**
A percentage ratio that varies with the engine's rpm measuring the difference between the air-fuel mixture actually entering a cylinder and the amount that can enter under ideal conditions.

**VOR**
An abbreviation for vehicle off road.

**VORAD**
An abbreviation for vehicle on-board radar.

**VORTAC**
Collocation of VOR and TACAN providing distance and bearing to station; a basic guidance mode, providing lateral guidance to a set of a VOR station and a TACAN station that are collocated.

**vortex oil flow**
The circular oil-flow path as it leaves the impeller, travels to the turbine, then through the stator and back into the impeller. A mass of whirling fluid within a torque converter when impeller speed is high and turbine speed is low.

**waddle**
> A term used for lateral runout or tire waddle.

**Warning**
> A signal which alerts the operator to a dangerous condition requiring immediate action (from MIL-STD-1472D); an annunciator that is the most critical (more than an advisory or a caution); Also, an indicator of potential failure soon; *Values:* none, hot, low-power, high-power, other.

**warning blinker**
> A term used for hazard system.

**Warning, Caution, Advisory (WCA)**
> *See:* warning, caution, advisory, annunciator, alert.

**warning flasher**
> A device found in the turn signal and hazard flasher circuit that causes the warning lamps to flash on and off.

**warning light**
> A light on the dash to warn of a problem.

**warp**
> A slight twist or curve in a surface.

**Wash-out filter**
A filter to smooth a transition due to change of input source, such as when changing modes; *See Also*: transient-free switch.

**washboard**
The corrugated surface of an unpaved road.

**washer**
A round, metal device with a hole in the middle to help secure a nut or a bolt.

**wastegate**
A turbocharger relief valve to prevent the buildup of too much pressure.

**Waste Oil Heating Manufacturers Association (WOHMA)**
An association of waste oil heater manufacturers that promote recycling used motor oil as a heating fuel.

**waste spark**
A spark occurring during the exhaust stroke on a computerized ignition system.

**water brake**
A type of absorption unit found on some dynamometers.

**water burnout**
The application of bleach or water to the rear wheels prior to a burnout to clean, scuff, and heat the tire surfaces for better traction immediately before a drag race.

**water column**
A manometer.

**water control valve**
A mechanically operated or vacuum-operated shutoff valve that stops the flow of hot water to the heater core.

**water cooled**
Using water as a heat transfer medium.

**water-cooled system**
A term used to identify a liquid cooling system such as one that uses water and antifreeze.

**water diverter**
A device used to direct the flow of coolant in a head or block.

**water filter**
A replaceable filter used to remove impurities from an engine-cooling system.

**water glass**
A common term for sodium silicate.

**water valve**
An electrical-, mechanical-, or vacuum-operated device that controls the flow of coolant to the heater core.

**water wash**
The forcing of exhaust air and fumes from a spray booth through water so that the vented air is free of thermal-sprayed particles or fumes.

**watt**
A unit of measure of electrical power.

**wattage**
A specific quantity of electrical power.

**Watt's linkage**
A three-bar arrangement of a live or de Dion rear axle to prevent lateral movement.

**wave scavenging**
Internal exhaust resonating that increases the extraction of exhaust gases.

**wax**
> 1. A compound to shine the painted surface.
> 2. To beat a competitor in a race.

**weld metal**
> The portion of a fusion weld that has been completely melted during welding.

**weld pool**
> The localized volume of molten metal in a weld prior to its solidification as weld metal.

**Western Union splice**
> The electrical connection made by paralleling the bared ends of two conductors and then twisting these bared ends, each around the other.

**wet bulb**
> A device, such as a thermometer, having a wet sock over its sensing element.

**wet-bulb temperature**
> The ambient temperature measured with a wet-bulb thermometer.

**wet-disk clutch**
> A clutch having a friction disk that operates in a bath of oil.

**wet liner**
> A cylinder liner that is in contact with the coolant.

**wet sleeve**
> A term used for wet liner.

**wet tank**
> A supply reservoir.

**whale tale**
> A large, horizontal spoiler at the rear of a vehicle.

**wheel**
1. A circular frame or hub of an axle to which a tire is attached.
2. A flight control operated by turning with hands in fixed-wing aircraft, primarily to control roll (heading) via the ailerons; wheel is connected to yoke.

**wheel adapter**
A metal plate that permits the use of a wheel having a different bolt pattern.

**wheel alignment**
A condition where the wheels and tires are in proper position on the vehicle.

**wheel-and-axle speed sensors**
Electromagnetic devices used to provide wheel speed information for an anti-lock brake system.

**wheel balance**
The equal distribution of weight of a wheel with a mounted tire.

**wheel base**
The distance from the center of the front wheels to the center of the rear wheels.

**wheel cans**
The wheel wells on a race car having a full width body.

**wheel centerline**
An imaginary line through the center of the tire, a vertical line if the tire is exactly in an upright position.

**Wheel cue**
A lateral flight director cue for fixed-wing aircraft, primarily to control heading, by changing roll; *Compare:* lateral cyclic cue; *Symbols:* Gamma sub 'LAT' ; *Typical Units:* percent,in.

**wheel cylinder**
A hydraulic cylinder device at each wheel of a drum-brake

system that transfers hydraulic pressure developed in the master cylinder to the brake shoes.

**wheel cylinder piston**
The device in a wheel cylinder that expands, causing the brake shoe to contact the drum.

**wheelie**
A wheelstand, lifting the front wheels off the pavement.

**wheelie bars**
A pair of long bars with wheels extending from the rear of the vehicle to prevent wheelstanding.

**wheel meter**
A chassis dynamometer.

**wheel nut**
Threaded nuts used to retain the wheel to the studs on the hub assembly.

**wheel offset**
The wheel rim offset from the center of the mounting flange.

**wheel rebound**
Downward wheel and suspension movement.

**wheel rim**
Circular steel, aluminum, or magnesium components on which the tires are mounted, manufactured from stamped, or pressed steel discs that are riveted or welded together to form the circular rim.

**wheel shimmy**
1. The wobbling motion during rotation of a dynamically unbalanced tire.
2. Rapid inward and outward oscillations of the front wheels.

## wheel-slip brake-control system

A system which automatically controls rotational wheel slip during braking.

## wheel-slip sensor

A device used in combination with the wheel slip brake-control system to sense the rate of angular rotation of the wheel(s) and transmit signals to the logic controller.

## wheel-speed sensor

A sensor on each wheel used to monitor speed for anti-lock braking systems.

## wheel spindle

The spindle on which a wheel is mounted.

## wheel tramp

The wheel-lifting action or hopping motion caused by static unbalance. Motion may be up-and-down or forward-and-backward, caused by centrifugal force acting on a heavy tire section located near the tread-face center.

## wheel tubs

Wheel wells installed to accommodate oversized tires.

## wheel weights

Weights used during the balancing process to equalize the weight mass around and across the tire; attached to the rim with clips or special adhesive.

## white flag

A signal to a closed-course race driver that she or he is about to begin the last lap.

## whoop-dee-doo

A bump or dip severe enough to make a vehicle airborne in off- road racing.

**wrist pin**
 A pin used to attach the connecting rod to the piston.

**wrist-pin bushing**
 A bushing that supports the wrist pin in a connecting rod.

**www**
 The World Wide Web is an Internet service consisting of hypertext-linked documents; included in most web site addresses.

**wye**
 A mechanical or electrical assembly connected in the form of a y.

**X-axis**
>The longitudinal axis around which a vehicle structure rolls from side to side.

**X-chassis**
>A conventional chassis design, used until the late 1960s, which narrows in the center, giving the vehicle a rigid structure that is designed to withstand a high degree of twist having a heavy front cross member to support the upper and lower suspension control arms and coil springs.

**X-drilled crank**
>A term used for X-drilled crankshaft.

**X-drilled crankshaft**
>A crankshaft having two oil passages at approximately 90 degrees apart in the main journals.

**X-frame**
>A term used for X-chassis.

**X-member**
>An X-shaped reinforcement member in a chassis or frame.

**XO**
>Exchange order.

**yaw**
1. The Z-axis.
2. The rotation of a vehicle structure around a vertical axis.
3. Angle of heading; *Symbols:* psi,Psi; *Typical Units:* rad, deg;

**Yaw rate**
Rate of change of yaw; time derivative of yaw; *Symbols:* r; *Symbols:* psi dot; *Typical Units:* rad/s, deg/s; *Dimensions:* 1/Time.

**Y-axis**
The lateral axis around which a vehicle pitches fore and aft.

**Y-block**
The block of a V-type engine having a deep crankcase.

**yellow bumper**
1. A freshman driver in NASCAR competition. Also known as yellow tail.
2. The color of the rear bumper of a first-year driver's car in NASCAR competition.

**yellow flag**
A signal to drivers that there is a hazard on the track in closed-course racing. Also known as yellow light.

**yellow light**

A signal to drivers in closed-course racing that there is hazard on the track. Also known as yellow flag.

**yellow line**

1. A line that separates the apron from the race track.
2. The rev limit of a tachometer before reaching the red line.

**yellow tail**

A freshman driver in NASCAR competition. Also known as yellow bumper.

**yield management**

The practice of adjusting prices up and down in response to demand in order to control yield. The process is usually computerized.

**yield strength**

The amount of force that can be applied to a material before it bends or breaks.

**Yoke**

A flight control operated by pushing and pulling with hands in fixed-wing aircraft, primarily to control pitch (altitude) via the elevators; yoke is mounted on a column between the operator's legs, positioned much like a steering wheel in a car; yoke control is achieved by pushing and pulling the wheel to move the column (yoke) fore and aft.

**yoke-sleeve kit**

A kit that may be used to rebuild the yoke.

**Yoke cue**

A vertical flight director cue for fixed-wing aircraft, primarily to control altitude, by changing pitch; *Compare:* collective cue; *Symbols:* Gamma sub VERT; *Typical Units:* percent,in.

**zap**
1. To defeat an opponent.
2. To over rev an engine to the extent that it is damaged.

**Z-axis**
The vertical axis around which a vehicle structure's front and rear ends swing back and forth.

**zener diode**
A diode often used in electronic voltage regulators.

**zerk**
A term used for zerk fitting.

**zerk fitting**
A nipple-like lubrication fitting through which grease is applied to a chassis or suspension joint with a grease gun.

**zero emissions**
A system or device that does not emit exhaust pollutants to the atmosphere.

**zero-emissions vehicle (ZEV)**
An electric vehicle.

**zero-gap ring**
A piston ring that does not have end clearance.

**zero lash**
No clearance between the valve lifter and camshaft lobe.

**zero toe**
Adjusting the wheels so they point straight ahead.

**ZEV**
An abbreviation for zero-emissions vehicle.

**zinc inner liner**
A thin zinc-metal leaf between the longer steel leaves of a leaf-spring suspension system to control sliding friction between the leaves, and prevent corrosion on certain models.

**zing**
To unintentionally over rev an engine.

**zirc fitting**
A zerk fitting made of zirconium alloy.

**Zone of confusion (ZOC)**
A circular area centered at a TACAN station in which bearing is extremely noisy.

**zoomies**
Exhaust headers that sweep back and up toward the top of the rear tires on an open-wheeled drag racer.

**Z-plane**
Discrete complex frequency plane; Z-plane is used in control systems engineering in the design of control laws *See Also:* Z transform.

**Z transform**
A mathematical relationship to model a discrete function in the complex frequency domain (Z-plane); Z transforms are commonly used by systems engineers to describe avionics systems; *Compare:* continuous-time equation, difference equation, differential equation, discrete-time equation, Laplace

transform, state-space model; *See Also:* first-order filter, second-order filter, unit functions.

## zyglow

A non-destructive system using a dye penetrant and an ultraviolet light to check non-magnetic parts for faults and cracks.